OUR
PASSION
FOR
JUSTICE

OUR PASSION FOR JUSTICE

*Images of Power,
Sexuality, and Liberation*

Carter Heyward

The Pilgrim Press
New York

Library of Congress Cataloging in Publication Data

Heyward, Carter.
  Our passion for justice.

  Includes bibliographical references.
    1. Woman (Christian theology)—Addresses, essays, lectures.   2. Liberation theology—Addresses, essays, lectures.   3. Feminism—Religious aspects—Christianity—Addresses, essays, lectures.   4. Hom.osexuality—Religious aspects—Christianity—Addresses, essays, lectures.
  I. Title.
BT704.H49   1984   261.8   84-4936
ISBN 0-8298-0705-5 (pbk.)

The Pilgrim Press, 132 West 31 Street, New York, New York 10001

TO

my mother
Mary Ann Carter Heyward,
artist
of irrepressible faith
in the whole human family,

my father,
Robert Clarence Heyward Jr.,
gentle man
who sees the power
in gentle people,

and
Suzanne Radley Hiatt,
prophet/priest,
because of whom the church
will never be the same.

Our good friends make justice.
By them we are blessed.

Contents

Preface

Our Passion for Justice is a collection of essays, addresses, sermons, homilies, and liturgical poetry composed over a seven-year period. Each was written for a specific reason and in relation to a particular group of people. As the author of these pieces, I decided to have them published for three reasons that illustrate three dimensions of the task of feminist liberation theology.

1. *To help make some theological connections among various human experiences of justice and injustice as well as among their social and political foundations.* In the overlapping realms of systematic, moral, and pastoral theology, there is nothing more critical than the need to recognize links among structures of alienation in our life together in this nation and in this planet.

By "structure" I mean the historically rooted organization of social power to the intentional effect that certain groups of people are more, or less, empowered as agents of people's lives in those institutions on which the dominant society rests (church, marriage, school, etc.). By "alienation," I mean the actual condition in which people live daily as individuals separate, cut off, from one another. This alienation is no *one's* fault. It is built, structured, into the social world—indeed, into people's psyches, feelings, dreams, and prayers. By "structures of alienation," I refer to specific historical "organizations" or patterns of social relations on the basis of alienation, in particular:

- White supremacy (racism), by which persons of darker colors have been denied social power to shape their own lives in this and many other societies;
- Male gender superiority (sexism) and its twin, the operative assumption in sexist society that the male-over-female relation is sexually normative (heterosexism);
- The accumulation of profit at the expense of human well-being (the effect of advanced capitalism in practice) and its structural corollaries: the mystified wounds of class (classism) and the business of war-making as profitable (militarism);
- National, cultural, and/or religious arrogance (imperialism), which, among Christians, has taken the form of a virulent antagonism toward Jewish people (anti-Semitism) and which is manifest also in the unholy alliance between the current governments of the United States and Israel in their treatment of Palestinian people;
- Public policies that dictate the isolation of elderly, sick, and differently-abled persons from full participation in society.

I do not speak directly to all these problems. I do suggest some association between, for example, militaristic machismo (the violence the United States makes so well at home and abroad) and eroticaphobia (the fear of the sexual, the sensual, the tender), connections between and among common experiences of power, body, spirit, gender, darker and lighter peoples, the need to control and to be controlled.

No structure of alienation in our life together can be uprooted unless we dig into the foundations of the separatism in which all our lives are fastened. Some people will insist that racism is, in fact, the foundation of our alienation; others will contend that sexism or capitalism is basic to everything else. I am persuaded that the problem is the dynamic interaction among the various structures, each of which can only be trivialized when studied as an autonomous phenomenon apart from the others.

To dig into the foundations of why we live in such fear and antipathy, scorn and apathy, in relation to most members of our global family is to make the connections among our diverse experiences of injustice and our various movements for justice. For each injustice in our common life is held in place in the everyday lives of women and men on the basis of race *and* class *and* gender *and* sexual preference *and* religion *and* age *and* national/ethnic/cultural heritage *and* a willingness or an unwillingness to conform to the ideologies and practices of those (usually Euroamerican men) who deny that *they* are alienated and, rather, perceive the rest of us as prisoners of our own alienation and ideological suspicions by which we are said to bring violence onto ourselves.

2. *To explore some connections between our interests in the larger social order and our relationships to those closest to us.* It may be especially hard for white Christians, who have been poorly nurtured on dualistic assumptions about "pastoral" as distinct from "prophetic" concerns, to come to terms with the urgency of our call to live justice-making lives and, in so doing, to work together as pastors to one another in our times of loss, grief, fear, confusion. Surely there is no more profound a spirituality than for us to stand in solidarity with members of this created world and, therein, to find our peace as well as our ability to act with compassion toward our enemies, those whose lived values we oppose.

We must learn how to experience, and cultivate among ourselves, the relation between the common good and the rights of the individual; the fabric of our lives as social beings and the patchwork of our own souls; the peace of god on this earth and the peace of god "which passes all understanding," said to be available to each man and woman through faith.

To assume that we can live as persons of good faith, good will, good works *in spite of—over and against—*social unrest and global conflagration is to live a lie. The theme of this book, connecting an assortment of writings that at first glance may seem unrelated, is that our faith, our will, and our works emerge *in, through, and because of* the alienation into which we are born—and which we are called by the god who empowers us to transform.

3. *To illustrate theological movement over a period of time as an example of how one white christian feminist liberation theologian works.* As someone who is not a social scientist but rather a theologian, I explore links between what large numbers of white Christians have called "God" and the ways in which we same Christians receive our daily bread and act in relation to other persons and earth creatures of many species. To express the relation between ourselves and our god is theological work. As such, the four sections of this book reflect theological movement, my own, in relation to those whose lives and deaths continue to touch and re-form me.

We are people of many relations/movements/revolutions/ resistances, and I am no more or less disposed than the next person to ephemeral "chances" of change and stagnation in my life and work. My purpose then in publishing these writings is not to demonstrate my personal/theological "growth" but rather to present images of commitments made, foundations shaken, reconstructions begun, and expanding circles of relations/ movements/revolutions that make both theologians and our theologies—ourselves and our images of god—different today than before, yet rooted in a certain sameness of purpose. The movements of our lives turn us round and round to meet ourselves again—each time different inasmuch as we are shaped afresh by the power in our relation to new people, times, places, opportunities; each time the same because what we affirm and what we denounce today is never entirely unrelated to whatever has touched us in the past. To that extent, this volume is a remembering, a recollection, and a moving on. . . .

Those who read this book from beginning to end will discover that in the later statements and essays I have learned some things about the world and god, myself and others, which are not apparent, except occasionally in embryonic form, in the early pieces. My comprehension of racism and classism, for example, as *structural* rather than as simply personal problems emerges only gradually, and then only in suggestive ways. For even now I am just beginning to see the extent to which I have failed to realize the ramifications of my own race and class biases in my theological work. I like to suppose that this does not render the positive significance of the earlier work null and void, but rather, to the contrary, may serve to sharpen the significance of theological movement in each of our lives, a value that can be assessed only insofar as we recollect our past—what we have seen, what we have failed to see—and proceed to learn from this history. It is in this process of transformation, and the theological development that accompanies it, that we are able to discern the spirit of a wise god/ess[1] at work in our lives. She compels us to keep moving, to bring with us all that we can bear to carry from the past that we think may be useful for the future, and to appreciate our lives, our relations, and our work with the revolutionary respect due to all living creatures. In this spirit, most of the entries in this volume are presented in the order in which they were composed. Wherever it has seemed apparent to me, and those working with me, that a particular contribution would make little sense without some information about the circumstances for which it was written, this information has been provided in a brief introductory note.

Two substantive stylistic decisions have been made that may confuse the reader looking for either smooth or consistent theological movement: (1) The repetition of certain themes and autobiographical material throughout the volume has seemed vital to an honest presentation of each piece in its own context as well as to the "connection-making" praxis of the book as a whole. Thus, seldom has material been removed from one entry simply because the same material has appeared earlier. (2) The reader should be warned also that s/he will at times encounter unfamiliar (uncapitalized) forms of the words "god" and "christian." The instances in which either of these words is not capitalized are meant to convey theological meaning and, in all cases, reflect the particular context of the specific piece.

Wherever "God" appears with a capital "G," the reference is to the deity of Western monotheism—either as "He" is presented traditionally in these religious traditions or as He, She, or It is, perhaps, able to be transformed into a more universally justice-making deity. Wherever "god" appears uncapitalized, clearly referring to our deity, I am speaking of that divine one who does not seem to me easily, if at all, compatible with the accounts of monotheism given in the dominant Western tradition.

Similarly, by the word "Christian," I allude to the Christian *church* as a historical, institutional agency. When "christian" is not capitalized, it points to those people who may or may not be members of the church, but who experience their own lives and faith in continuity with the life and faith of Jesus.

In short, the lower case reflects a protest against the imperial claims of white ruling-class Christian men in the name of their God. I suspect we christians might do well to "think small" in our god-talk and our ecclesiastical business.

The production of this work has been collaborative from beginning to end. A grant from the Episcopal Church's Conant Fund enabled me to begin work on this project. Without Norene Carter and Peg Hall, I doubt that I would have found the confidence to pursue this work. These two women, each a teacher and an inspiration to me, read these and many other pieces and discussed with me which should be published and why. Some of these essays are more honest and probably more constructive because Peg and Norene asked questions and made incisive criticisms. I asked these two friends in particular to help me because I have never known persons any more fully committed to justice. For your brilliant integrity of intellect, Norene, and your candid imaginative power, Peg, I am enormously grateful.

At the outset, when this book lurked in the realm of possibility, Staley Hitchcock—ever a brother and a source of support— not only typed more than three hundred pages for me but kept saying "Now, *when* we go to press . . ." Thank you, Staley, for your stubborn faith.

My editor at The Pilgrim Press, Marion Meyer, believed in this work and persisted in her efforts to have it published, for which I give thanks.

Anne Gilson joined me in researching footnotes and revising

and retyping much of the manuscript. Anne also helped me rework some grammatical and stylistic difficulties that seemed to haunt several of the more complicated pieces. Anne has been a source of fine-humored wisdom, patience, and labor. In all this, and in your poetry and your courage, Anne, I rejoice.

Somewhere on the New York State Thruway, my friend Joan Griscom told me that the originally proposed title of this volume ("Passion for Justice") struck her as arrogant. Joan and I, together with our friends, spent the next twenty minutes tossing titles back and forth—to return to the original, as amended to suggest that the passion belongs to no one of us, but rather is ours together. Thank you, Joan, for claiming rightly that many of us are at work here.

For providing encouragement in all my work, and especially for some of the efforts reflected in this publication, I am grateful to my wise friend John Craig, and to Robbie Heyward, my humanistic brother/gutsy soul-mate/fellow struggler against all manner and means of severe spirits.

For pushing, nudging, stretching, insisting; for frustrating me, puzzling me, comforting me, learning and teaching with me, I appreciate my feminist theological colleagues in Cambridge, Boston, Toronto, Berkeley/San Francisco, Chicago, New York, and elsewhere. And I am continually touched, empowered, and encouraged in my teaching and learning with my students at the Episcopal Divinity School. I think especially of the Liberation Group, whose participants push and pray/pray and push for a justice that is often so utterly elusive.

The work of four sister-theologians and ethicists in particular has been critically bound up with my own. Katie Cannon, who introduced me to the structural character of "my" racism as a fundamental theological issue; Dorothee Sölle, whose activist spirituality has inspired me to struggle *because* of my faith; Delores Williams, who has helped me see how fully creative theologizing is the only truly constructive theologizing; and Beverly Harrison,[2] who has brought me such personal comfort and has helped me discover wellsprings of vision, into which I am able to dip and draw afresh the sacred awareness that this earth and its diverse peoples, creatures, and cultures are worthy of deep respect.

Three good friends—Chris Blackburn, Sydney Howell, and Early Thompson—worked hard with me in reading the final manuscript, and for this I am grateful.

For all of you and for our many blessings, opening me/ opening us more and more to our passion for justice, I give thanks.

Carter Heyward
Cambridge, Massachusetts

PART I

Digging

To forgive is not to forget, but rather to re-member whatever has been dismembered. We must recall as many, and as much, and as far back as we can bear.

· 1 ·

On Behalf of Women Priests*

I am here to speak for many women priests, and by the power of
the Holy Spirit, I trust, on behalf of all women priests, deacons,
and seminarians studying for ordination. I am here as a woman
speaking for women, and as a Christian, speaking for the soul of
the church. I am here to speak of woman's strength, woman's
power, and woman's pride—to speak well of pride and power
and strength of woman, our greatest assets, and to suggest that
our greatest sin—that which separates women from God—has
always been our failure to take ourselves seriously as strong,
powerful, autonomous and creative persons.

The time has come for churchwomen, and particularly for
women priests and those who intend to be priests, to channel
our prayerful energies into the active realization of our power as
persons of God. We are planted here on this earth, and in this
church, to grow and to bloom, and to make no apologies for
being who and what we are. The time has gone when we could
make a gracious and responsible attempt to discuss the pros and

---

*This address was given in a meeting with Episcopal women interested in ordi-
nation, Diocese of Los Angeles, April 1977. It reflects the spirit of feminist
methodology, ecclesiology, and theo-politics fundamental to this book.

cons of women's ordination with those who oppose it, including the Presiding Bishop. The time has gone when we could attempt politely to "justify" ourselves—our vocational calls, our various appearances, personalities, marital statuses, and sexual persuasions—to those who wonder if, how, and under what circumstances women can be priests. The time has come and gone when we could fruitfully spend our energy attempting to convince our own denomination that God is with us, moving through us, offering new creation to the church. We have better things to do. We have vocations to live, ministries to fulfill, selves bursting open with God's own possibilities for us, for the rest of the church, for the world, and for God. As for the Presiding Bishop, the Evangelical Catholic organization that is formed in opposition to women priests, and the newly formed Anglican Church of North America whose position it is that women cannot be priests, we must be humble and realistic enough to let them go their respective ways. We must let the dead bury the dead, and do what we can among the living.

And what we must do—we who are priests, deacons, seminarians, and laywomen—is this: We must realize, actively, that we are meant by God, in whose image we are created, to come into our own, and to help others do the same. If we take the risen Christ seriously as alive, and well, and active among us, then we know well what Paul meant when he proclaimed that "there is neither Jew nor Greek, there is neither slave nor free, there is neither male nor female, for you are all one in Christ Jesus [Gal. 3:28]." We know well that this cannot be written off as "the way it will be someday—in heaven," but rather that this is a statement of the gospel's radical affirmation of the power and the value and the worth and the rights of all persons within and without the church. And that it is to this end—this deeply spiritual and profoundly political end—that we are called by God to live, and, if need be, to die.

We must let no one convince us that "women's rights" do not belong in the church, or that "women's rights" are less urgent and less critical than other human rights. It may well be that many of us will live our entire lives to make one point: that women are people of God. To the extent that this point is made, the church and the world will be more fully human, more truly holy, arenas of human life and divine movement.

Finally, I am here to say that we go on. There is and will be no turning us back. Women are priests. We are a fact. We are an irreversible reality. And we are, in the words of a sister priest, a gift to the church. They who have eyes to see, see what is given. They who have hearts to discern, know that the church has an opportunity—to discover God in its midst, being born of woman, transforming, recreating human experience. We who are women are called to celebrate this, to proceed as we must, to pursue and live our vocations, regardless of the opposition we meet, and to thank God each day for the grace and the wonder of the call that we share. We must be bold. We must be "wise as serpents and innocent as doves [Matt. 10:16]." We must make no peace with any oppression—our own or that of others. We must speak out. We must risk offending, not for the sake of offense, but for the sake of God. We must pray, and trust, that the Spirit will teach us as we go, giving us the words that we often cannot find or speak on our own. And we must believe that they who have ears to hear, will hear.

· 2 ·

Feminist Theology:
The Early Task and Beyond[1]

In the winter of 1975, I received a letter from a woman in Atlanta who had been present during a house communion in which I had been a celebrant of the eucharist. It was the first time she had participated in a service in which a woman priest had presided.

> I did not expect to be so personally affected by your presence here. I was unaware of the ways that I have felt excluded from God's inner circle of love until I experienced being included—both by the obvious fact of your inclusion and by you, as God's representative, including me. *Somehow I feel I've spent my life trying to be God's son, only to realize at last that I am God's daughter.*[2]

"Only to realize at last that I am God's daughter." This sums up well the early work of feminist theology: helping women discover themselves as daughters, mothers, and sisters in relationship to God; the discovery that we are not "men of God," we are not "brethren," we are not "sons of God"; the discovery that this makes a difference. We are "personally affected." We feel included. And it is good. It is also just a beginning.

I want to say a little about what I have referred to as the "early task" of feminist theology. In 1972 I might have described feminism as women's realization of our own power. Today I would say that it is a movement, initiated by women's realization of our own power, toward a transformation of fundamental assumptions about the created and social order. Earlier, I might have defined theology as disciplined reflection on the nature of God. Today I would suggest that theology is a capacity to discern God's presence here and now and to reflect on what this means. Then and now, I would have maintained that both feminism and theology are grounded in a realization of our own experience; and that the capacity to be aware of, and to reflect upon, the experience of being human—of being female, in this instance—is the cornerstone upon which feminist theology is constructed. An experiential foundation is what we have in common. While we have different experiences, we *all* have experiences. As such, we all have access to the material out of which theology is constructed. And it is this capacity to experience, our common denominator, that cuts through the barriers that otherwise divide us: male/female; black/white; gay and lesbian/straight; rich/poor; conservative/liberal; capitalist/socialist; Christian/Jew; theist/atheist.

The early work of feminist theology is rooted in women's discovery of ourselves as daughters, mothers, and sisters in relation to God. The shape that this work has taken—and in 1972 this was full-time work for most feminist theologians—has been that of "proof-texting" on behalf of women. By that I mean that, in relationship to such issues as women's ordination, the Equal Rights Amendment, abortion laws, and equity in employment practices, Christian and Jewish women have attempted to "prove" in whatever ways we can that we are fully human, created in the image of a God who created male and female in "his image." Many Christians, for example, have been learning to use exegetical tools with precision in order to show that the New Testament does *not* mandate women's subordination, that Galatians 3:28, in which Paul proclaims that there is "neither male nor female . . . in Christ Jesus," must, for us, take precedence over his more restrictive teachings about women being silent in the churches, precisely because as the "declaration of

Christian independence," Galatians proclaims a gospel that pushes toward the transcendence of the cultural limitations of first-century Roman and Jewish ruling-class custom, which militated against the liberation of gentiles, slaves, or women.

The early task of feminist theology, therefore, emerging out of women's awakening to ourselves as fully human, has been—and, for those of us in the church, continues to be—to "prove" our full humanness in relationship to God, men, and one another. This experiential and informed witness, in the context of ecclesiastical and secular opposition to women's rights, has demanded the energy of most feminist theologians up until very recently. Certainly Mary Daly's first book, *The Church and the Second Sex* (1968), testified to women's creation in the image of God and women's rights in the name of God, as did earlier works by such women as Rosemary Ruether, Letty Russell, and Peggy Way. A similar motivation lay behind the early work of Sarah Bentley Doely, who edited the first feminist Christian compendium (1970)[3]; Emily Hewitt and Suzanne Hiatt in their fine book on women priests (1973)[4]; male theologians such as Krister Stendahl; and Leonard Swidler, whose article "Jesus Was a Feminist" has become a classic among feminist Christian resources.[5] Each of these theologians has been engaged in an effort to show not only the worth and value of women, but to "prove" the legitimacy of this perspective by scriptural authority. In 1976, my own book, *A Priest Forever*, reflected my effort to show continuity between the life and teachings of Jesus and contemporary events among women in the church.

But many of us have been discovering that this proof-texting will not do. Our need is for something more than the realization that we are affirmed in "the faith of our fathers." In 1977 three of my students presented a project in a Feminist Credo class at the Episcopal Divinity School. They asked:

> How do we come to answers if we do not formulate questions? The questions we ask determine the type of lives we live, the kind of answers we seek. If we have only answers to meaningless questions, what good are they to us? . . . Can we be both feminists/liberationists and still be faithful followers of our religious traditions? Indeed, what does it mean to "follow" a tradition? What does it mean to "lead" a tradition? Do we want to be convinced to stay, or

encouraged to leave our traditions? . . . How do we overcome the temptation to remain innocent—not to deal with ultimate questions—not to eat of the tree of the knowledge of good and evil? Can we be innocent and responsible persons at the same time? Is not innocence a demonic goal? . . . Will our questions not lead us to conflict with others? Can we *love* without experiencing conflict? Will not this kind of questioning lead us to heresy? What is heresy? If Dorothee Sölle is right when she points out that the tradition in the Church has been synonymous with the status quo, then is not heresy a vital part of the tradition? . . . How far are we willing to go?[6]

One of our sister theologians has gone so far as to suggest that women should leave the church.[7] The response among many men to Mary Daly's *Beyond God the Father* has been one of horror; among many women, the response has been fear. For what Daly has done, in the tradition of Aristotle, has been to challenge the assumptions behind the issues that most of us have been struggling with as "givens." For example, to Leonard Swidler's thesis that Jesus was a feminist, Mary Daly suggests that an appropriate feminist response is, "Fine. Wonderful. But even if he wasn't I am."[8] The "given" with which women have had to contend here is that Jesus is the Christ; Jesus is the Son of God; Jesus is the Son; Jesus is—ultimately and uniquely—divine; and that, therefore, everything Jesus did or said, everything that Jesus did not do or did not say, is to be taken as exemplary for all Christians. Since Jesus apparently did not call women to be among "the twelve," women have had to contend with this as an argument as to why women cannot be priests. And while many have attempted to combat this argument by suggesting that Jesus "had" to choose those persons whom he knew would have some credibility in his own time, Mary Daly's response to this dilemma has become, "So what if Jesus didn't choose women?" She is challenging the assumption behind the givenness of Jesus Christ as authority:

> The idea of a unique male savior may be seen as one more legitimation of male superiority. . . . To put it rather bluntly, I propose that Christianity itself should be castrated by cutting away the products of supermale arrogance.[9]

For Daly, there is no more proof-texting, no more defensiveness in relationship to the church, but rather the possibility of a theological offense in which women, departing from the church, go our own way, beginning at the beginning, to re-name God, to re-conceive ourselves, together, as sisters. Regardless of where one stands in relationship to either the content or the style of Daly's work, her significance for feminist theology has been extraordinary.

I have not left the church, for reasons probably both good and bad—and perhaps for reasons that I do not know. I do not agree with all Mary Daly has written, but I do recognize Mary Daly as a sister whose vision of theological possibility has helped me, and many others, realize increasingly that one of our theological tasks is to scrutinize the assumptions that lie beneath the "givens." In so doing, we are moving beyond "the early task" of feminist theology.

No longer is it enough to maintain that I am a daughter of God. No longer can I believe simply that God is my Mother as well as my Father. No longer am I content simply to change the language of our liturgies in order to be able to speak of, and affirm, myself and other women as sisters. Changing pronouns from "he" to "she" is fine, and it must happen—and it is now beginning to happen here and there in the church. But it is not enough.

What must happen, and what *is* happening now among feminist theologians, is that we are digging into assumptions that have undergirded the givens in Christian tradition. We are moving beyond the early task—digging, sifting, probing. For some of us, this is our theological vocation.

To give you examples of what I mean by givens and the assumptions that undergird them, let me cite several givens in Christian tradition and then note the assumptions that lie beneath each of them.

Given: Christian tradition is itself a set of givens, a set of doctrines and practices from which no "true" Christian can depart.

Assumption: According to Vincent of Lérins, there is a set of doctrines that has been believed "everywhere, always, and by all."

This given and, apparently, the assumption undergirding it is cited as fact by that body of Episcopalians who have now left the Episcopal Church in opposition to the ordination of women and to other changes which, they believe, are contrary to that which has been held as true in every place and time, by everyone.

Given: God can be best discerned and articulated as Trinity.

Assumption: God reveals Godself within the parameters of language and symbolism that we have inherited from past generations and past cultures.

Another assumption: Trinitarian symbolism is essential to Christian faith.

Given: Jesus Christ is God the Son.

Assumption: The divinity of Jesus is inherent and necessary to Christian faith.

We, and many Christians, have assumed such givens are simply the way it is. Many of us have never thought seriously about the assumptions we bring to such faith statements, assumptions that may or may not be constructive in our lives and work as people of God.

I understand our work as feminist theologians to be that of explorers, diggers, artists, re-formers. We do not work to tear down symbols and structures that have been, and continue to be, meaningful to Christians throughout the world. We do not "do theology" for the sake of "doing theology," but rather because we who experience God moving within, between, and among us believe that we must try to articulate what it is that we experience, in order to point to and lift up the presence of God here and now and in order to live and speak *in* God, *through* God, and *by* God, rather than simply *about* God. We are coming to realize that God is present, acting, moving, creating, here and now among us—revealing Godself to us, compelling us to act and speak, to live and sooner or later to die, on the basis of God, just as surely as God was living and acting among those who penned, compiled, and canonized holy scripture.

Whereas the early task of feminist theology has been to enable our self-discovery as full persons of God and to "prove" that this is so, our more fundamental work may be rooted in our realization that, as full persons of God, we have more compelling tasks than to attempt to "prove" ourselves to anyone. Thus, our task becomes one of probing the assumptions behind the givens that have shaped our consciousness; of celebrating the realities of holy movement in our midst; of realizing our essential connectedness to all persons whose lives have been shaped, and often perverted, by sets of dehumanizing givens (hence, our awareness of our fundamental relationship to other liberation theologies emerging in Third World communities, in black communities, in gay communities). We need to risk offense—rather than defense—for the sake of who we are and what we are discovering about God and about ourselves.

Increasingly, we realize that what we are about, we who are feminist theologians, is not self-fulfillment as individuals, but rather a heightened sense of who we are, *we our-selves, in relation to others.* Feminist theology is born of *community.* You will seldom find, among women who would call ourselves feminist theologians, a "hero," a "guru," a leader to whose every word we cling because feminist theology is centered in *communal responsibility* and *sharing collective wisdom.* It is a give-and-take, learn-and-teach process, in which each of us is always teacher, always learner. Feminist theology is not competitive. Nor do we seek *a* feminist theology, which our daughters and sons and those who follow will be able to cite as normative for all feminist theology. Feminist theologizing reflects gracious, spacious, moving processes of diverse being and diverse becoming. It is rooted in a God whose being is dynamic and moving within and among human beings and all created life. Feminist theologians speak in, to, and of this God. Feminist theology is not a system of dogmas, doctrines, and categories, but rather a revelation of a living God whom we believe to be Godself defiant of all static, rigid categories and concepts. Feminist theologians cannot accept any dogma or theological concept in and of itself—that is, outside the context of in what ways it enhances and supports human life and women's lives in particular.

We ask why the Trinity, when as a symbol it explicitly excludes the possibility of articulating God's own female-being,

God's relationship to women as chosen, and the holiness of woman. We ask why the divinity of Jesus, when, as it seems to some of us, Jesus himself tried his best to shift focus from himself to God and to get his friends to take themselves—their power—as seriously as he took his, by the grace of God. We ask why we should be expected to take seriously the "advice" or "admonitions" of bishops and other "church fathers," when it is increasingly clear to us that the vast majority of bishops do not care as much about women's vocations and women's affirmation as they do about an unattainable, hypothetical, and altogether imaginary "unity of the church"; more importantly, that even if the bishops did care about women, our most loving stance in relationship to them would not be one of obedience or deference, but rather cooperation with them, steeped in mutual recognition of one another as sisters and brothers, not as daughters accountable to fathers. Many of us, including some of us who are priests, might even ask why ordination at all. As our sister priest Sue Hiatt has warned:

> Like women pioneering in any field that has been male dominated, we need to be especially vigilant about the dangers of becoming part of, rather than merely the object of, the councils of the church. The great danger for women in the ministry is the danger of "out-clericalizing" the male clergy. If we let ourselves become part of the system as it is, we will simply compound the oppression of women.[10]

It is to this end that feminist theology is being done: in order that we who are theologians, teachers, ministers and priests, clergy and laywomen, might not "compound the oppression" of women, but rather participate with one another and with our brothers in a transformation of fundamental assumptions about the social order within and without the church.

In the last few years, many of us have begun digging theologically. With students at the Episcopal Divinity School, with faculty colleagues, with other church people, as well as with women who have left the church, I am being led ever more critically toward the heart of related theological issues, such as authority and Christology.

In 1974 eleven women deacons were ordained priests in a service that shook the Episcopal Church at its foundation. I am convinced increasingly that the ecclesiastical convulsion fomented by the Philadelphia ordinations was not simply a misogynist reaction against women, but rather sexism compounded by an anxiety response to the breakdown of authority in the church. Most people who opposed this ordination said just that. The Presiding Bishop of the Episcopal Church, in calling an emergency meeting of the House of Bishops to respond to the Philadelphia ordination, noted that the issue before the bishops was "order, not orders": authority, not women. What the bishops and many others in the church failed to understand at the time was that the participants in that ordination had come to realize that the issues of ecclesiastical *authority* and ecclesiastical *sexism* are inseparable.

"Authority" may be understood both as a source of power and as a manifestation of personal confidence. In the image of a Father God, who himself is Authority—Source of all Power— fathers, brothers, and sons have learned to embody a confidence in themselves as the source of social power. Men have assumed that theirs is the "right" to possess this double-edged authority. They have been educated to see themselves as the source of women's and children's power; and they have been trained to compete for positions of "greatest" power within realms of ecclesiastical and other social relations.

The most powerful ecclesiastical authorities have been men, who—by mystical rite—have been designated by God, through his Son Jesus Christ, to bear God's authority here on earth. These elite functionaries, or bishops, are assumed to have authority, to be themselves sources of power and influence. They are to be obeyed, as Fathers in God who are responsible for shaping the attitudes and behavior of their children in God. The given here is *order:* the hierarchical ordering of authority, a downward chain of command among human beings, from men, to women, to children. Indeed, the issue in the Philadelphia ordination was that of a disruption of sexist order: women saying NO to the divine authority that has been assumed by men as their own; women daring to claim the right and the power to stand in defiance of this authority, which had become, historically, a strong, tenacious given.

In the image of an authoritarian Father God, men—Fathers in

God, parish fathers, family fathers—decide what women can do, or may do. In Philadelphia, women were perceived by such men to be acting like naughty daughters, rather than as the good girls they had assumed we were. Our message to these men was that we are *not* good daughters; we are not daughters at all to our bishops. We are not little girls. We are adult women. And we will live our lives accordingly. Our vocations are rooted in our yearning and our intention to share God's authority, to pass on God's authority, to extend our birthright—in which we are given authority by God's grace—to others, so that they too may realize the authority that God has given all persons. In saying NO to the hierarchical order of creation and governance, by which men have assumed the right to say NO to women's full participation in the various ministries of the church, we were saying YES not only to women's birthrights and vocations but also to the possibility of men being our brothers, of men's letting go of their needs to oversee us and one another so that men, too, might discover more and more what it means simply to be human.

There are probably few Christians who would argue with the suggestion that *God* is, or ought to be, the authority, the source of power and influence, in our lives. We might all agree that the authority given us by God has something to do with being like God, of living for God, and of possessing a confidence, a freedom if you will, to live for God in the face of whatever obstacles. Many might agree that our gift to others—God's gift, through us, to others—is to help others see that the authority granted to us has been granted also to them; and that we thereby can, and ought to, pass on God's authority. We might all agree, then, that God, who is Godself Authority, is to be shared, an assertion on which presumably such Christian rites as baptism, confirmation, and ordination are based. But this, so far, is a rather safe theological assertion. It is the grist for the mill of safe sermons.

I want to push farther into the dilemma that most of us encounter when we consider the issue of authority: the very real, existential tension that we experience between personal freedom and communal responsibility. Christian theology, particularly at its catholic roots, has tended to affirm the subordination of the individual person to the good of the whole. Individual and community are assumed to be fundamentally different phenomena.

In terms of personal freedom and communal responsibility, from whence comes the assumption that these two "goods" are necessarily in destructive tension—even in opposition? How is it that we experience this dichotomy? Have we grown accustomed to believing a faulty assumption about ourselves in relation to others? Does my freedom to be myself within the parameters of God's love actually threaten to undo the well-being of my community? No. An understanding of the compatibility of personal freedom with community responsibility necessitates a different way of perceiving who God is among us and what God is doing. For an affirmation of the creative relation between individual liberty and communal accountability must be grounded in the experience of a God who is both very personal and a cosmic, mysterious, unifying principle moving not only in our lives but beyond our lives, relating each and all of us, personally, to God's own way of being in the universe. Such a concept of God must be grounded in our experience of God as one who cares for us, you and me in all our individualities, and who cares also—and is immersed in the being of—every created person, animal, plant, rock, cell, and space. To believe that our personal freedom can go hand in hand with our responsibility to others requires our acknowledgment of others' freedom; and so the personal (*my* business) becomes transpersonal (*our* business); and the transpersonal and the personal become *im*personal in the sense that God is Godself moving and growing throughout the universe, related no more to any one of us than to all others.

I do not expect that we would always agree on who God is, or on what God is doing among us. But I do expect that within community women and men will be open to encounter, exchange, conflict, and shared decision-making, and that we can live within the tensions created by difference until such a time as anyone among us can no longer consider her/himself responsible to the community, at which point one's personal freedom may rightly take her into some new place to find or build community. In the meantime, freedom to be honestly who one is is essential to corporate life. To be oneself is the only truly responsible way to be in community.

We are so afraid of chaos—disorder, disunity, things falling apart—that we go to great lengths to insure ourselves against it. Our fear of chaos is steeped in our angst, a state of existential anxiety, about our "non-being" (Tillich). Disintegration of self, falling to pieces, loss of center, out-of-controlness, orgasmic terror—experiences pressing into a semiawareness that we are dying, and that we will in fact die. As things go, very little really helpful theology is written, because most theologians are too afraid of dying to speak boldly of living. We are afraid of nonbeing, of losing control, of disintegrating into chaotic nothingness. We insist upon tight, clear systems. Holding on to our controls—our canon law, moral law, clerical authority—we become stiff and corpselike. And what of Jesus' words about letting go: "[The one] who loses . . . life . . . will find it [Matt. 10:39]"? And Paul's witness to the same: "We are treated . . . as dying, and behold we live [2 Cor. 6:8–9]"? What of the possibility that, in giving up authority, granting others the right to their own power, we ourselves may manifest more fully a quality of being both powerful and confident?

And what of Jesus? For my life—relationships, ministry, prayer, teaching, studies—Jesus was someone who lived to reveal us to ourselves as we are meant to be. In Jesus, God showed us how it is to be in relation to God. In the life of this Jesus, God's being was manifest fully in relation to human being, thereby revealing to us a harmony between divine being and human being—a dynamic relatedness that we call "Christ." What might be the meaning of "Christ"? Whether or not Jesus believed himself to be the Jewish Messiah—the one to bring salvation—he seemed to perceive that his work would involve a radical shift in consciousness (perhaps his own, certainly that of others) from an emphasis, for example, on ritual to right-relationship; from salvation as "deliverance-from-enemies" to salvation as "right-relationship-with-God," which might involve deliverance into the hands of enemies. This being so, might it be that Jesus, by his manner of life in relationship to God, redefined that hypothetical one for whom Israel had been waiting? Might it be that, by his life with God, Jesus showed us that

"Christ" is the love relation between the human and the divine, manifest in human life that is lived in right-relationship to God? Just as Jesus himself lived as this "Christ," and in so being, becomes our Christ, we ourselves can discern in him who we are at our best, in right-relation to God. Or, as we affirm at the end of the Eucharistic Prayer, "by Christ, in Christ, with Christ," we come to know ourselves as we are meant to be.

Such a christological possibility (which calls for a reexamination of the place of Jesus Christ in Christian community) puts the responsibility for living our lives, dying our deaths, and taking ourselves seriously as daughters, sons, and people of God squarely on our shoulders. Jesus did not do it for us. Jesus' life does not spare us the need to live our own or to discover ourselves in relationship to God. Jesus has shown us the way. In his life, we find clues—if we are looking—as to who and where God is, and as to who we ourselves are. Such faith may spill over with possibilities for us. Rather than proclaim the mystery of our faith as we Episcopalians do in our new liturgy by focusing our attention on a singular and unique Christ-being—Jesus of Nazareth—when we say, "Christ has died. Christ is risen. Christ will come again," we might well sing out in celebration that "Christ is dying. Christ is rising. Christ is here again," manifest in and through our own lives, in our own times, revealing God's being to us, and us to ourselves.

I am amazed and frightened by what is happening now among women in seminaries, church, and the rest of society: Amazed by the power and pride and strength and grace I see among my sisters. God is full of wonder, filling us with energy and hope and faith and showing us what it means to love—a harsh, jubilant, bittersweet, painful love of God, moving in us as we come to know God, ourselves, and our sisters and brothers, as we are meant to be. Frightened, because letting go is scary. The future is open. The sands shift. The light breaks unpredictably through the forest in different spots when we least expect it. A matter of no small wonder. In it all, it is a matter of finding God, and of "loving her fiercely."[11]

· 3 ·

Passion*

The church has become a passionless institution—a body without depth, without intensity of experience, involvement, relationship. Church leaders have projected their passion onto women and homosexuals, equating passion with sex, and "broads" and "queers" with passion, making them scapegoats, virtually the bearers of the passion of the church.

That we who are feminist women (lesbian and straight) and gay men have come to symbolize passion is in its own way a tribute to us. It is, in fact, a tribute that many of us do not merit, for there are of course many women (lesbian and straight) and many gay men who are not passionate people. But through the eyes of ecclesiastical authority—Roman Catholic, Protestant, Episcopal—we are viewed as the archetypal carrier of passion. We are seen collectively as the character for whom Equus is God and lover: the boy who relates orgiastically—with sweat, panting, screams, and semen—to the created world around him. We are blown up into child-devouring monster proportions, living to lure, seduce, destroy whatever is pure, hence good.

---

*Address given on March 6, 1976. Heyward does not remember the exact occasion. It is included because it seems to have been the first occasion in her work that she used the concept of "passion."

And all around us, those who fear passion in themselves project it onto us gay men, lesbians, and other women, who in many cases also fear passion in ourselves and have nowhere to project it. So we swallow it. And like all fear swallowed whole, it contributes to emotional dis-ease, which in women is often labeled "depression" and in gays and lesbians "inversion." And people gawk at us and give us names not of our choosing, like "chick" and "doll" and "broad" and "fag" and "femme" and "butch" and "queer." They have called us names for so long that we begin to answer when we are called, to jump when the finger snaps, believing these names to be our own.

Feminist women and gay men have become a terrifying "other," a passionate "not-me" to many practicing heterosexual men and women; to many self-denying, self-denigrating homosexuals who cannot celebrate themselves because they have learned well to despise themselves; to many people writhing in the tension between active genitals and celibate psyches; and conversely to people caught in conflict between celibate genitals and sexually active psyches.

The Passion of Jesus—a term that traditionally has marked the period of time between, and including, the Last Supper and the crucifixion—was exactly that: a time during which Jesus bore the passion of his time, his culture, his religious heritage: Jesus, through whose passion his friends began to recognize their own; Jesus, for whom being human involved immersion in choices of real life and real death; Jesus, the passionate—lover of brothers and sisters, brother of many moods, person for whom all relationships bore bonds of intimacy; Jesus, whose passion—capacity for life and death—was a challenge, a threat, to those around him who were willing to settle for less than passion; less than living life and dying death; less than being full, abundant, electric with contemplative and relational energy; less than being fired up about matters of justice and dignity. Jesus, the compelling and terrifying Christ, to whom people are often drawn and from whom we simultaneously step back, because passionate people get clobbered. Like Jesus.

Taking cues from the very cultural forces that crucified Jesus, the church cultivates passionless people—more accurately, people who must deny their passion, their full capacities for living and dying—in order to be acceptable as priests, ministers, mothers, fathers, sons, daughters in the church and the rest of society. The church has hailed the dispassionate Logos—Word of a patriarchal Lord governing his earthly manor, whose sterile and pallid Son was born painlessly by an untouched Virgin—as that which is divine. Conversely, that which is *not* God—*not* the One in whose image we are created; that which is, for Christians, "not-me"—has been branded satanic, demonic, evil, passionate. For early Church Fathers, evil, woman, and sex were the same passionate phenomenon. "Evil," "woman," "sex," and "passion" became, in the history of Christian experience, different words for the same experience, the same demon, against which holy men believe they must contend for the sake of an antiseptic God, in whose pure image they are created and whose fatherly work they strive to accomplish—to curse passionate bodies and bless dispassionate souls.

What does this mean for us now in the church? It means, I believe, that the ordination of women and homosexuals, the Equal Rights Amendment, equal pay, equal employment opportunity, and equal rights for homosexuals and women—within and without the church—are worthy goals. It also means that, while these goals for basic rights are good ones, it is imperative that those of us involved in these struggles keep clearly in mind that the attainment of such goals is not enough. Ordaining women is not enough. Blessing gay/lesbian relationships is not enough. Open housing for homosexuals and equal employment for women are not enough. Women priests and gay/lesbian relationships can be every bit as passionless as many male priests and straight relationships have been; every bit as devoid of depth, humor, pain, joy, and fullness of capacity to really experience living or dying. We want more than this.

What we in the church must be about, I am convinced, is a return to religion of passion—a way of being in which anything less than spilling over with the Spirit of God is not enough; spilling over with desire to know and do the will of God in our daily work and play; with righteous and active indignation at injustice, with careful caring for others and self, with courage to stand up and be counted—when it counts; spilling over with integrity in relationship and with awareness of our oneness with all aspects and persons of creation, filling up and spilling over with the Passion of Jesus. This is what we must be about, within or without the religious institutions we have known.

A fair number of our ecclesiastical brothers accuse us of being radical feminists, lesbians, witches, anarchists, revolutionaries. These angry brothers do not realize what compliments they pay us! They do not realize (they do not care to realize) to what a long, strong line of passionate women they allude when they toss these epithets at my sisters and me. They do not know (they do not care to know) the strength and sensitivity of women who have cared more about honesty than seduction, and who have known that love without justice is not love at all. Those who curse us do not see (they do not open their eyes to see) the creative loving of women who have loved themselves not as shadowed half-reflections of male egos but as human beings created in the image of a holy God of power, wholeness, passion. The men who fear us have not felt (they have not dared to feel) the wise affections of women who love women and men not as sex objects but as sister and brother sojourners along a common way.

No, those who call us names, thinking they do us harm, do not know of whom, or to whom, they speak. They do not know us, and they shall not know us so cheaply. They do not know Mary, the mother of Jesus, woman of strong will, who stood in defiance of custom, Mary the strong mother of Jesus. They do not know Sappho, whose poetic spirit nurtured wounded souls by giving them power, Sappho, eloquent Sappho, who empowered those conceived and cultivated specifically to be powerless. They do not know Sojourner Truth, wise old Sojourner whose truth cut through the crap of the ecclesiastical and educational elitism that booed her, and issued forth in relationship between black and white, poor and rich, women and women, as sisters. My frightened brothers do not hear (they do not try to hear) what Gertrude Stein and Alice B. Toklas were saying to each other. They do not hear the passion of the Pankhursts, Virginia Woolf, Amelia Earhart, Mother Jones, the One and the Many who have cooked the meals, sown the gardens and sewn the clothes, borne the children, contemplated in convents, worked in factories, fought in wars, made love to sisters and brothers; women who have read and written and learned and taught and cared and cried and held on and held up those around them—and have stood there and listened to men tell them that they are unfit, too weak, too emotional to be taken seriously this time.

Those who say these things to us or behind our backs may, one day, any day, today, open their eyes and see that we move on. We are not waiting passively to be either understood or affirmed. We go on, rejoicing as we move, into the unknown, drawn passionately into the heart of Christian faith.

· 4 ·

The Enigmatic God*

Elie Wiesel, incarcerated in a concentration camp during World War II, tells of having watched a young boy his own age (about ten) and two adults being hanged by the Nazi soldiers. The adults cried out "Long live liberty!" And the child was silent. One of the witnesses asked another, "Where is God?" The response was silence. The boy struggled between life and death, dying an agonizingly slow death because his light weight prevented an immediately effective hanging. The prisoners—forced to march by the hanging site—passed the barely-clinging-to-life boy. The same witness asked again, "Where is God now?" And a voice within Wiesel replied, "Here God is—God is hanging here on this gallows." Wiesel speaks of the *utterly helpless* God.[1]

What of this God, this terrible good, this holy terror, this Father, Son, and Holy Spirit Trinity? This Mother Goddess giving us birth and taking us back again into her womb, the earth? This God of many faces, to whom has been ascribed many names? *Who is our God?* I ask believing, to quote one of my students, that "God does not mechanically answer our questions, but rather moves us to ask them." And unless we en-

*Adapted from a sermon given at Duke University Chapel, Durham, NC, winter 1977. The original sermon was published in *The Witness*, April 1978, and in *Spinning a Sacred Yarn* (New York: The Pilgrim Press, 1982), pp. 107–15.

counter God honestly—probing, seeking, risking offense—we do not encounter God at all.

In the beginning, long before there was any idea of God, something stirred. In that cosmic moment pulsating in possibility, God breathed into space and, groaning in passion and pain and hope, gave birth to creation. We cannot remember this easily, for we cannot easily bear to remember the pain and the hope of our own beginning. But it was good.

It was far better than we can imagine. For coming forth from God / in God / with God / by God, we were shaped by God, in God's own image, formed in the being of God, daughters and sons of God. With all created beings, we are reflections of / witnesses to God's own possibility. It was very, very good. For being created meant being *with* God. (To be *without* God would be not to be at all.)

James Weldon Johnson suggests that God created us because God was lonely. Various process theologians suggest that God created us because God needed us to help God continue to become. It may be that God created us simply because it is the nature of God to create, or that God created us because God, having begun to come to life Godself, realized that the only way to experience life is to share it.

And so we were created in God's own being, to move with God / in God / by God, into the passion and the pain and the wonder of creation.

Long after the dawn of creation, a small group of people in the Middle East began to speak to one another of God. Other people believed there were many gods: gods of rain, of sun, of war, of fertility, vying for supremacy. The people of Israel believed, however, that there is in fact one God who is the creator of all and who has created us in God's own image: to be one.

Now, God promised the people of Israel to go *with* them on the earth, empowering them to do what it is in the being of God *and* humanity to do: to love, to reach out to one another and to creation itself, aware of the worth and value of every created person and thing. God showed the people of Israel that God is not a far-distant God, spinning holy wheels off high in the sky, but rather is involved in creation, history, and human activity.

Long before Jesus, God made Godself known as One immersed in the affairs of being human. Human history is sacred history, the story of God's own being moving in creation itself.

The people of Israel wanted to know more about this God in whose being they were bound up. So Moses spoke to God and asked God what he, Moses, was to tell the people God's name was. For the Israelites there was much in a name—the revelation of a person's true character.

And God responded. God did not give a long list of credentials or a speech about power, authority, and might. God did not spell things out, but responded simply, "I AM WHO I AM" (Exod. 3:14; or, in other translations, "I AM WHAT I AM," or "I WILL BE WHAT I WILL BE").

God could hardly have given a more enigmatic reply, the sort that would be totally unacceptable to most of us, to admissions committees, teachers, or psychiatrists. We would be likely to hear "I am who I am" (in response to "Who are you?") as an impudent, defiant response. Certainly it was evasive. *God* was evasive. Moses could not pin God down. Approaching God in fear and tremors, seeking clarification, he is met with a riddle. *I am who I am.*

What about God is God saying?

Could it be that God is *not* being evasive, but rather clear, straightforward, and to the point? And that the point is that God *is*, in fact, evasive, elusive, not one to be pinned down, boxed into categories and expectations? God will be what God will be:

God will hang on the gallows.

God will inspire poets and artists.

God will be battered as a wife, a child, a nigger, a faggot.

God will judge with righteousness, justice, mercy those who batter, burn, sneer, discriminate, or harbor prejudice.

God will have a mastectomy.

God will experience the wonder of giving birth.

God will be handicapped.

God will run the marathon.

God will win.

God will lose.

God will be down and out, suffering, dying.

God will be bursting free, coming to life, for God will be who God will be.

If this is so, then God is suggesting to the people of Israel and to us that the very minute we think we "have" God, God will surprise us. As we search in fire and earthquakes, God will be in the still small voice. As we listen in silent meditation, God will be shouting protests on the street. God is warning us that we had best not try to find our security in any well-defined concept or category of what is Godly—for the minute we believe we are into God, God is off again and calling us forth into some unknown place.

God is saying something prickly to any of us who believe that our way is God's way—hence, the only way. God is alerting us to the fact that God's own growth and movement will not be stunted by our low tolerance for ambiguity and change. God will not be confined to our expectations of who God "ought" to be.

And God surely knows that most of us cannot bear much God. When God says, "I AM WHO I AM," our characteristic response is one of utter denial. We do not easily hear what God is saying. Instead, we opt for the creation of our own idol, one in which we can believe; a god-idol who, as Sister Corita Kent said, is "like a big Bayer aspirin." Take a little God, and you'll feel better.

But, what if:

In seeking to feel better, we are avoiding God's moving us toward growth?

In seeking God always as light, we are missing God as darkness?

In avoiding change, we are missing God's plea for us to move into the wonder of some unknown possibility?

In perceiving God as our Father, we are refusing to be nurtured at the breast of God our Mother?

In seeing God only in our own colors, shapes, styles, and ways of life, we are blinded to God's presence in others' colors, forms, and ways of being?

In looking for God in the magnanimous, that which is great, we are overlooking God in the most unremarkable places of our own lives?

In running from death, in trying to hold onto life, we are utterly missing the presence and power of God in aging, in letting go, in dying itself, in moving graciously in time with God?

In perceiving God always in that which is sacred, holy, otherworldly, religious, we are failing to see God in the secular, this world, the office, the home, the classroom, our day-to-day relationships, work and play?

What if, in seeking God always in the Bible, we are missing God in newspapers, novels, poetry, and everyday speech?

What if simply to be with God, live with God, know God, love God is enough—in living and dying?

The people of Israel had to struggle with this enigma. Their expectations of a Messiah who was to save the nation, beat down the enemies, rout out the wicked, suggests Israel's needs, and ours, for a God we can count on to bring us light, life, and victory. I AM WHO I AM is hard to bear. For being in this image/being WHO WE ARE is both a terror and a wonder, an adventure in living and dying—all with God, in God, in which terror and death do not lose their sting—but are experienced graciously.

And Jesus Christ did not clarify the enigmatic God. Jesus did not offer to help us put God into an incarnate box to be carried around and shown off as "God." Jesus did not come to reveal God's power, God's might, God's victory. Rather, Jesus came as one created in God/by God/empowered to move with God, into the pain, the passion, and the wonder of creation itself. Jesus accepted the vocation of being truly human in the image of an enigmatic God.

In Jesus, we are able to discern a person in whose human being God was made manifest, and a God in whose holy Being human life was lived fully. "Christ" is that way of being in which God and humanity, the creator and the created, the infinite and the finite, are experienced and manifested as One way of being.

Jesus Christ lived and died to show us what being human is all about. In Jesus, we see what it means to be a daughter or a son of God, to bear God's name; in Jesus, we perceive that being human, in the image of I AM WHO I AM, means simply that *we are who we are.*

As God's namesake, Jesus was who he was, free of all expectations and categories, defiant of any expectation that would stunt his growth as a person of God.

Jesus lived and died allowing himself, by God's grace, the freedom to be himself, regardless of customs, laws, and expectations that he be some other.

The people who wished him to be a political zealot found him to be a person of prayerful spirituality; those who wanted him to be a pious, sweet man discovered they had on their hands an offensive activist. To those who wanted him to be Messiah, he retorted, "Get thee behind me, Satan." And in the presence of those who wanted him to explain himself, he stood silently: enigmatic God reflected in enigmatic personhood.

When I probe the story of Jesus Christ, I realize that as Jesus was who he was, so too am I put here by God to be who I am. Jesus could not be who I am. I cannot be who Jesus was. My vocation as a person of God is not to imitate Jesus—not to try to recreate the being of a person who lived in a different world, in a different time, with different life experiences and possibilities. My vocation as a person of God is to live with God for God in God, in my own time, as graciously as I can.

Our business, our birthrights, and our beings are in God here now. As such, with individual interests and persuasions, we are together in One Christ: a way of being in which God's being and human being are experienced as one.

There are four qualities which, I believe, are ways of being with in God. No one of the four can stand alone. They are overlapping pieces of a whole cloth, the tapestry of creation itself: Wisdom, Passion, Justice, and Prayer.

Wisdom. Wisdom is a virtue close to the heart of God, we are told in scripture. Wisdom is the perception of the wholeness of all that is. The wise person knows that there is more to life than her/his own little world; that there is more to living than pursuing happiness. The wise person will face reality, ambiguity, and tension. S/he is able to live into, not flee from, matters of life and death.

Moreover, she will do everything she can to deal creatively, realistically, empathetically, with conviction, in her everyday comings and goings. She is no fool. She is aware that she is, God with her, put in this world, here and now, to participate fully in the affairs of this world, loving this world as God does, and using everything at her disposal to work cleverly and carefully, for the good of the whole.

Passion. As wisdom allows us to perceive the breadth of God and of creation, the wholeness of it all, so passion allows us to discern the depth. To be passionately involved in God, in life itself, is to be immersed in enigma—to experience one's own dying as the boy hangs on the gallows; to realize one's own shortcomings and capacities for wrongdoings when a President of the United States resigns; to realize the extent to which our lives are related—socially, politically, spiritually. In passion, we find our resources, our courage, our motivation, a way of being human as Jesus was human—in touch with others. In passion, we are aware that we—*all* of us (not just folks like ourselves)—are infused by the Spirit of God. This is what birth is all about, what creation is, and what baptism signifies. The human race is a holy-spirited people.

And the wise passionate person will know that Christ has as much to do with the secular arenas of our lives as the sacred; as much to do with the profane as with the holy; as much to do with the sexual, the political, the social, as with the spiritual. The passionate person who is wise will realize that God is just as present in the kitchen, the classroom, the hospital, the prison, the bed, as in church. The passionate person is one who can cut through to the heart of the matter, whatever the occasion, and discover God.

Justice. Suppose Jesus' friends had advised him to speak only of God and to stay out of religious and secular politics. Suppose they had warned him not to offend people. The Bible as a whole speaks of justice as "right-relationship" between and among people. Justice presupposes community as fundamental to human life with God. In justice, there is no such thing as a person living simply for him/herself. I am suspicious of anyone who tells me she or he has "found the Lord," or been "converted to Christ," or is "committed to Jesus" if that person is not committed to justice for *all* people—black, yellow, red, white; poor, rich; straight, gay, lesbian; sophisticated, simple; well educated, poorly educated; sick, healthy; male and female.

Some years ago, yearning for justice, I was saddened and angered by white governors blocking the doors to schools and universities to prevent black people from entering. Today, although the racial crisis in this country is far from resolved, other related crises continue to emerge among us. And I am fired up by, and compelled to call to account, state legislators who willingly put their own reelection, economic interests, and insecurities above clearly and simply affirming that "equality of rights under law shall not be denied or abridged by the United States or by any state on account of sex." I do not believe that a person who is truly aware of his/her birthright and responsibility to be with God in ongoing creation can sit back silently in this world. I believe we are compelled, and empowered, to risk whatever we must risk to create with God a climate in which all people can be who they are. It is a matter of doing justice, of standing up to be counted, a stand infused by the passion of the Holy Spirit; informed by wise perception of the wholeness, the breadth, the interdependence of the issues at hand; and empowered by prayer.

Prayer. The gospel that speaks most explicitly about social activism, Luke, is also the gospel in which Jesus is most often portrayed at prayer. Prayer is the opening up of oneself to the presence and power of God, perceiving what is invisible to the eye, and hearing what is inaudible to the ear.

Without prayer, passion may become restless, manic activity. Without prayer, wisdom is empty and becomes mere intellectualizing, the spinning of conceptual wheels to no particular end. Without prayer, for example, theology may be *about* God, but seldom draws us farther *into* God. Without prayer, justice is doomed to disillusionment because we are unable to see beyond what the eye can see, and all we see is injustice, a terror of vision that leads us eventually to rage, to futile outcry, to apathy; to feelings of helplessness, to violence, to suicide. In prayer, we hear and see that something is happening, stirring, moving, coming forth out of the awful pains and groans of labor and travail. Something is being born again and again wherever there is any justice, any wisdom, any passion among us/others. And, in prayer, we know well that this something is God—in us/with us/for us, carrying us along.

· 5 ·

Lesbianism and the Church[1]

Going with God is like unto a woman seeking goodly pearls; and, having found one pearl of great price, she went and sold all that she had, and bought it.

—Matthew 13:45–46 (paraphrase)

I am interested in lesbianism, specifically the situation of lesbians in the church: an issue, an experience, an existential process of being and becoming among many women who are going with God and who, in so doing, are participating, knowingly or unknowingly, in shaking the foundations of the Christian church: its theology, its ethics, its liturgies and polities, its structures. We see through a glass darkly that ecclesiastical foundations are being shaken so relentlessly by the issue of sexuality that within the next few decades, we who care will find (1) that we have given in to ecclesiastical anguish and made peace with an institution whose ways are not ours; (2) that we have departed the ecclesiastical institutions rather than sell the pearl of great price; or (3) that the church—through words and action—will be in a process of divesting itself of certain ancient theological, ethical, and political norms in order to invest itself in the ongoing, creative being with God, who is Godself the source, the giver, the essence of all that we name as sexual.

I am a person essentially defiant of categories. I remember myself as a child who (like many children) lived with a wisdom (Sophia): an imaginary playmate, in my case, named Sophie Couch—whom I outgrew. My experiences, buoyed by imagination, permitted few categories or lines of clear demarcation between who I was and who I was not, or between the values of being a human, an animal, or a plant as member of God's creation. I was not bound early or easily by such categories as white and black, child and adult, male and female, let alone by such arbitrary concepts as masculine and feminine. Only later, much later, was I to learn that such boundaries are necessary to the maintenance of the established social order; that in order to function "normally" in this society, I had to be clear on what I was, category by category, what I was as distinct from what I was *not*: "colored," male, communist, atheist, "common." Such clarity about the lines that divide us enables us to develop strong egos and stable personalities, and to become "normal" individuals. Or so we are led to assume. A lack of clarity surely manifests itself in the disintegrated, pathological, "abnormal" self. The categories were abundant. My clarity was keen: I was Christian, white, "refined," good, smart, talented, female, and, with God's help, hopeful of being very, very "feminine." My wise little friend, Sophie Couch, had long since departed with my imagination, and there I was, at age thirteen, within a stone's throw of becoming the All-American Girl, cheerleader, class president, debutante, *Who's Who*, dean's list, church leader, Girl Friday to the clergy, and, farther along, by the grace of the divine Patriarch, the wife of a priest and the mother of his sons.

Many secret crushes on strong women and men came and went, people in whom I yearned for reunion with Sophie Couch. Many offices, honors, and awards passed. Many pastors, counselors, and therapists came my way. Several proposals for marriage came too. Many years of clarity and confusion passed—times of thrills and heartbreaks, moments/days/weeks/months of running fast toward some goal and even faster away from it. And, after more than a decade of searching for goodly pearls and for some sense of relatedness that made sense to me and of me, there—tucked away deep within me—I found my soul. My Sophie soared imaginatively through my being, toward all that has been, all that is, all that will ever be, within me, beyond me, around me, in awareness of my relation to all members of creation. I found myself, both unique in all the world and involved, organically/inextricably, in the living and dying of all persons and creatures. I found myself, my being in relationship to that One/God who moves among us all, together. I found the pearl of great price. And I realized that my relatedness to God, and to all, is at once spiritual and sexual. And there was no way, and there is no way, for me to know sexuality as that fundamental human yearning for meaningful relationship without knowing that, to the extent that I am yearning for meaningful relationship with people who are men, I am yearning sexually for men; and that to the extent that I am yearning for meaningful relationship with people who are women, I am yearning sexually for women; and to the extent that I am open to and yearning for relationship with God, or with people, or with other aspects of creation, I am alive and yearning sexually—period.

For it is not just with my intellect or with my emotions that I yearn, but with *myself*—every bone in my body, every nerve under my skin, every orifice in my being, everything that I am—that I reach out, and take in, and give out, and hold onto, and let go, and move with, whether in bed with a lover, on my knees in prayer, in class with students, at the altar in Holy Communion, or romping in the yard with my dog. And so that is who I am, one in whose life the categories are confluent rather than definitive or divisive: spirituality and sexuality are a common relational current; homosexuality and heterosexuality may be descriptive dimensions of a human being/any human being/the *same* human being; and that which we name "divine" is also that which we name "human" when any person reaches for meaningful relationship. It seems to me that we are talking about incarnation and atonement. God is with us, yearning to be born again, and again, in relationship within, between, and among us.

The dominant themes in Christian tradition have undercut in no small way our capacity for such yearning. Because yearning implies some *unknown* One for whom we yearn, it is an almost unintelligible quest for meaningful relatedness. And Christian thought—what the church has taught—has from its early days attempted to locate, define, and map out the "right," and only, way to God. Consider the ongoing battles the church has waged against various heresies and practices, agnosticism, and even questions that might suggest alterations or evolutions in the orthodox rendition of Yahweh as our God and Father: God is *not* darkness, God is light. God is *not* death, God is life. God is *not* irrational, God is rational. God is *not* Mother, God is Father. God is *not* of the flesh, God is of the Spirit. God is *not* sexual, God is spiritual.

In each and every case, "God" is in whatever those who have done the defining in a patriarchal religion and culture perceive to be, essentially, that which controls chaos—and creativity. God, in light, overcomes darkness; God, in life, conquers death. God, as rational Logos, brings logic to irrationality. God, in spirit, is stronger than the flesh. God the Father penetrates and uses, at his will, the female recipient of his initiative. And spirituality is a weapon employed tenaciously against death, darkness, chaos, woman, and sexuality, which have been defined, implicitly or explicitly, throughout the history of the church, as evil. And our anxieties about our sexual selves have been hardly less great than our fear of death, the final and absolute phenomenon beyond our control.

I offer these observations to suggest that the ecclesiastical tremor toward sexuality is formidable, and that we who ask that church polity and theology be reformed in celebration of women and sexuality are, in fact, asking that a vast cosmic consciousness be raised and opened to its own revolution. It is no wonder that countless thousands, perhaps millions, of women were burned as witches during the Middle Ages—usually for sexual offenses. We should have expected that many Christians would go into convulsions over the ordination of Bill Johnson (the first openly gay man to be ordained as a minister in the United Church of Christ), and that the Episcopal Bishop of New York would be subjected to greater harassment after his ordination to the priesthood of Ellen Barrett (an open lesbian) than he received either about controversial civil rights advocacy or as he ran through the streets of Saigon. It is much more amazing that you and I would assume that we can help change the church's teachings about homosexuality. But some of us believe that we can do something, and that something must be done. And we who do believe that change can happen and that we must participate in it will suffer much and long, whether we call ourselves gay or lesbian or straight or bisexual, whether we are single or married, older or younger. The extent of our commitment depends on how much we value the pearl of great price.

Feminism is a cultural revolution steeped in values that are shared by many women and some men. We believe that woman's equality to man is a matter not simply of raising women's pay, providing women with child-care centers, ordaining women, or addressing women as "Ms." Rather, the feminist commitment is to work collectively toward the transformation of all cultural assumptions about the inherent nature of woman and of man, the purpose of sex, and the role of gender in relationships between the sexes and among members of the same sex.

It should come as no surprise that, with feminist impact, significant numbers of men and women (including many who are not or would not claim to be feminists) are more open now than a decade ago not only to intimate relationship with members of the same sex and to the possibilities of expressing this intimacy in physical ways, but also to acknowledging to self and others that this is so—and that it is good. There is an enormous difference between consciousness expressed about homosexuality in such films of the past decade as *The Fox* and *The Boys in the Band* (in which homosexuality is dealt with sensitively and poignantly, but as a rather pathetic grasping after straws)—and current celebrations of homosexuality as really very fine, heralded publicly in such slogans as "Gay is good"/"Gay and proud" and, increasingly, in feminist music, poetry, paintings, and prose.

In discussions about homosexuality with gay men, I have learned how little I understand the experiences of male homosexuals. And so, I will not attempt to say much about gay men in particular. I can make few constructive comparisons between the situations in which gay men and lesbians find ourselves. I believe our commonality to be deeper and stronger than our differences. For while our differences derive from the separate cultural expectations in which women and men have been steeped, the commonality lesbians and gay men share is that all of us are yearning for meaningful relationship in a society in which we are absolutely forbidden to seek and to find such relationship with members of our own sex.

The situation that lesbians and gay men share is difficult enough outside the boundaries of institutional religion. Witness the sentiments expressed in antihomosexual campaigns spurred by those who seek to "protect" society; the fights and plights of gay men and lesbians in the armed services; the struggles of lesbian mothers for custody of their children; and the struggles of lesbians interrogated and jailed by grand juries. Within the church itself, the situation is more complex, for not only do we contend with the norms of civil religion, whose standards of sexual morality are strong and effective both within and without the church, but, moreover, the entirety of the church's theology and structure is held fast and firm by the ancient proscription of sex outside marriage as destructive, evil, and a sin against God. Then too, church law is fastened more deeply than civil law in a ban against adventuring into the unknown or the uncontrollable ("God" is synonymous with Ultimate Control). Increasingly, small step by small step, in the secular arena of our corporate life, women and homosexuals have civil law on our side, while in the sacred arena of corporate life—in institutional religion—men with power are likely to fight ferociously against any significant advocacy of women or of homosexuals. Churches will attempt to strangle every effort of women, lesbians, and gays toward an active, lively, and celebrative expression of who we are.

I will go so far as to suggest that while the churches lead occasionally in our work for justice in society as a whole, among institutional leaders church leaders will be the last to venture into the celebration of sexuality as good and right, so strong is the historical Christian theological mandate against sexuality and against woman, who is held, if only preconsciously, to be the bearer of sexuality *to* man.

Lesbians, unlike gay men, thus bear the burden not only of being homosexual in a church in which sexuality is held to be evil, sex outside marriage indefensible, and homosexuality itself perverse, but moreover of being female in a church in which woman has long borne the psychological, social, and theological burden of being what is—by definition—chaotic, irrational, mysterious, unknown, uncontrollable, and deadly: i.e., sexual. Make no mistake about it, as homosexual, yes, but even more significantly, as *woman*, Ellen Barrett is carrying the burden of sexuality for many gay men who are able to sit back and cheer quietly as she is engulfed by a rage and a terror that priests and bishops throughout the Episcopal Church have spent their lives eluding in the corners of their closets.

In every happy lesbian, the church is encountered by a woman who has said *no* to traditional marriage; *yes* to her own body and to sexuality; and *yes* to what has been traditionally defined as chaotic, irrational, mysterious, unknown, uncontrollable: *woman*.

In the untransformed Christian consciousness, lesbianism is an implicit and bold NO to the God that is limited, by definition, within the categories of light, Logos, and Father. The unrepentant lesbian, by her very being—proud and gay—is a sign of new religion/new consciousness/new faith, in which there is no patriarchal authority and no space for male definition of who or what woman is, should be, or will be. This much we should remember, whether or not we who are lesbian want to signify such transformation, whether or not we wish to signify such change. Regardless of how orthodox or heterodox an individual lesbian may be in her faith and practice, if she is happy, bold, and clear about herself, her very being is a threat to the Christian church as we know it. Ellen Barrett is a mild-mannered Anglo-Catholic, whose intention has not been to revolutionize the theology of the Episcopal Church. But because she is a lesbian, Ellen Barrett is perceived to be wielding a sword at the throat of the orthodox faith and practice of catholic Christendom.

I think we should not take lightly the ramifications of who we are, but rather live into these embodied implications, for the sake of both ourselves and the Christian church. For we are participants in a slow but positive transformation of the ecclesial institution from being an antisexual misogynist space to a Body at once human and divine, spiritual and sexual. What then might our tasks include in this work of transformation?

1. To cultivate ourselves as people open to/yearning for meaningful relationship—with God, with one another, female and male, female and female, male and male, relation of mutual respect, freedom, and love for the very process of the yearning that takes us always into new discoveries within, between, and among ourselves. It is not easy to live with integrity as relational process, but I believe it is impossible to really live without it.

2. To express thoughtfully and boldly this experience in our theology, our liturgy, and certainly in our lives as ministers, teachers, pastors, counselors, friends, and lovers, not accepting the concept of a closed/finished Christian tradition as viable for open, changing people. I can only speak for myself when I say that it is precisely because I do *not* believe the life, teachings, death, and resurrection of Jesus Christ to be categorically contained within a closed system of symbols and thought that I remain within the institutional church. I am finding the most radical position to be *within* the church, for only from within can we search for and find those roots that have as much to do with contemporary daily experience as with the tomes and teachings of the past. As we dig, we press into a vision of what we are meant to be about as people of God.

3. To stand defiant of all external, and most internal, attempts at categorizing ourselves—except insofar as we must state, again and again, as our sisters and brothers are harassed and punished, deprived and humiliated, because either they or others call them gay or lesbian, that *we too are gay/lesbian.* Insofar as we have any idea of what it means to love people because they are people, *we are gay/lesbian.* Insofar as we refuse to accept passively the clinical and ecclesiastical definitions of "normality" and "righteousness" in sexual relationships, *we are gay/lesbian.* Insofar as I am open to the possibility of reaching out and touching deeply the life and being of a sister, *I am a lesbian—and I am good*—and in that one single affirmation, the groan of good Christian "gentlemen" can be heard echoing back two thousand years. And we must say again and again that we are good, and not simply our feelings or our caring, but also our activity, our

flesh, the lovemaking that may ensue between/among us. Our passion—the whole of who we are—is good in our yearning for relationship, in which there is no dualism between body and soul, flesh and spirit, desire and activity, doer and deed.

4. To work hard, together and alone, for justice for women and homosexuals in and beyond the church. This will mean education, caucusing, taking risks, losing face—maybe jobs—and receiving pleas for caution in our activities, usually in the guise of political expediency, such as being told that what we are doing or saying is counterproductive—the favorite charge, I have learned, from liberal churchmen.

5. To be on guard against the wiles, however unintentional, of people who say they are "liberal"—which is most of us much of the time—and who, therefore, must "study" the issues some more before taking action; or who want to get a clear "consensus of the faithful" before making an unequivocal statement; or who have other issues that "take priority" over sexuality, which after all is a "concern of only a few people." No battle in the church on the issue of sexuality will be won without the liberals, but few liberals will take a firm and just stand on this (or any other ethical issue) until *we* make the issue more trouble to overlook than to confront. We must make clear and visible the fact that sexuality is good—by the boldness, visibility, and articulateness of our lives as we yearn for relationship, and, as we find it, of expressing it, among ourselves, in our theologies, in our liturgies, our teachings, our questions.

6. To struggle against the acting out of the old sex-role norms in our relationships with same and other sex, in order to diffuse, in our own lives—for our sake and for others' sakes—the uses of power and control to avoid intimacy and to master the unknown. Each time we are captivated in a power-laden struggle for domination and control, or for submission and being controlled, whether in bed or in church, we short-circuit the yearning for relationship into which we flow, and we instead participate in the ongoing building of a world order, an ecclesiastical order, and personal relationships founded on an inability to appreciate the mystery and the process of becoming at one with God and creation itself. In so doing, we further cement the

concepts and reality of domination, control, and categories—all to the demeaning of women and sexuality, of human life and God.

7. To seek community with gay men and to refuse to allow ourselves to be used as the scapegoat for their sexuality. We should not forget that we are just as vulnerable in the church as women as we are as lesbians. We can support our brothers, but we cannot give them the pearl of great price.

8. To come into self-discovery in discovering the roots of the yearning for meaningful relationship. We need time and space by ourselves to appropriate the fresh sense of our worth and value as persons rooted in love with all living things. In discovering these common roots, we find God-with-us, She who has been there all along. And coming home, at the bosom of God, embraced by friends and lovers, delighted with our shared work and pleased to have our separate rooms, we are well on our way.

· 6 ·

Theological Explorations of Homosexuality[1]

In the beginning, I AM WHO I AM created everything that lived and grew and changed and wondered and tried and stretched and cuddled and recoiled. Every plant, every rock, every animal, every person. Everything created was to realize itself the relationship of all created things to I AM WHO I AM. This process, of realizing oneself and all creation in relationship to the Creator, people began to call "spirituality."

The Creator, I AM WHO I AM, could find no adequate word for this process except "love." I AM WHO I AM realized that loving means changing and becoming something new, and that in loving, the plants and the rocks and the animals and the people were changing and becoming a new creation, and that it was good. I AM WHO I AM began to realize that even Creators change and that, in loving, I AM WHO I AM had become I AM BECOMING WHO I AM BECOMING.

A young person with assorted ups and downs—run-of-the-mill problems, dreams, pipe dreams, goals, fantasies; sexually and spiritually potent, a well-adjusted and intense child and teenager—I did not experience my sexual adolescence until my early twenties. This was not atypical among my female peers. I had no active sexual relationship even of a "petting" variety until I was twenty-two. Prior to that, I had experienced only mild anxiety and curiosity about sex. I was not sure what it entailed. I imagined it to be rather disgusting and not something to which I should look forward. Theoretically, I had surmised that sex was basically wrong, except maybe in marriage, and I was not even sure about that.

During these teen years, when sex was for me a nonissue, I moved into what I would characterize now as my spiritual adolescence. I loved "God." And even more than "God," I loved the church—in my case, the Episcopal Church and its Anglo-Catholic traditions—the priests, the vestments, the smells and sounds and silences in the church. I prayed the rosary. I made confession. I was immersed in a spirituality that despises physicality. If I could not be a priest I would be a nun, and for several years I planned toward this vocation.

What spirituality had been for me as a teenager—*a yearning for meaningful relationship of deep significance*— sexuality soon became for me as a young woman. In both instances, my adolescence was marked by my need to locate and secure an object for my yearning as quickly as possible and as indiscriminately as necessary. So, what the "God" of my spiritual adolesence had been—a wholly Other, magical, beautiful Superman, manifest in ecclesiastical splendor—so too did a variety of men and women become, in my sexual adolescence, objects of adoration, of projection, and of a complete absorption of my being.

I do not now look upon my spiritual adolescence and my sexual adolescence as unfortunate, but rather as necessary steps along the way in my own becoming. In fact, I recall these experiences with gratitude. What they taught me is that the yearning within me for meaningful relationship to help me validate my own being is, in fact, simultaneously a sexual and a spiritual yearning for relationship and that this yearning is not only good, but that which brings me to life, to risk, to courage, to commitment, to passion, to vocation, to feelings, to sisters and brothers, and, yes, to God.

The experience I can cite as an initiation into coming of age, spiritually *and* sexually, was my ordination to the priesthood of the Episcopal Church in Philadelphia. The integrity in which spirituality and sexuality are realized as one flow of being, relating us both to God and to sisters and brothers, enables self-validation. It is God-with-us as opposed to a dependence on validation by ecclesiastical mandate or by persons to whom we have given over the power and authority to tell us who we are, be they lovers, spouses, or institutional leaders.

Coming of age, I find that I am resistant to categories, including sexual categories such as homosexual, heterosexual, bisexual. I resist categories not primarily, I think, because of what may happen to me when people realize that I yearn for and find relationship—spiritual, sexual relationship—with people who are women; not because I believe my sexuality to be my private business (sometimes the opposite of "private" is not "public" but rather "communal responsibility"). Rather, I resist categories because, to quote a friend and student, "Being human—being sexual—is not a matter of 'qualitative analysis,'" in which relationships of highest value are genital equations: "Woman plus woman equals lesbian; woman plus man equals straight."

God's being is in loving—that is, in involvement in, immersion in, in passionate relationship to, God's own creation, respecting and cherishing that which makes each member or aspect of creation uniquely who, or what, it is and is becoming. God is Godself defiant of categories and qualitative analysis.

God is not alone as lover—the one who loves. Fundamental to the doctrines of creation and incarnation is the *human* capacity to love. Being human means being self-consciously (not necessarily rationally) able to love and be loved: involved in, immersed in, related passionately to God and to human beings, respecting and cherishing that which makes each loved one uniquely who she or he is and is becoming—be this loved one male or female, black or white, old or young, sick or well.

Loving is one flow of being, stirred within us by the power of the Holy Spirit. One has only to read the prayers of Christian mystics like Julian of Norwich, Teresa of Avila, and John of the Cross to encounter the *eroticism of agape: the sexuality of spiritual love.*

But what of the separations we have made between agape

and eros? between sexuality and spirituality? between the flesh and the spirit? and, derivative of the same, between sexual orientation and sexual behavior?

I believe the theological root of the problem to be a dualistic world view, in which lines of demarcation are drawn between the sacred and the profane, the religious and the secular, heaven and hell, God's realm and the arenas of this world. One example of this dualism is manifest in a press release by the Evangelical Catholic Congress, in which its leaders decry "the invasion of the church by the world," the implication being that the church is good and the world bad.

Whether our incarnational theologies are focused finally on Jesus as the unique and singular revelation of God to the world, or on Jesus as the representation of our own possibilities to bear Christ to the world, in Christ we perceive what we believed to be "divine" (out there, far away) and what we believed to be "human" (us, here, now) together in one reality. In Christ, God and humanity are, in a single glance through a glass darkly, perceived to be in unity. The dualism is shown for what it was all along: a delusion. And the value-laden schism between sacred and secular, spirit and body, is seen as false.

To speak negatively of sexuality, which the larger body of orthodox tradition has done, is to portray a cosmos in which God and spiritual things exist "up there" and creation, humanity, and physical things exist "down here." Spiritual things are above and are intended to overcome physical things. The Creator and the creation are seen to be at odds.

Historically, sexuality has been the living symbol of that which is physical, of this world, of the flesh, uncontrollable, orgasmic. Within the Judeo-Christian tradition, heavily influenced by Hellenism's Platonic dualism, sexuality has been posited as the enemy of spiritual development.

But theological propositions such as this do not fall out of the sky. They are rooted in experiences of sexuality and of spirituality. And one is left wondering what experiences prompted Jerome, for example, to say that since angels have no sexual organs and that since we someday are to become angels, we ought now to model ourselves after angels and act as though we have no sexual organs. I find myself wondering if sexuality is experienced as nonspiritual because God is experienced as non-physical; and, if so, how seriously these early Church Fathers really took the incarnation. Or is the fear of sexuality, perhaps, a fear of losing control? Ultimately of losing *all* control (dying)? Or, again, is the rejection of sexuality built by these men upon a rejection of women? Indeed women are held, theologically, to be nearly synonymous with that which is "not God": evil, tempting, uncontrollable, seducing men into "fall" and bringing men to death. It is hard to know which is cause and which is effect.

But it is not hard to know or imagine why homosexuality has been considered such an anathema. It is sexual. It is not in marriage (the only possible legitimating parameter for sexuality). It is for pleasure in companionship rather than for the duty of procreation (sexuality's theological justification). Moreover, homosexuality is seen to be orgasmic, wild, uncontrollable, hedonistic. It is viewed by men as men's attempts to be "like women" (read: sexual, physical, nonspiritual) and as women's attempt to reject men (read: that which is good).

I would characterize homosexuality not as a matter of sexual preference nor simply as sexual activity between persons of the same sex, but rather as a way of being in relationship to persons of the same sex that is rooted in one's yearning for relationship that is meaningful. Like heterosexuality, homosexuality may find expression in acts of relationship that would naturally include touching and being touched by one's friend, one's lover, whether the touch be a physical expression as in an embrace or in genital contact; a matter of emotional vulnerability; an essentially spiritual affinity, or all three.

It is possible, of course, to deny one's homosexuality just as it is possible to deny one's heterosexuality, to the effect that homosexuality involves an aversion to touching or being touched by persons of the same sex—whether the touching be physical, emotional, spiritual. This denial, or refusal to be one's own sex, or the opposite sex, I believe to be unnatural, unhealthy, and unholy.

The fundamental ethical questions regarding sexuality— questions of commitment and loyalty between people, of mutual responsibility in relationship, and of participation in the shaping of a society in which people can be nurtured with justice as individuals in community—are rooted, I believe, not in people's refusals to touch or to make contact with one another. Whether one's experience is homosexual, heterosexual, or both, the immorality in relationship results primarily from a fear of really being known by and knowing another. Hence, the inability to make commitment; to be vulnerable to another; to be honest either in conflict or at peace; to sustain interest in loving relationship once it is found; or to realize actively that loving does indeed involve fear and loss and death, and that these experiences within relationships are givens. They are reality to be entered into and experienced, not to be fled from. Loneliness, separation, promiscuity. The boxing off of genitals from really touching and being touched. These things are more often than not the results of our alienation from ourselves as lovers—of God, of each other, of creation itself.

We have a long way to go. It is a frightening time of spiritual and sexual transformation, in which our consciousness of who we are—individually and collectively—is expanding. We must be careful. We must be tender. We must be open to new discovery. We must keep our courage, which is to say that we must keep in mind that God is with us. Whenever we believe that we are right, we must claim no authority over others, realizing that those who make no claim to authority over others are those in whom true authority may be perceived. We must not forget that we—like the lilies of the field—are becoming who we are becoming in the image of a God who is becoming. Finally, in this present crisis, we may find it helpful to remember that the Chinese ideogram for "crisis" is "a dangerous opportunity."

· 7 ·

Blessing the Bread: A Litany[1]

In the beginning was God
In the beginning
    the source of all that is
In the beginning
    God yearning
    God moaning
    God laboring
    God giving birth
    God rejoicing

And God loved what she had made
And God said,
    "It is good."
And God, knowing that all that is good is shared
held the earth tenderly in her arms
God yearned for relationship
God longed to share the good earth
And humanity was born in the yearning of God
We were born to share the earth

In the earth was the seed
In the seed was the grain

In the grain was the harvest
In the harvest was the bread
In the bread was the power

And God said,
    "All shall eat of the earth.
    All shall eat of the seed.
    All shall eat of the grain.
    All shall eat of the harvest.
    All shall eat of the bread.
    All shall eat of the power."

God said,
    "You are my people,
    My friends,
    My lovers,
    My sisters,
    And brothers
    All of you shall eat
    Of the bread
    And the power
    And shall eat."

Then God, gathering up her courage in love, said,
"Let there be bread!"
And God's sisters
her friends and lovers
knelt on the earth
planted the seeds
prayed for the rain
sang for the grain
made the harvest
cracked the wheat
pounded the corn
kneaded the dough
kindled the fire
filled the air
with the smell of fresh bread

And there was bread!
And it was good!

We the sisters of God say today,
    "All shall eat of the bread,
    And the power.
    We say today,
    All shall have power
    And bread.
    Today we say,
    Let there be bread!
    Let there be power!
    Let us eat of the bread
    and the power!
    And all will be filled
    For the bread is rising!"

By the power of God
Women are blessed
By the women of God
The bread is blessed
By the bread of God
The power is blessed
By the power of bread
The power of women
The power of God
The people are blessed
The earth is blessed
And the bread is rising!

PART II

Touching

Don't be duped by folks who talk about "God" all the time. It's more critical to make the connections among ourselves. And a hell of a lot more honest.

· 8 ·

Ruether and Daly: Speaking and Sparking / Building and Burning[1]

Rosemary Ruether speaks. Mary Daly "sparks." Ruether builds bridges to the future church and Daly burns them. Ruether takes care to be tender and Daly traumatizes. Ruether tosses us lifelines and Daly pulls them in, leaving us to swim or to sink. Ruether evokes my nod, my commitment, my Yes! Daly provokes my fist to clench, my stomach to spasm, my silent voice to shriek No! Two women with something to say that is worth our hearing, each writing out of a Roman Catholic heritage, each engaged in "the service of passionate commitment" (Ruether) to liberation, having at a not-so-distant time shared the vision Daly articulated in 1968.

> In the exercise of a self-transcending creative activity, inspired and driven forward by faith and hope, sustained by courage, men and women can learn to set their pride beyond the sexual differentiation. Working together on all levels they may come at last to see each other's faces, and in so doing, come to know themselves.[2]

Today Daly and Ruether have become probably the most prominent representatives among North American feminists of two radically disparate theological positions. Daly has left the church and has begun to construct a postchristian world in which she and her sister "Amazons" are "spinning" and "sparking" their lives as separate from the world of men and non-feminist women.[3] Ruether has remained in the church and, with other feminist Christians, is attempting to untangle the mangled sexist roots of the Judeo-Christian tradition on the basis of her lingering hope that church people will join in working together for a redeemed humanity, involving ourselves in the future of God.[4]

It would be simplistic and incorrect to assert, as some do, that Daly has "moved" while Ruether has not. In the past ten years, both have moved radically—Daly into postchristian feminist spirituality, Ruether into liberation theology inclusive of various oppressed peoples. Nor is it correct to suggest, as some do, that Daly's movement out of Christianity has been motivated by an overwhelming and irrational bitterness, while Ruether's apparent stability within the church is sustained by a patience of spirit.

Both are tough women. Neither is patient with injustice. Each has a record, well established among feminist theologians, of professional struggle for women's rights. And, to be sure, both Mary Daly and Rosemary Ruether continue to bear the burden of male projection onto them of all that is terrorizing and most threatening about women in search of sexual liberation.

We would need to know more than we do about the respective biographical journeys of these two women to begin to understand when, how, and why their current differences began to develop. This information I do not have, so I am in no position to speculate as to the causes of their theological divergence. I can, however, discuss the consequences of their positions as these affect me, other feminists, and other church people.

Epistemological Starting-points

First, I want to examine some apparent presuppositions—assumptions and implicit values—in the works of Daly and

Ruether, beginning with an inquiry into their respective methods of doing theology. Theological method—the way in which a theologian goes about her work—is founded, most basically, on her presuppositions: What does she most value? What assumptions—examined or unexamined—does her work reflect? To begin at this point is to begin to unravel or "a-maze" (Daly) some of the significant differences between Ruether's and Daly's theological postures.

I must confess my own bias. I am fond of Rosemary Ruether. I am moved by her sensibilities as well as her commitment to justice in all quarters of human life. I have some difficulty with Mary Daly. This is partly a matter of personal history in relationship to Daly, an earlier relationship marked more by my curiosity than by any mutuality between us as sisters. But it may be also a matter of anxiety-laden resistance to the theological tenets of this "Female Fury," this "revolting Hag."[5]

In this essay I have attempted to take Daly with the same seriousness and appreciation that I give to Ruether. I am aware that just as I am drawn to Ruether—in part because in her work I recognize aspects of my own with which I am comfortable (such as working to reform the church)—it may be that I am put off by Daly in part because in her work I encounter aspects of my own with which I am uncomfortable (such as the possibly infinite incapacity of the church to take women seriously in a fundamental way).

Some years ago I wrote, "I am unwilling to participate in a game of plastic smiles, new committees, old study projects; a game of watching and waiting as my sisters and I suffocate in coerced compliance . . . a game called 'church.' "[6] Still today I suffocate. I watch. I wait. And I participate. Ruether speaks to me as she always has, and Daly calls me to spin.

The most basic presumption and value that any of us brings to the doing of theology falls under the philosophical rubric of epistemology: How is it that we know what we know? On what basis does the theologian claim to know anything—about God, and Christ, about the meaning of history, and so forth? How does the theologian see herself—the knowing subject—in relation to other people, the world, the cosmos—the known object? The lasting value of any theology is dependent in large measure on the credibility of the theologian's epistemology—her capacity to convince her readership, students, or audience that her knowledge of the relationship between the human and the divine is grounded in her own integrity.

For the purposes of this essay, two epistemological positions should be noted: subjective idealism and Marxist realism. Idealist epistemology is an Enlightenment-conditioned theory of knowledge, which holds that all knowledge is literally "in the mind of" the knower. All knowledge is dependent on the autonomous reason and sense perception of the individual theologian, whose ideas are themselves the shapers of reality. Karl Marx challenged this theory with his epistemologically revolutionary thesis that the purpose of knowledge is not to understand the world but to change it, and that the world is not changed by ideas (central to the idealist position), but rather that ideas are changed by the work of people in the world.

Marxist epistemology is grounded in a post-Enlightenment recognition of the social reality of specific groups (classes) of people who, in their daily work, give shape to ideas or expressions of social reality (including religion and theology). The idealist emphasis is on the individual theologian and her power of right perception. For Marx, the emphasis is on the community as context of the theologian's work and on her involvement in the work of the community. The idealist expresses primarily herself, her own ideas. The Marxist attempts to articulate the meaning of the work of her people.

It seems to me that Mary Daly, like most traditional Catholic and Protestant thinkers, operates primarily on the epistemological assumptions of a subjective idealism; and that Rosemary Ruether, like a number of Latin American liberation theologians as well as politically radical European theologians such as Dorothee Sölle, does her work on the basis of a Marxist understanding of knowledge. If this is true, issue might be taken with Carol Christ's labeling of Daly as "revolutionary" and Ruether as "radical reformist," for it would seem that a theologian whose operative foundation is that of social praxis is revolutionary in a more realistic sense than an idealist whose revolution rests on the power of her ideas.[7]

Clarifying as such labels may be, however, they can also be

deceptive. In this case, they are. For while I perceive the epistemological distinctions as set forth above to be accurate, I would maintain also that Daly is creatively revolutionary (or, in her word, "revolting") in some ways that Ruether is not experienced to be, and that Ruether's theological praxis is not yet as fundamentally critical of and offensive to Christians as it must become if she (and we with her) are effectively to challenge—and change—the domination-submission motif of what she has called the "phallic cult" of Christendom, even insofar as to create among ourselves within the church a community of powerful sisters.

A-Mazing the Phallic Myth

Daly is a philosopher and myth-maker first, a theologian second (if at all, according to her definition of theology as that which legitimates patriarchy).

> If the word "theology" can be torn free from its usual limited and limiting context . . . then my book can be called an effort to create theology as well as philosophy. For my purpose is to show that *the women's revolution, insofar as it is true to its own essential dynamics, is an ontological spiritual revolution, pointing beyond the idolatries of sexist society and sparking creative action in and toward transcendence.*[8]

Essential. Ontological. Spiritual. Pointing beyond—toward transcendence. These words suggest a metaphysician who may be more closely akin to the classical Greek tradition than to her own Thomist heritage. It is difficult to imagine what "revolution" means for Daly apart from her own suggestion, in both her later books, that she is primarily committed to the revolutionizing of women's consciousness whereby we can "transcend" the limits of patriarchy (read: world, church, culture itself), "spinning and sparking" within and among ourselves in our own paradise.

> Our beautiful, spiral-like designs are the designs/purposes of our bodies/minds. We communicate these through our forcefields, our auras, our O-zones. We move backward over the water, toward the Background. We gain speed. Argonauts move apart and together, forming and reforming our Amazon Argosy. In the rising and setting of our sister the sun, we seek the gold of our hearts' desire. In

the light of our sisters the moon and stars we rekindle the Fore-Crone's fire. In its searing light we see through the fathers' lies of genesis and demise; we burn through the snarls of the Nothing-lovers.[9]

From metaphysics to mythology: The creation of transcendence, rising above languages and images of world, church, culture itself.

> Gynocentric writing means risking. Since the language and style of patriarchal writing simply cannot contain or carry the energy of women's exorcism and ecstasy, in this book I invent, dis-cover, re-member. At times I make up words. . . . At times I have been conscious of breaking almost into cantations, chants, alliterative lyrics.[10]

As a myth-maker, Daly looks like an inverted Rudolph Bultmann, having come to believe that the only way to comprehend our authenticity, the Depth of our Selves, is to mythologize Being. In so doing, Daly does not deny historical or social reality but rather subordinates it to the primacy and power of transcendence, which finds expression in prehistorical mythology (parallel to Bultmann's existential anthropology).

By patriarchal standards, Daly is mindless of historical reality—out of touch with the reality of our fathers. As such, she is in touch with an aspect of reality—human experience, her own experience—that has been, in fact, written, burned, and beaten off by our forefathers. To this same extent, traditional theology—especially, perhaps, "liberal" theology—does not acknowledge as valid theological data the human experiences of ecstasy, rage, and visionary dreaming as expressed in mythology and yearning. (Wolfhart Pannenberg is a contemporary representative of those theologians for whom rational, scientifically verifiable data are normative for theology.) Nor can the case be made simply on the basis of Daly's myth-making that she is ahistorical. A myth is a historical expression of a historical reality—even if the reality is one's own dream or pain.

Given that Mary Daly is speaking of real human experience and that myth-making is not in and of itself ahistorical, in what sense might we assert that Daly is creating a "state of mind" rather than a movement for significant social change in history?[11]

The answer is traceable to her epistemology: Daly has chosen to remove her mind from the world and do philosophy (myth and metaethics) as a subject who is shaping her object—transcendent time-space for women: "The radical be-ing of women is very much an Otherworld Journey."[12] Daly has chosen to be "prehistorical"—prior to patriarchal history (world history as created by men), in terms both of chronology and of importance. She has chosen to focus—fully and finally—on the creation of a transcendent time-space for women who do not want to engage in any way the male-defined processes of world and church history.

Daly has chosen to be a woman-defined woman among women for women. Noting with Simone de Beauvoir the extent to which women within patriarchy exhaust ourselves attempting to change patriarchal institutions, Daly has chosen to leave patriarchy in the only way possible—short of suicide—by "surviving" ("living above," from *supervivere*) it all. Hence, she seems to lack interest in social change, including movements of class and race, which she perceives to be, at best, distractions from the women's revolution; at worst, movements dominated by patriarchal interests, methods, and goals.

But this stance is made problematic for Daly by her existential roots, reminiscent not only of Paul Tillich's ontology of being but also of the typology of hero as rebel, up against the world. Existentialism—the awareness of existential alienation, pain, life in the real world—sets her on the horns of a dilemma. On one hand, such existence and her awareness of it provide her with the last vestige of relationship to patriarchy (life in the nontranscendent world of men and nonfeminist women). On the other hand, it is bound also to provide the basis for her apparent contempt for men and for women whom she does not consider to be A-mazing Amazons.

Daly's existential affinities serve as her ticket both into the arena of conversation with those who read her books, attend her lectures, and share the patriarchal environs of her body, and into the arena of bad press among those who feel personally trivialized or demeaned by her "heroic" contempt for the inhabitants of the world who have not learned to a-maze patriarchy, Christianity, and heterosexist values. This seems to me the dilemma of a subjective idealist whose self (correction: mind) is the creator and norm of all Be-ing: a contemporary manifestation of Gnostic dis-embodiment?

Dualism and Oppression

Ruether is a Roman Catholic historian and theologian. Her posture as a feminist scholar, teacher, and writer is that of a Christian woman and an analyst of the roles, work, and symbols of women in Christian history. Complementing her feminist commitment and research is her interest in, and research of, the historical situations of other powerless groups of people, especially in relation to the church and Christian theology.[13] She writes from within the church and often addresses issues of particular concern to church women—for example, the issue of Mariology.[14]

Although, for Ruether, "the oppression of women is undoubtedly the oldest form of oppression in human history"—and as such can be historically paradigmatic for all other forms of oppression—she is unwilling to lift women's liberation out of the context of human oppression in such a way as to essentialize women as the first and final cause (see Daly). To the contrary, Ruether believes that oppression is itself the manifest result of historically essentializing or ontologizing groups of people in terms of dominance and submission—an ontological dualism founded on the ascription of essential givens to people on the basis of "nature." Hence, Ruether's primary theological target is the problem of dualism.

> Christianity . . . inherited from its syncretism of Jewish apocalypticism and hellenistic gnosticism a series of polarities [dualisms] which now stand as basic barriers to not only a theology of liberation, but the *praxis* of liberation as well.[15]

Recognizing with Daly, Alfred North Whitehead, and Tillich that dualism is a fundamental theological problem related directly to the human experience of self and other, subject and object, Ruether goes a step farther than the others in her assertion that ontology (the effort to comprehend pure Being, ultimate reality) is also a fundamental theological problem related directly to dualism. In this she is joined by a number of other liberation theologians—European, Latin American, North American feminist—such as Sölle, Gustavo Gutiérrez, Tom F. Driver, Nelle Morton, Elisabeth Schüssler Fiorenza, and Beverly Wildung Harrison, who writes: "We go from *duality* [a fundamental dynamic of personal development, the me/not-me experience] to *dualism*, from *difference* to *subordination and subjection*."[16]

To ontologize is to "naturalize" to construct a "natural" hierarchy of value and worth that is not distributed equally among the various levels of the hierarchical superstructure.[17] Accordingly, dominant-submissive relations become normative for human life, a norm legitimated—mythologically, theologically, and historically—by religion of transcendent dualism (Christianity), in which there is no possibility of cooperation, mutuality, or reciprocity between the higher and the lower parties (God-humanity, men-women, Christians-Jews, rich-poor, white-black, etc.).

Ruether therefore challenges dualistic theological concepts, such as creator and creature, individual and collective, nature and grace. More basically, given her particular scholarly interests, she has set out to spot and analyze the historical manifestations of dualism at work between and among the peoples of the earth (for example, men and women in the church; rich and poor in Latin America; white and black in North American society) and to relate one manifestation of oppression to the other.

Like Daly, Ruether believes that the male-female dualism comes first—chronologically. Like Daly, she acknowledges the availability of resources for a prehistorical reconstruction of this dualism.[18] Unlike Daly, she rejects such prehistory as "unhistorical" and chooses to "sketch out . . . the lines of the historical development whereby the female person . . . was subverted and made to appear physiologically and intellectually inferior."[19]

Methodologically, Ruether combines a critical assessment of anthropological resources on primitive culture with a Marxist understanding of the role of work and distribution of functions as basic to social organization. She concludes that "history has been the holocaust of women," an arena of irrational and primitive male taboos about women, blood, mother, death, the earth itself, which becomes the ideological wheel on which social organization, work, production, and institutional relationships are molded. Sexism is rooted in a dualism which, in turn, is rooted in the essentializing of fear, the unknown, and mystery.[20]

A basically Marxist epistemology supports Ruether's contention that just as sexism has a historical context, so does liberation from sexism have its context in patriarchal society; moreover, that the entire purpose of theology is to change the world/church. In its narrow sense, theology must verbalize a challenge to dualism, such as that of Reinhold Niebuhr's private-public split. In a broader sense, the theologian must work, not simply speak, for concrete changes in institutional structures, be they changes in ordination policies that exclude women or transportation policies that maximize gasoline consumption.

Fundamental to her work is Ruether's sense of commitment to the very patriarchal society and church she challenges. The world/church sets her theological agenda by way of the expressed needs of the oppressed, especially women. Like Daly, she takes seriously the social construction of patriarchal reality. Unlike Daly, she also takes seriously both the social construction of matriarchal reality, whether myth or history, and the necessity for the social demolition of patriarchal reality if, in fact, there is to be any significant new creation, new women, new earth. Transcendence, subjective idealism, the creation of a state of mind—none of these is, in and of itself, enough for Ruether. The immanence of God in and with humanity, the significance of world/social/church history as the only significant arena of realistic be-ing, the creation of justice in society—these are Ruether's values.

> The theological model for this liberation cannot be merely the apocalyptic, sectarian Armageddon, *nor yet the flight of the soul from the body and the outer world to infinite inner space, for these have become too much a part of a problem to be a credible part of the solution today.* Nor can we seek liberation merely in the romantic, primitivistic "body grope" of some aspects of the human potential and "encounter" movements, nor the escape from civilization to the uncultivated primal paradise of the utopian ecologists. Rather a perspective on liberation must emerge from a much more deeply integral vision which finds a new unity of opposites through transformation of values.[21]

Having named and explored the most critical methodological assumptions that distinguish the work of Daly from that of Ruether, I want to examine—in summary fashion—the deception of this distinction, because this curious twist is absolutely crucial in the work of feminist theology. Turning the tables somewhat, I suggest that Daly is doing work that Christian feminists who share Ruether's epistemological assumptions need not only to take seriously but also to share, and that Ruether's work, as a historian, lacks Daly's devastating "sparking" power—a power critical to fundamental change in the world/church. It is unfair to ask more of any one woman than she herself can give as theologian. But it is not unfair, and it is important, to ask feminist theologians (ourselves, alongside Ruether and Daly) to consider what each of us, as individual representatives of others, needs to bring to feminist theologizing in terms of insight, courage, and vision.

I will lay my cards on the table at this point: As our brothers in the world, individual men cannot be held personally responsible for sexism's demonic and bitter history. In both past and contemporary history, men as a caste must be acknowledged as the human agents who are responsible for what they have done, and do, to us—and to themselves. This is, I think, the only way we can hope to love them as we do ourselves.

Daly's perception of the depth of the historical problem of patriarchy and sexism is more unequivocal than Ruether's. She names the systemic demon, not as a theological construct, but rather as a *human agent*—that is, *men*, the creators and rulers of the patriarchal world. But she then flees inward, for a personal exorcism of the mind. Ruether does not name the demon with the same unmistakable clarity: she suggests that it is a theological concept ("dualism"). Ruether, however, does not flee inward; rather she joins her sisters and brothers in the world for the corporate task of exorcising a historic, systemic demon whose human name and face remain elusive.

To put it another way, Daly's sense of the problem seems more realistic than Ruether's, while Ruether's sense of the solution is stronger than Daly's. Or, yet again, Daly perceives initially through Marxist eyes ("This planetary sexual caste system involves birth-ascribed hierarchically ordered groups whose members have unequal access to goods, services"[22]), and then proceeds to reject the social and historical challenge in what she sees, thereby opting for an idealistic posture vis-à-vis reality as an Other-world.

Ruether, in contrast, much in the tradition of philosophical idealism, does not seem to plumb the immense depth of the sociohistorical, but for all practical purposes irreversible, depravity in which, for example, Mariological symbols were brought into being and are maintained. To attempt to revise Mariology—even upon communal mandate—may be to participate farther in the social and historical oppression of women. Most of us who are still Christians will realize that we falter with Ruether at this very point.

It may be that Ruether's strong and valuable sense of commitment to her people, her community—especially Christian women—is militating against her assumption of a more revolutionary prophetic role within the community—the role of one who speaks *as an individual to the community instead of as a member of the community for the community.* Daly's voice is prophetic, but she has chosen to stand outside the very community (Christianity) to which she could most forcefully speak prophetically. Prophets get killed, and Daly has chosen survival. Ruether stands within the community that needs the prophecy, but she is not "sparking" the same terrifying and devastating warning. She has seen more clearly than Daly that prophets must belong to community. But Daly is heard to echo more urgently the voice of the One whom I would call "God," as she means to pierce, rip, and shatter the patriarchy that is operative at all levels of our lives.

Ruether's Marxist epistemology is incomplete, for she does not always apply the same methodological analysis to Christian *practices* related to theism, christology, Mariology, worship, ordination, etc., that she applies to the sociohistorical criticism of the *ideas* that express the practices. Ironically, then, Ruether, as Carol Christ points out, may appear to be less than revolutionary in her critique of the world/church, despite her epistemological appreciation of collectivity and the formative power of activity, work, and reflection (praxis) in the creation of ideas.

Daly, however, despite her idealism—the power she appears to ascribe to ideas *qua* ideas—may read as the more radical, if not revolutionary, of the two analysts, as she names the demonic work of the social construction of the patriarchal reality.

> Women's minds have been mutilated and muted to such a state that "Free Spirit" has been branded into them as a brand name for girdles and bras rather than as the name of our verb-ing, be-ing selves. . . . Moronized, women believe that male-written texts (biblical, literary, medical, legal, scientific) are "trues." . . . Patriarchy has stolen our cosmos and returned it in the form of *Cosmopolitan* magazine and cosmetics.[23]

Theologizing in Patriarchal Time/Space

This is the stuff that must be said—*within and to the church.* Daly may be "spinning" off into her own space of female idolatry and isolation, but her radical naming of the demonic destruction of women's Selves in the name of Free Spirit, *Cosmopolitan*, and Christ is absolutely vital, I am convinced, to the work that Ruether is attempting to do—significant and enduring reformation of the church and meaningful restoration of the world.

What is at stake for feminist theology is no less than our Selves. Our survival is at stake, not in Daly's sense of "living above" history and patriarchal reality, but rather in the sense of *our absolute refusal to compromise or equivocate our experience of being alienated, "other," Furious Females, as the basis for our participation in the world/church.* I believe that it is *not* an either/or—Daly's fury or Ruether's fortitude, imaginative spinning or historical analysis, hard-nosed prophecy or analytical teaching, what might be or what is. It is, rather, a both-and: Daly's remarkable clarity and prophetic boldness of "telling it like it is," and Ruether's vision for unity through a transformation of values; both an appreciation of the individual as fundamentally creative, and an awareness of the social dimension of all creativity; both the realistic vitality of being alone with and loving our sisters, and the realistic necessity of critical engagement with our brothers and sisters alienated from us; both the imaginative work of dreaming dreams and creating new myths and the indispensable work of probing history—not only for what is given but also for what is not given—as a tool for understanding, and changing, the world/church; both a vision of what might be (and even today is, in some important ways, among us) and the acceptance of what is—this patriarchal time-space, here, now, as our context, our challenge, our history, and our home.

We who join the theological work of feminism need urgently to function on the basis of Daly's courage to name and rage, and Ruether's courage to live in the world on the basis of a utopic (nowhere yet) vision. Like Daly, we need to risk defying any attempt to make us minimize women as our focus, our passion, our lifetime commitment. Like Ruether, we need the breadth of vision to see that humanity is one—first and finally—and that as change happens, it will be more by how we relate and what we stand for concretely, actively, in patriarchal history, than by what we write, publish, or imagine we have done as a-mazing women.

Our other options are, on one hand, *to move into our Other-world* via our own minds (Daly) or our bodies (Jonestown), or on the other, *to lose our Selves* in an attempt historically, psychologically, or otherwise to justify patriarchal reality at whatever subtle and deceptive levels we must—in order to keep our place as marginal participants in the world/church (Ruether's position carried to its logical end by women and men with much less sense than Ruether of the severe malaise of Christianity).

To immerse ourselves in theology and ministry of *radical participation* may be to survive in a sense that Daly has a-mazed as impossible.

· 9 ·

Looking in the Mirror:
A Response to Jonestown[1]

On November 18, 1978, five persons were shot to death in Guyana by members of the People's Temple. Shortly thereafter, at the directive of Temple leader Jim Jones, hundreds of his followers drank a cyanide-laced potion and died within minutes. Many did so apparently without physical coercion. The death toll was over nine hundred.

It would be easy to write it off as an anomaly, a macabre exception to an otherwise good rule: to feed the hungry, clothe the naked, work for the common good, take seriously the life and teachings of Jesus. Many Christians will declare with the air of certainty that the problem was Marxism; that Jim Jones was a phony Christian, a socialist manipulating Christianity as a recruitment instrument. Jones's wife Marceline said as much in a 1977 interview: "Jim used religion to try to get some people out of the opiate of religion."[2] Marxists and socialists, in contrast, may well contend that the problem was religion, an illusion of spirituality permeating the American culture out of which Jones and his people came and which they attempted to purify in Guyana—a spirituality that duped Jones and, finally, more than nine hundred others, shielding them from the lessons of history itself.

There was much buck-passing. What happened at the airstrip and later in the commune was lamented as the result of socialism, communism, capitalism, religion, the churches, moral decline in a rootless society, the jungle, the U.S. government, the Guyanese government, the cults, the parents, narcissism, masochism, homosexuality. Or, as most contended, the psychosis of one person, the Rev. Jim Jones.

Early that Thanksgiving week as reports began to trickle in, I found myself distracted from the work I had intended to do over the holidays—reading contemporary theology. As the news from Jonestown mounted, so too did my distraction. I wanted to talk about Jonestown—constantly. Yet in conversation my friends and I would find ourselves uneasy about what felt like our voyeurism: gawking at the scene of an accident; gasping, repelled by what we saw and heard, yet drawn again and again to see and hear.

For the first time, I experienced panic about a close friend's involvement in a fundamentalist biblical group centered around one charismatic male leader who champions abundant living in the name of Jesus.

I was also enraged that the People's Temple had defined itself as both Christian and socialist, and was perceived as such, thereby undercutting two complementary perspectives that seem to me critical to ministry in the world.

Moreover, I knew that we would begin to hear much about the sexual mores of the commune and the sexual attitudes and practices of Jim Jones himself, thereby feeding into the already hysterical anxieties of Americans about sexual "abnormality."

Related to these concerns was my own sense that it could have been me. Far from distancing the Jonestown affair, I felt aware somewhere in the deep recesses of my own consciousness that Jim Jones and his people had "acted out" my own capacities to participate in destruction, to live into the transformation of good to evil.

Needless to say, through issues raised by Jonestown, I discovered that far from being distracted from contemporary theology, I had been immersed in it all week. Jonestown helped me to confront issues with which I had been struggling.

Vision

What went wrong? How did it happen that a Christian vision of a socialist utopia became so grossly distorted? It is inadequate to lay the blame on the inner workings of the leader, to suggest that Jim Jones was all along a power-hungry and paranoid individual suffering delusions and indulging in self-deification. All of this may be true, as is often the case with "successful" religious leaders. But it is an inadequate explanation of what happened not only to the nine hundred others, but also to Jim Jones himself.

We need to take very seriously the "social construction of reality" (Peter Berger)—e.g., of ideologies such as Marxism, Christianity, utopia, sexism, racism, classism; and ways of experiencing and organizing reality, such as work, sexuality, worship, leading and following, economic distribution, social/racial relations, male-female relations, and even mass suicide. Jonestown made clear, if ever there were any doubt, that the vision is neither pure, nor enough.

The vision is not pure. The dream is constructed out of pieces of the historical-cultural situations of the visionary and cannot be extracted from the context of social reality. To paraphrase Margaret Mead, the dreamer, the leader, and the follower cannot remain uncontaminated by any knowledge of the people in the United States, Guyana, the world, without cutting him/herself off from the possibility of making a constructive difference to the people of that world, including him/herself. Jonestown blows the lid off the illusion of a constructive separatism from the world—whether its theoretical impulse is the Word of God, pure theology, socialist utopia, radical feminism, mythological reconstruction, or psychological-spiritual retreat.

The vision is not enough. Jim Jones's dream, as he articulated it some twenty years ago, was a Christian dream that cannot be surpassed. It is regrettable that it was rejected by many on the basis of Jones's inability to persevere toward its fulfillment. The problem was not his religious socialist vision, but rather his incapacity to sustain it. The end did not sustain the means. The goal did not produce the methods. The vision was not enough.

The final Jonestown vision—bloated, decomposing bodies, layered in circles, linked arm in arm—was dramatic and nauseating witness to the incapacity of either the Christian or the socialist dream to sustain itself in the absence of engagement with historical realities and in the absence of thoughtful means by which to affect these realities from a participatory position. To rely upon the vision to sustain itself is to betray the substance of Christianity and the method of Marxist analysis.

Disengagement. Isolation. Contempt for the people of the world and the realities of opposition and struggle. Passion for one's own commitment without compassion for others in the society whose commitments are different from one's own. Within the People's Temple, this defensive contempt undercut the historical possibilities for the making real of a dream. As such, it rendered almost predictable the mass suicide as the final act—itself a liturgy of defensive contempt for the realities of human life in the world. Perhaps this was the only way the visionary people could opt for the last word. The other option would have been engagement, communication, taking responsibility for relationships to those outside themselves.

Authority

> Where the world is understood biblically, that is, as moving toward an end, a goal, an authoritarian obedience cannot adequately express the will of God for the world. It is interested solely in the preservation of order and consequently displays hostility toward the future.
>
> —Dorothee Sölle[3]

The most apparent problem was the manipulation of people by a demented leader. But the most basic problem was the willingness of the people to submit themselves totally to the authority of a leader—sane or insane, creative or destructive.

Throughout the Jonestown week the media raised the question of authority from a variety of perspectives. The U.S. government was accused of not interfering, undoubtedly by many persons who have otherwise pleaded, worked, and voted for less interference by government in their lives. Parents were televised lambasting cults and yet lamenting the lack of structured authority in the lives of their children; indeed, some of the same parents who, before the deaths, had spoken of the beautiful sense of purpose and meaning Jim Jones had given their children were shown after the fact to be outraged by Jim Jones, whom they called a dictator, a fascist.

The *New York Times* and other media reported that what began as a commendable and effective social mission in the 1950s and 1960s turned bizarre as Jones began to focus on his own messianic role, denouncing all opposition within and without the Temple. Finally, it was reported, Jones claimed to be Jesus, "God's incarnation." And the people were willing to give him ultimate and absolute authority over their lives—and their deaths.

What is extraordinary about this is that it is not at all extraordinary. Depending on the individual perspective, there are some noble and some deranged historical precedents for murders or suicide pacts inspired by religious conviction (e.g., Masada, the phenomenon of holy wars, and smaller-scale acts such as those of the Manson cult). More significantly, the willingness of people to submit totally to the judgment and the world-view of others is commonplace.

Today we see this abdication of personal responsibility in Christian groups in which the biblical interpretations of one leader are assumed to be the truth and are given their legitimation under the guise of the infallibility of scripture (not of the leader, who characteristically disclaims all authority for what he says). Psychologically, it is a small step between humility such as this (even if genuine) and others' perception of such a leader as godlike, perceptions which in turn are bound to affect the leader.

Authoritarian harassment is characteristic not only of the so-called cults, but also of all churches that commend personal submission in the guise of obedience, tradition, discipline, or scriptural authority. Roman Catholics are expected to obey the dictates of papal authority. Ordained priests and ministers take vows of obedience to superiors. And baptized Christians are expected to submit to Christ, whose person and will is interpreted by those in authority.

Such submission is manifest also in the many forms of patriotism, such as anticommunism, militarism and defense, national security, the equation of God with country, the capitalist system of economy, the nuclear family, the headship of men over women, and obedience to authority (of parents, teachers, husbands, bosses, bishops, generals), regardless of whether the authority is just or unjust, beneficent or cruel.

Many of us in the liberal contingents of the church are ready to name the problems inherent in authoritarianism and mindless obedience to a leader, whether civil or ecclesiastical. But Jonestown pushes us farther. Because many of us—feminists, blacks, liberationists, liberals, postliberals, radicals, democrats and socialists, gay/lesbian and gay/lesbian advocates—have shared and struggled within the context of the People's Temple's antiauthoritarianism. We too have been resistant to the policies of the U.S. government; we too have been ridiculed and written off for a lack of patriotism; we too have been denounced as blasphemous and perverse by Christians who have been scandalized by our searches for new ways of living in community and by theologians who have been scandalized by our relativization of biblical authority.

We can despise the People's Temple. We can denounce its methods. We can distance ourselves from its death. But the People's Temple and the Jonestown incident was us. It was not the enemy. It was not antiblack, anticommunist, antigay, antisocial change. It was us, our vision and our values, stripped to the terrifying bareness of our own vulnerability either to manipulate or to be manipulated by the madness of our passion for a better world.

And so Jonestown invites us to reconsider the norms of our authority. From what, or from whom, do we take our cues for the shaping of our values? the positing of our goals? the means by which we intend to move toward these ends? the doing of our deeds? the definitions of ourselves as meaningful, productive, worthwhile people? These questions are fundamental in doing theology as well as in living life.

· 10 ·

Coming Out:
Journey Without Maps*

In an article published in 1979,[1] I spoke of my resistance to all categorizing of human beings, including the use of sexual categories such as homosexual, heterosexual, and bisexual. The reason I cited for resisting is that "being human—being sexual—is not a matter of 'qualitative analysis'" in which relationships of highest value become genital equations: "Woman plus woman equals lesbian; woman plus man equals straight." In my view, the labels we use do not express, but rather distort, the most important things we can know and say about our own sexuality and human sexuality in general.

If I believe this—and I do—why then break through my own resistance and "come out"?

The answer does not come easily. The difficulty here does

---

*The author wrote this article in the late spring of 1979 as a means of "coming out" as a lesbian. It was published in *Christianity and Crisis*, June 11, 1979, pp. 153–56. In order to underscore her sense of the theological/moral tension inherent in the use of sexual labels, she made public at the same time the text of an earlier address on sexuality. The earlier address was published by *The Witness*, June 1979, and begins in this book on page 43.

not rise out of diffidence, for the article was not primarily biographical but rather an analytic attempt to make sense out of biographical journeying. Quite apart from personal meanings, however, the subject being addressed does not yield readily to our efforts for comprehension. We live, all of us, in uncomfortable ambiguity. We live with contradictions and partial truths. In ambiguity we seek the meaning of ourselves and of the world, and the words to communicate the meanings we find. In its enormous, vital complexity, sexuality may draw us as close as we ever get to the heart of ambiguity. It is to escape from anxiety-producing uncertainty, I think, that we so readily accept labels and resist our own questing and questioning.

People tend to think of sexual identity (or preference, or orientation) as something innate. I do not believe this is true. It seems to me that our sexual feelings and behavior are shaped by a variety of interweaving factors. Biology—our glands and their powerful secretions, along with anatomy itself—is one, but only one of these factors. We are shaped also by our ethnic, religious, and class heritages, by our schooling, by the events in our early experience, and certainly by our parents—by the specifically sexual models they provide, by their values, and by the ways they relate not only to each other, but also to us, and to others.

In my opinion, we are born sexual; our sexuality is indeed a given. But it is from a myriad of sources, and by a process closer to osmosis than to either inheritance or deliberation, that we *learn* how to feel and act sexually. That is why we ought not identify the categories of sexual identity with sexuality itself, as though the categories were fundamental and fixed, as though they too were gifts to be accepted and valued without question. To celebrate our sexuality is to make a theological and anthropological affirmation of the pulsating dynamic of created life, the force within us that moves us beyond ourselves toward others. But this powerful affirmation of both creation and creator is diminished in its truth when sexuality is equated with such categories as "gay/lesbian" and "straight." For these categories can be boxes; they can be imposed from without, not truly chosen, not reflective of who we are or might have been or might become.

Yet these categories—boxes—are real. We live in them. We are in some significant part creatures of the social structures in which we participate; the boxes we call our sexual identities can be not only influenced, but even determined, by them. These structures, then, demand recognition and responsible attention. With regard to sexuality, what must be realized is that historically the predominant effect or cultural conditioning has been to squeeze all humanity into a single large box labeled "heterosexual." This social structure, this box, is so huge and so all-pervasive that we cannot easily see it; because we are enveloped by it, we cannot often find the distance we need to see and examine it. We accept this boxing of our sexuality as natural, the way things are and therefore ought to be.

Thus the heterosexual box becomes god of our social structures (including the church), our relationships, and our self-images. Functionally the heterosexual box becomes critical to and definitive for patriarchy, nuclear family, private enterprise, male headship and derivative boxes such as "masculine" and "feminine."

The social order is thus constructed on a box largely invisible to its inhabitants. The moment a boy child learns that little boys do not cry, the instant a girl child learns that little girls do not fight, the child takes a step farther into the heterosexual box. If, for reasons that may have little if anything to do with sex or gender, the child is drawn to protest against boxes, specifically against the heterosexual box designed to transform vulnerable little boys into big, strong men and feisty little girls into soft, sweet ladies, the very social effort to implant a heterosexual identity may begin a contrary process. The point is that the result in either case is that the sexuality within is confined, shaped, limited, perhaps diminished, by the container built around it.

The reason this is important is that sexuality drives toward relationship. It is a movement shared by all creatures and the Creator, an impulse that we are capable of celebrating in every aspect of our lives. A significant aspect of sexuality is that it brings us to physical and emotional ecstasy in partnership. The ecstatic power of the sex act can lead us to identify it wrongly with the whole of sexuality, when in truth sexuality is, I believe, the one most vital source of our other passions, of our capacities to love and to do what is just in the world. I would go so far as to suggest that the capacity to celebrate sexuality is linked inextricably with the capacity to court peace, instead of war; justice, instead of oppression; life, instead of hunger, torture, fear, crime, and death.

Sexuality, which finds its most intimate expression between lovers, moves us into an active realization, and great relief, that we are not alone; that we are, in fact, bound up in the lives of others; and that this is good. That is why, I think, many (but too few) Christians speak of love and justice together; justice is the moral act of love.

This has personal meaning for me. Recalling my past, I can see now that coming out has been a long and puzzling journey out of the heterosexual box, in which I was no more comfortable at age five than I am now. The experience is hardly rare, as we are coming to know from testimonies of women and men who, when they were girls and boys, were continually reminded that anatomy is destiny and that sex-role expectations are not to be evaded. My own parents made no conscious attempt to teach me rigid sex roles. Yet both they and I lived in the heterosexual box that was far larger, and more deeply formative, than either they or their children could realize. Accordingly, I experienced the larger social order as squeezing something out of me, pressing something in on me, and eventually depressing into me feelings of shame about wanting to do things and be things that "weren't for girls."

Why did I want to be Superman and not Lois Lane? Matt Dillon and not Miss Kitty? Because Superman and Matt Dillon were more interesting to me. They led exciting lives. They made things happen. They were confident, assertive, energetic. Somewhere inside I knew (and knew rightly) that unless I felt myself to be an interesting, confident, and assertive person, completely capable of exerting as much will and leadership as the next person, I could never really love, or allow myself to be loved, by anyone. Not mutually. Not really. I knew also that any effort I might make on behalf of justice would be triggered by my own lack of self-esteem and by the painful inclination to identify with the underdog, rather than by the human *and sexual* impulse to work for justice on the basis of a strong confidence both in myself and in the power of God to love.

In our history, our society, our churches, the heterosexual box is that into which girls are pressed into ladies who *should* marry and who *must* be held within the social order as subordinate to husbands, fathers, or father surrogates—regardless of the unique and individual capacities, needs, and desires of either women or men. There is too little room in this enormous, socially constructed box for real mutual love between the sexes and no support at all for mutual love between women or between men. There is too little room in the heterosexual box for either spouse in a marriage to develop fully her or his capacities for loving humanity and God out of a sense of self as both strong and gentle, confident and vulnerable, assertive and receptive, equally able to lead and to follow. As a social structure, the heterosexual box intends to permit no androgyny or gynandry, nor does it encourage us to cast off the burden of sex roles—because the heterosexual box is built entirely out of sex roles.

New Priorities

Feminism challenges the legitimacy of sex roles. Along with other social movements, feminism is rooted in the critique that a society so constructed that certain people and groups profit from inequalities—between men and women, rich and poor, black and white, etc.—is a society in which money is more highly valued than love, justice, and human life itself. Feminism moves toward the reversal of these values: human life must be first; all else, second. As sex roles fall, as more and more women and men refuse to play along for profit and social gain at the expense of our true selves, the heterosexual box begins to weaken. This is exactly what is happening today in our society. The box is collapsing: women and men are coming out.

For many women, and I am one, coming out means that we are beginning to value ourselves and our sisters as highly as we have been taught to value men. Coming out means loving women, not hating men. Coming out means beginning to feel the same attraction, warmth, tenderness, desire to touch and be touched by women as we have learned to feel in relation to men.

For many years I have been coming out sexually, experiencing my attraction to women as well as men to be a valuable dimension of myself—as friend, lover, Christian. I have been aware that there is a box, another box, a less constrictive box, for people with this experience: bisexual. As boxes go, bisexuality is not bad. It may be (if unknowable truths were known) the most nearly adequate box for *all* persons. The problem with bisexuality in my life (and I can speak only for myself) is that it has been grounded too much in my utopian fantasy of the way things ought to be and too little in the more modest recognition of myself as a participant in *this* society at *this* time in *this* world, in which I have both a concrete desire for personal intimacy with someone else and a responsibility to participate in, and witness to, the destruction of unjust social structures—specifically, the heterosexual box.

If our world and civilization have a future, it may be that in some future decade or century sex roles will be transcended; persons will be defined as persons and modes of relationship will be chosen, not imposed. It has been my experience that to live now as bisexual is to live somewhat abstractly in anticipation of a future that has not arrived. That is why, for several years, I have been coming out of bisexuality, coming out of utopian vision in order to focus my sight on the urgency and immediacy of the concrete present.

I am a teacher in a seminary in which both women and gay/lesbian people have to struggle fiercely to keep themselves from being squeezed into the heterosexual box in which women must submit, and gay/lesbian people must repent. I am a priest in a church which, like most churches, threatens to collapse under the weight of a perverse notion of a sexuality that is to be neither celebrated nor related to other issues of love and justice. I am a woman in a church and a society that patronize women with reminders of how far we have come and of how much we have been given. And I am a lesbian—a woman who has come out of the heterosexual box and into another box, which, as boxes go, is far superior for my life as a responsible person, a Christian woman, in this world at this time.

Coming out, I come into the realization of myself as best able to relate most intimately—to touch and be touched most deeply, to give and receive most naturally, to empower and be empowered most remarkably, to express everything I most value: God in human life, God in justice, God in passion, God as love—in sexual relationship to a lover who is female.

It is with another woman in this world at this time that I am able to experience a radical mutuality between self and other, a mutuality we have known since we were girl children, a mutuality that has shaped our consciousness of female-female relationships as the first and final place in which women can be most truly at home, in the most natural of social relations. It is, moreover, with other lesbian feminist Christians that we can witness to the power of God's presence in mutuality—relationship in which there is no higher and no lower, no destructive insecurities fastened in the grip of sex-role expectations, but rather a dynamic relational dance in which each nurtures and is nurtured by the other in her time of need.

A romantic portrayal? No, it is not easy. There are tensions, fears, the possibility of cruelty and abuse—just as in any relationship. It is not that lesbian relationships are always, or even most often, characterized by mutuality. It is just that, in the present social order, lesbian relationships offer an opportunity for a mutuality of remarkable depth. Lesbian relationships can make prophetic witness within and to society; a witness not on behalf of homosexuality per se, but rather on behalf of mutuality and friendship in all relations.

Gains and Losses

Coming out, there are things lost: the likelihood of bearing my own children and learning how to live better with male lovers. But the gain outweighs the loss: Coming out, I begin to envision and embrace the children of the world as my own and the men of the world as my brothers, whom I can better learn to know and love as friends. Coming out involves a recognition of the co-creative power I have always experienced in relation to women. Coming out is a confession that I need and want intimacy with someone whose values and ways of being in the world can support and be supported by my own. Coming out means realizing and cherishing my parents' way of loving and of being in the world, of valuing who they have been and who they are, and of knowing myself both as bound to them and as separate from them in my journeying. Coming out means remembering my other relatives and early friends in the hope that they can trust and celebrate the parts we have played in the shaping of one another's values.

Coming out is a protest against social structures that are built on alienation between men and women, women and women, men and men. Coming out is the most radical, deeply personal and consciously political affirmation I can make on behalf of the possibilities of love and justice in the social order. Coming out is moving into relation with peers. It is not simply a way of being in bed, but rather a way of being in the world. To the extent that it invites voyeurism, coming out is an invitation to look and see and consider the value of mutuality in human life. Coming out is simultaneously a political movement and the mighty rush of God's Spirit carrying us on.

Coming out, I stake my sexual identity on the claim that I hold to be the gospel at its heart: that we are here to love God and our neighbors as ourselves. Each of us must find her or his own way to the realization of this claim. I have given you a glimpse into my way. Where the journey began, where it will end, I do not know.

· 11 ·

Sexuality, Love, and Justice[1]

> The role of the artist is exactly the same as the role of the lover. If I
> love you, I have to make you conscious of the things you don't see.
> —James Baldwin

If I love you, I have to make you conscious of the things you
don't see. I read and understand this to be our common voca-
tion.

My understanding of myself continues to evolve—often very
roughly, sometimes abrasively even to myself, peppered with
surprises about myself and others. I do not understand myself
primarily in categories that suggest that anything about me is
static, unchanging, finished. Even those categories that most of
us assume to be basic—such as female or male gender, such as
racial identity, such as the *Homo sapiens* species itself—seem to
me more elusive, less static, than we often assume. I am
tempted to say, and will for now, that nothing is fixed; nothing
in the world is so essentially what it is today that tomorrow may
not surprise us with something new—whether in the nations,
governments, religions, economic and political structures of our
own country, or in the ways in which we live our lives among
friends, lovers, colleagues.

And yet, there is something basic among us, something evolutionary—and revolutionary; something more basic than femaleness or maleness, whiteness or blackness, gayness or straightness; something more basic than Christianity or any religion. Something that is unchanging, stable, constant, precisely in its dynamic, revolutionary movement in the world. I am speaking of the human experience, and perhaps also the experience of other creatures, of love—or, of our human experience of God in the world. And so, if there is one fundamental category that can be appropriately descriptive, even definitive, of who we are—of what we are here to do in the world—it is that of *lover.*

Because the word love has become a catchall for sweet and happy feelings; because we have learned to believe that love stories are warm and fuzzy tales about dewy eyes and titillating embraces; because we have been taught that love and marriage go together like a horse and carriage and that love means never having to say you're sorry; because, in short, love has been romanticized so poorly, trivialized so thoroughly, and perverted—turned completely around—from what it is, we find ourselves having to begin again to re-experience, re-consider, re-conceptualize what it means to say "I love you." What does it mean to believe that God is in the world, among us, moving with us, even by us, here and now? What does it mean to be a lover?

It occurs to me that it may be the special privilege of lesbians and gay men to take very seriously, and very actively, what it means to love. As lesbians and gay men, we have had to fall back on the category of lover in order to speak of our most intimate, and often most meaningful, relationships. Deprived of the categories that are steeped in the tradition of romantic love—categories like husband and wife, fiancée, marriage, masculinity and femininity, bride and bridegroom—deprived of the symbols of romantic love, such as rings and weddings and public displays of affection, both verbal and physical; deprived of the religious legitimation of romantic love—the blessing of our relationships; deprived of celebration, acceptance, even acknowledgment, of our relationships, we have had no other common word for ourselves, and for those whom we love, except the word lover. Deprived of civil and religious trappings of romantic love, we may well be those who are most compelled to

plumb the depths of what it really means to love. Our depriva-
tion becomes an opportunity and a vocation: to become con-
scious of the things we have not seen, and to make others con-
scious of these same things.

What might it mean—to love? I want to tell you what I am
discovering, in the hope that you—each of you, all of you—will
be moved to consider carefully your own experiences. There is a
time, occasionally, for us to come to a consensus, for the pur-
pose of corporate action. But my intention is not to gather a
consensus on what it means to love, or even to suggest that a
consensus would be helpful to us, or to anyone.

At this point, the last thing we need is a new set of com-
mandments writ large in stone. I believe it is time to tell our
stories, to listen carefully, to begin to experience our experience,
to risk realizing and sharing our own senses of confusion, fear,
frustration, anger, even rage, about what is done to us, and
about what we do to ourselves and others, all in the name of a
"love" that is too often not love at all, but only a sham. A
perversion. A corruption of ourselves and of the God that is
with us.

And so I speak personally, as a *lesbian feminist Christian priest
and teacher*. I use each of these words to describe myself, because
each of them has grown in an evolving sense of how I might best
be a lover of sisters and brothers in the world today. Lesbian.
Feminist. Christian. Priest. Teacher. Either these dimensions of
my identity enable me, as a lover of human beings and of crea-
tion itself, or they are destructive, dysfunctional dimensions of
who I am that would best be somehow outgrown or discarded.
For now, these overlapping, at times interchangeable, senses of
myself ignite me, excite me, infuse me with a sense not only of
what love means, but also that who I am—and who you are,
and who we are together—matters. If we love the world, we
matter. Lovers make all the difference in the world. Lovers re-
create the world.

We must begin to see that *love is justice*. Love does not come
first, justice later. Love is not a "feeling" that precedes right-
relation among the persons in a family or the people of the
world. We do not feel our ways into right-relation with other
races, other people. We do not feel our way into doing what is

just. We act our way into feeling. This was, by the way, the raison d'être of the Philadelphia ordination: a conviction shared by many that we act our way into new feelings, new emotions, new ideas. And the act is love. The act is justice. Good feelings about love and justice may come later.

The same thing is true in friendship. The more just a personal relationship, the more loving this relationship, the more mutual, honest, beneficial, and creative for each friend, the more intense are the feelings of love between us. Speaking personally, the better the friendship, the more sustained and deeper and more precious to me is the erotic flow of energy that bonds us together. I find this terribly confusing, as you might imagine, in the context of a social order in which there is historically a great divide between friendship and sexual love—between philia and eros. Most of us have been out of touch, from the beginning, with the eroticism that draws us into friendship with persons of both sexes. Our sexuality is our desire to participate in making love, making justice, in the world; our drive toward one another; our movement in love; our expression of our sense of being bonded together in life and death. Sexuality is expressed not only between lovers in personal relationship, but also in the work of an artist who loves her painting or her poetry, a father who loves his children, a revolutionary who loves her people.

Sexuality is the undercurrent of the love that flows as justice in close friendship; in the victory salutation of a Sandinista rebel in Nicaragua; in the poetry of e e cummings, Emily Dickinson, Adrienne Rich; in the celebration of the Maundy Thursday Eucharist on behalf of Maria Cueto and Raisa Nemikin; in the genital embrace and ecstasy of two women, or two men, or a woman and a man, who are doing their best to make justice in their relationship. Where there is no justice—between two people or among thousands—there is no love. And where there is no justice/no love, sexuality is perverted into violence and violation, the effects of which most surely include rape, emotional and physical battering, relationships manipulated by control, competition, and contempt, and even war itself.

Love is passionate. If I love you, I am invested in our bonding. You are important to me, deeply so. Passion is a deep realization of our relation, of the significance of who we are together, of the fact that you matter / I matter / we matter. I may not always be able to show you or tell you. I may even be afraid of you. I may hurt you or be hurt by you. But I *care* about us, whether or not I "feel good" about us right now, and I do not want to leave you comfortless and without strength. If I love you, I am your advocate. If I love you, I will struggle for you/myself/us. My passion is my willingness to suffer for us, not masochistically, but rather bearing up who we are, enduring both the pain and the pleasure of what it means to love, to do what is just, to make right our relation. A person of passion, a lover of humanity, is she or he who enters seriously and intentionally into the depths of human experience, insists upon its value, and finds God in "the exchange of glances heavy with existence" (Elie Wiesel); or in refusing to live any longer with "someone's feet upon our necks" (Sarah Grimke); or in the vision of a promised land in which we are "free at last" (Martin Luther King Jr.), a land in which love as justice is humanity's common experience.

Our passion as lovers is what fuels both our rage at injustice—including that which is done to us—and our compassion, or our passion, which is on behalf of/in empathy with those who violate us and hurt us and would even destroy us. Rage and compassion, far from being mutually exclusive, belong together. Each is an aspect of our honesty—and our integrity—for just as our rage is entirely appropriate to our experience of lovelessness in our own lives and elsewhere in the world, so too is our compassion the ongoing acknowledgment and confession of our own refusals to make love, to make justice, in the world— beginning in our own homes, in our own beds, at our own altars. How, in the name of either God or humanity, can we hear the frustrated and fear-laced protests against us raised by bishops, priests, and laypersons of our own church without experiencing both rage at what is being done to us in the name of love, and compassion for those who—like us, and with us— act, in some way, every day, on the basis of fear, projection, denial, scapegoating, and contempt for those who threaten us?

I am not suggesting that we be marshmallows. To the contrary. I would like us to continue to toughen up in our work for love and justice at every level of human life. And the way to move on through these trials by fire, being shaped by courage and passion, is actively to realize our own participation in fear and denial, in injustice and lovelessness; and to do what we can each day "to go and sin no more." Regardless of our good intentions, our feet will always be placed squarely on someone's neck—perhaps when we least realize it. And it is the loving, just vocation of those whom we put down to ask us to remove our feet from their necks; if need be, to tell us; and, finally—if we refuse—to knock us off.

We, lesbians and gay men in the church, are in a social situation in which we are asking ecclesiastical authorities to remove the feet of a predominant theological tradition—both sexist and heterosexist—from our necks. Some of us are telling these institutional authorities. And, if it is not done, our loving and just vocation is to knock them off.

We need to remember something. Both as *oppressor* (white, male, upper-middle-strata people, capitalist dupes in a world yearning for common sources, unjust lovers in one-to-one relationships) and as *oppressed* (females, homosexuals, poor, blacks, other colors and racial/ethnic minorities, victims of domination in personal relationships)—we need to remember that the oppressed set both the timetable and the agenda for liberation. If we say now is the time, *now is the time!* Our compassion is chastened and sustained by our rage.

Love is full of such yearning, such adamant insistence for right-relation, such compassion, such rage. And it is absolutely irrepressible.

In a society, essentially a contemporary world order, built upon sex roles; an economy—namely capitalism (although Marxism has a similar set of sex-role problems)—maintained upon sex roles; a religion—Christianity—thoroughly patriarchal and rooted in sex roles, the deepest currents of women's liberation and gay/lesbian liberation merge in radical feminism and threaten to bring down the entire social/economic/religious structure of reality.

Many fear that lesbian feminism poses a threat to the nuclear family, the economic order, the religious assumptions about marriage as the blessed state, the fatherhood of God and the motherhood of women, the procreative norm of sexuality, and the high value of dominant-submissive relationships beginning with male property rights and extending to God the Father. Those who fear that this is what we are about fear rightly. As lesbian, feminist, christian, I believe that our vocation is to bring down the sacred canopy that has heretofore prevented our active realization of love and justice in human life as the only sacred—godly, right, and normative—dimension of our life together on earth. If economic structures do not support love, justice, mutuality, and cooperation in human life, they should be undone.

Heterosexism is built and maintained upon patriarchy: patriarchal definitions of what it means to be female and male and of what it means to have sex—fantasies that rigidly delineate the male from the female, the masculine from the feminine, the animus from the anima, the top from the bottom, the initiator from the receiver, and the power of the phallus from the gratitude of the womb. Heterosexism is a social structure pervasive in our culture and worthy only of being undone.

And yet, to participate in its undoing is to feel a little crazy. For I, like you, like us all, have been raised and instructed in heterosexist values. I have come to realize that these heterosexist assumptions all but complete our sense of who we are in the world. To reject them privately is difficult and tedious, and leads us toward strange senses of schizophrenia. To reject them publicly is to take a step none of us is ever prepared to take. It is to begin to act our way into what we hope, believe, or trust will be new ways of feeling and thinking about ourselves and others in the world.

To state publicly that we are lesbians or gay men is to enter, for a time at least, into a sense of ourselves as crazy. Such has been my experience. By craziness, I mean that my own sense of what is important, of who I am in relation to others in the world, of what my vocation as priest and teacher is, even my sense of what is happening in my closest relations—with friends and lovers—is called into question, often as much by me as by others. To feel crazy is to wonder if I am concocting a reality meaningful only to me and a few folks who are crazy enough to agree with me; it is to feel as if I have stepped outside the arena of what is not only acceptable, but also intelligible—even, at times, to myself. My decision (years in the making) to state publicly that I am a lesbian was a decision central to my vocation as a teacher (of students, for whom sexuality is usually a primary concern); a priest (in a church in which sexuality is a bedrock of the entire corpus of theological tradition and praxis); a feminist (in a society founded upon unjust assumptions about female and male roles); a christian (who believes that the command to love neighbor as self has as much to do with eros and philia as with agape, and that such love knows no gender confines); and a lover (a person in pursuit of friendship, justice, co-creativity in the world, including our most immediate and intimate relations).

To say I am a lesbian is to make a statement at once personal and political. It is to acknowledge the fact that, in our present social order, mutual sexual relationships are available largely in same-sex relationships. I have come to believe that it is unwise to expect true personal equality—mutuality of common benefit—between women and men in a sexist society. And, while I can appreciate the efforts of women and men toward this end, this is not where I choose to invest my self, my energy, my passion.

The lesbian relation, as I experience it, may be mutual, and as such may offer a glimpse into a way of being in the world that is as instructive for women and men in relation as for women and women and men and men. To be a lesbian is, for me, a way—the best way for me—of being lover.

To be a lesbian is to begin to untangle myself from the "lies, secrets, and silences" (Adrienne Rich) that have been draped as a shroud over our life together on earth. It is to invite projections onto myself, to trigger anxiety, to learn to bear—with others—a common pain, a common yearning, a common responsibility to make each other conscious of the things we do not see. It is to suggest that eros, philia, and agape are different words for the one experience of what it means to love. It is to affirm that lesbianism is a political act, a spiritual affirmation of God, the power of relation, in the world.

We are just learning to name ourselves, to experience our experience, to speak of these things without trembling or even apology. For me, lesbian sexuality is *loving* sexuality. It is *just* sexuality, rooted in and expressed between peers who have work to do together in the world—specifically, the liberation of women. It is to linger on the particularity of being women in patriarchal society. Lesbianism is cultivated in a vital intensity between/among women, an intensity vital at least for some of us—if all of us are ever to take ourselves and our sisters as seriously as we were born to believe we should take men: whether Church Fathers or natural fathers, employers, husbands, or sons, the Sonship of a Redeemer, or the Fatherhood of a Creator. Lesbian feminism is shaped in the struggle against the structures of male dominance—including such structures of one-to-one relationships as mating, dating, marriage.

And we who are lesbians—and perhaps gay men as well—need to be on guard against being washed away by the torrents of craziness (which is what has happened to many of our foremothers and forefathers), or—worse yet—finally engulfed by the powers that be, and convinced that the only way we can survive in the world is to accommodate ourselves—passively and invisibly—in conformity with the norms of the present order.

This is not a call to "come out." It is a call to be aware of what you are doing and why. It is a call to realize the depth of the dilemma in which feminists, lesbians, and gay men find ourselves—whether we are 100 percent in the closet, 95 percent out, 50 percent both ways, completely unclear on whether we are in or out, or even on whether or not we are gay/lesbian! It is a call to realize that what homosexuals are perceived to be about (and what some of us are about intentionally) is not simply the right to lead our own private lives, but rather an overhauling of the social structures of our time.

Those who resist us have good reason. The stakes are high. True sexual liberation—for homosexuals and for women—will happen only when our economic, religious, educational, business, and other structures and customs do not operate on the assumption that men will lead and women follow; that men work away from home and women in the home; that only a man and a woman constitute a creative couple; that only procreation is truly creative; and that in order to have a social order, someone must be on top and someone else on the bottom—

economically, religiously, sexually, otherwise. To challenge these assumptions is, in some very real sense, to go mad. The "Fathers" are not with us. Our families do not know how to be with us. Our church believes it must be against us. The Bible admonishes us. Jesus was silent about us. The authorities that be despise the threat that we pose—and despise it all the more if we happen, or appear to be, wise and happy people. It is much easier to tolerate a sad and pitiful homosexual than a proud and creative gay man or lesbian. If we affirm ourselves, we are seen as sick; if we renounce ourselves, we are called healthy. And we think *we* are crazy!

All of which is to say that, for me, lesbianism has been, and is, a tedious but important way of my learning to love—myself, my friends, my God. Lesbianism is a sign of justice for women. Lesbianism signals the opportunity for creative cooperation among women on behalf of a humanity of women and men in which cooperation often gives way to competition, and love to coyness, manipulation, and contempt.

If our common vocation is to be lovers, perhaps we can be more conscious of what justice is in our own lives and in the world; conscious of our own passion with and for each other, as each of us seeks to make love; conscious of our own feelings of craziness—learning to see that we are not "out of our minds." We are beginning to live with integrity, to reclaim our minds as our own; integrity, in which personal life-style and political conviction converge; in which friendship, sexuality, love, and justice are a common stream flowing into righteousness at home and elsewhere in the world; in which we begin to understand that loving is always a revolutionary act. Among lovers and friends, as well as in our passion for justice for women, blacks, Native Americans, the poor in the United States, Latin America, the Middle East—true love is the *most* revolutionary act. It is exactly the opposite of romantic love. To really love is to topple unjust structures, bringing down the principalities and powers of domination and control at all levels of human social relations. Such loving needs no church blessing—although it is good when it is forthcoming, whether for a gay or lesbian couple, civil rights, or the revolution of the people in El Salvador.

To say I love you is to say that you are not mine, but rather your own.

To love you is to advocate your rights, your space, your self, and to struggle with you, rather than against you, in our learning to claim our power in the world.

To love you is to make love to you, and with you, whether in an exchange of glances heavy with existence, in the passing of a peace we mean, in our common work or play, in our struggle for social justice, or in the ecstasy and tenderness of intimate embrace that we believe is just and right for us—and for others in the world.

To love you is to be pushed by a power/God both terrifying and comforting, to touch and be touched by you. To love you is to sing with you, cry with you, pray with you, and act with you to re-create the world.

To say "I love you" means—*let the revolution begin!* God bless the Revolution! Amen.

· 12 ·

Being "in Christ"?*

Into a situation much like ours today came a brother. Into a revolutionary situation, a troubled generation, a society beset with injustice and alienation between classes, sexes, and ethnic groups; a time of impersonal government, high taxes, and low morale; a world marked by violence and by violation of the human spirit as well as by some sense that organized religion might be irrelevant to everything else; into this situation came a young Jew, rabbi/teacher, fellow seeker, whom we know by the name of Jesus. Jesus' life seems to have been steeped in his own strong sense that many human beings, in their common quest for God, had been searching in the wrong direction for the wrong kind of God, and hence had found neither God nor themselves.

Seeking God, many had studied, memorized, and idolized scripture. Seeking God, many had been immersed in religious traditions that they held precious. Seeking God, many had obeyed the ten commandments and other tenets of religious law. Seeking God, many had observed religious rituals on the

*This essay is taken from a sermon preached at Myers Park Baptist Church, Charlotte, NC, November 1979.

sabbath, attempting to be faithful practitioners of their religion. Seeking God, many had tried hard to be good Jews. Seeking God, they had looked to the past, in which God had done "mighty acts" (like delivering the children of Israel out of Egyptian captivity), and they looked to the future, in which time God would send a Messiah, a "Christ," a divine one, to save the world from pain, injustice, and distress. Seeking God, many people in Jesus' time, much like many today, had looked to heaven rather than earth for something divine rather than human.

And among them came Jesus, himself a good Jew, whose burning passion was to redirect the people's search for God, because Jesus seemed to know that God was to be found, known, and loved on earth, in whatever is fully human, rather than in the tomes of religious, sacred, or divine tradition.

If there is one overarching theme in the New Testament, it is, I believe, that what Jesus called "the kingdom of God" is *with us,* among us, here and now, immediately. Notice I said "us," because I am not speaking only of the people of Jesus' time. It seems to me that we today are in a very similar situation. Seeking God, we still look up, rather than down—toward heaven, rather than earth—to find what is most precious, most meaningful, most ultimate in some other time or place rather than among us, here and now, in this world.

Jesus revolutionized the human quest for God by bringing it down to earth, thereby signaling the holiness of the very ground on which we stand—in society; in our communities, churches, homes, and relationships; in our choices and actions; in our most simple and honest conversations. This is the meaning of in-carnation. God is in-flesh, brought to life through us, by us, between/among us.

> And Jesus went on with his disciples, to the villages of Caesarea Philippi; and on the way he asked his disciples, "Who do [people] say that I am?" And they told him, "John the Baptist; and others say, Elijah; and others one of the prophets." And he asked them, "But who do you say that I am?" Peter answered him, "You are the Christ."
>
> —Mark 8:27–29

This episode, "Peter's Confession," occurred at the point in Jesus' ministry when the tide of public opinion was beginning to turn against him. The religious leaders were not pleased with this uppity young rabbi who kept doing things that good Jews simply did not do: breaking Jewish law, healing on the sabbath, going around with whomever he pleased, acting on the power of his own authority rather than clearing his actions through institutional religious channels. This was, in modern parlance, "unacceptable behavior." Good religious folks do not do those things. But Jesus was concerned about ethics, not etiquette; relationships, not religion—although he was careful to point out that he had come not to destroy religion, but to fulfill it. And so, the religious leaders were up against the wall. Jesus fit neither "in" nor "out." If he had not claimed to be a faithful Jew, he would not have been a problem. He could have been written off as a crazy. If he had not taken the religious leaders seriously, they could have dismissed him as a hostile alien, assuming that if they gave him enough rope he would hang himself. But they gave him plenty of rope—many opportunities to heal at the wrong time, eat with the wrong people, use scripture in the wrong way; and he did, and in so doing, drew people to him. Moreover, he continued to meet the religious leaders on their own ground and took them seriously enough to engage in dialogue with them, rebuke them, and preach to them.

By the time of Peter's confession, Jesus knew these leaders were going to do whatever they had to do to undo him, probably by continuing to generate public disapproval of his defiant, blasphemous behavior. Jesus was bound to know the gravity of his dilemma: in order to go with God on the earth, to make God in-carnate in the world, Jesus had to do everything in his power to help people see that the power of God is here, now—active and transforming—wherever and whenever people choose to believe it, claim it, use it, share it, take it seriously among us. It is called faith, and it creates the common-wealth of God on earth. Jesus knew this and was driven by faith to participate in bringing God to life on earth. But Jesus knew also that human institutions, secular and sacred, do not tolerate such passionate faith. To do so is to acknowledge a power on earth, a power in human life—God—that is greater than that attributed to any institution, including synagogue or church. Sooner or later, Jesus would be crucified. This he surely knew.

Knowing this, he asked his friends, "Who do people say that I am?" And the disciples gave an interesting reply: "Some say John the Baptist. Some say Elijah, or one of the other prophets." They were saying that people considered Jesus to be a prophet in the tradition of Israel, a heritage in which people like Elijah, Isaiah, Jeremiah, Hosea, and Amos had spoken to the Jews about what was to come in the future; about what was to happen when God acted later.

Then Jesus asked, "But who do you say that I am?" Jesus was saying, "Regardless of what others think of me, what do you think? You're my friends. Who am I to you? That's what I really want to know." And Peter responded, "You are the Christ." Now all good Jews, including Jesus and Peter, knew the difference between being one of the prophets and being Christ. "Prophet" means God will act *in the future;* "Christ" means God is acting *now.* Prophets speak of what God will do farther down the road; Christ makes things happen in human life immediately, here and now. Prophets say that God is coming; Christ means God is here.

That is the difference, and it makes all the difference in the world. "The time is at hand. The common-wealth of God is among you." It is what Christ is all about, and it is what Christian life is all about. It is not sitting around waiting for a "Second Coming," or to die and go to heaven and be with God then, or to try to escape from the "real world" into a "spiritual realm" of holiness; but rather to make God incarnate among us, wherever we are, in whatever we are doing, here on earth. With us, God is at home. This is what Peter meant. And wherever God is at home, here with us, there is no higher authority—no scripture, no religious tradition, no government, no commandment, no institution, no church. For God is who God is, God will be who God will be, God does what God does, without necessarily calling a meeting and checking it out with scribes and pharisees, the Vatican, the Episcopal House of Bishops, Christian theologians, the Pentagon, or the Ayatollah Khomeini.

To be in Christ, to be with Christ, to know Christ is to be in touch with what is, in Greek, our *dunamis*—raw, spontaneous power, unable to be controlled, boxed in, or possessed as our own; *able only to be shared* and, in so being, to re-create the world. *Dunamis*, the power with which Jesus healed and drew people to him, is God's power, a relational power released only in the making of right-relation: justice/righteousness. To be in Christ is to share this power of God which drives toward justice, the moral act of love between people, black and white, Jew and Christian, rich and poor. To be with Christ is, necessarily, to live dangerously—because changing the world is a turbulent process and because people who take seriously their embodiment of God's power often get hurt: Jesus of Nazareth, Joan of Arc, Martin Luther King Jr.

To be in Christ is to love with passion, which involves our willingness to suffer, or bear, the power of God in our choices and actions; to insist that God's power moving among us in the world effects love in relation, justice in society, food for the hungry, liberation for the oppressed. To be with Christ is to live with our feet on the ground of ambiguity and confusion every day, and to know that our decisions make a difference—in our homes with family and in our most intimate relationships, in our jobs, in the ways we spend money, in the ways we eat, in the priorities we establish for our lives, in our investments, in our commitments. Our lives count, and where we act in love— that is, in a sense of being related deeply to others—we are in Christ. To be with Christ is to realize that God's relational *dunamis* is *the* authority under which all other authorities—laws, scriptures, traditions, governments, religions, and institutions—rise and fall.

I want to say again, emphatically, what I believe to be the most pervasive and troublesome difficulty in being Christian: namely, that most Christians have made of our religion the same kind of religion Jesus and his friends were radicalizing in their time. Like many of Jesus' contemporaries, we tend to worship the past. We too are inclined to idolize scripture and religion, as if God lives and moves and breathes within the pages of a holy book, on papyrus scrolls, or on stone tablets. Needing some security blanket, we take irresponsible refuge in the letter, rather than the spirit, of religion and ethical teachings. The letter of the law tells us what we should or should not do—what to eat, what to wear, with whom to be seen, with whom to sleep, what to say, when to say it, when (if at all) to kill, etc. The spirit of the law draws us repeatedly to the one and only commandment Jesus himself accepted as essential for life together on the earth: "You shall love God and your neighbor as yourself."

To be in Christ is to believe in God's grace and power to help folks like you and me use every available resource in our lives, including some common sense, and some courage, to do what we can to establish justice between and among ourselves, in our own homes and throughout the world; nothing is left untouched by God's power, God's justice, among us. No one is left untouched: not starving children, battered women, boat people, tortured prisoners, harassed sexual and religious minorities, black people, races/classes/sexes/nations/religions of people whose losses of food, home, money, and life are devised systematically by an ugly greed for profit on the part of the privileged peoples of our world, among whom you and I may count ourselves.

To be with Christ is to say *No more!* and to seek ways of stopping this destruction of human life. This travesty depends on our feelings of helplessness, which take the insidious shape of indifference. What will it profit us to gain the whole world—through national pride, multinational corporations, or Christian moralisms—if we have lost our soul, which is God-with-us empowering us for one purpose: to love God and humanity with a power and passion that can raise the dead?

Jesus asked, "Who do you say that I am?" Peter said, "You are the Christ." May we say, "Amen!" German theologian Dietrich Bonhoeffer, who was martyred by the Nazis in 1945, called us to live a "religionless Christianity"—to cut the jargon, the piety, the platitudes, the preciousness, and instead to live God, to make God in-carnate in the world. This is not simply the "social gospel." It is the only gospel: to visit the sick, feed the hungry, care for the old and the weak and the downtrodden, liberate the oppressed—not only by prayer, but also by choice, commitment, and action in the world, which becomes the most profound of prayers. It is what we are here to do, you and I, to re-create the world so that younger generations may inherit an earth that is more fully the common-wealth of God, and so that God, too, may find a place to be at home—even in the grubby mangers and cluttered closets of our lives.

PART III

Coming into Our Power

By the power of bread
The power of women
The power of God
The people are blessed
The earth is blessed
And the bread is rising!

· 13 ·

Latin American Liberation Theology: A North American Perspective[1]

Sociopolitical Context

In the year 1511, Fray Antonio de Montesinos preached to his wealthy congregation in Hispaniola:

> You are in mortal sin . . . for the cruelty and tyranny you use in dealing with innocent people. . . . By what right or justice do you keep these Indians in such cruel and horrible servitude? Are they not human? Have they not rational souls, are you not bound to love them as you love yourselves?[2]

Viewed politically, in terms of the dynamics of power, Latin American history for the past four hundred years has been a picture of vast numbers of people kept dependent on a few others, so that the few on top—both those in foreign lands and their puppets at home—might expand their own economic and political interests. In essence, the majority of Latin Americans have been slaves to the interests of Spanish colonialization and later to the interests of the Western world itself, which in our time have taken the shape of multinational corporate interests of economic imperialism, planted most deeply in the soil of the United States and protected most fastidiously by the U.S. military and its allies.

Jose Miguez Bonino, Protestant theologian and teacher in Argentina, encapsulates the meaning of Latin American economic and political history in his attempt to show why the Northern hemisphere's plan for the "development" of Latin America has been and will be forever a failure.

> The rise of the Northern countries took place at a particular moment in history and was built on the possibilities offered by the resources of the dependent countries. Development and underdevelopment are not two independent realities, nor two stages in a continuum but two mutually related processes: Latin American underdevelopment is the dark side of Northern development; Northern development is built on third world underdevelopment. The basic categories for understanding our history are not development and underdevelopment, but domination and dependence. This is the crux of the matter.[3]

Miguez Bonino is saying that the United Nations' and Western world's plan for the "development" of the Third World, implemented in the 1950s and 1960s, is a sham. The point is this: there can be no economic "development" of the "have-nots" without significant, systemic, and intentional sacrifice of economic privilege on the part of the "haves." History indicates that an already developed nation like the United States will not allow, much less encourage, the "development" of a nation like Chile, because this means letting go of what we have and of what we believe is ours to keep by privilege—the "privilege" of hard work, God's grace, or some other special and exclusive "right." As Robert McAfee Brown, white North American Presbyterian theologian and teacher, suggests, "We fail to perceive [the injustices of capitalism] because such an admission would be too costly for us."[4]

The Latin American movement from economic "development" to "liberation" is founded on the assumption that the "haves" will not give up voluntarily what we have, and that the "have nots" must take what they need in order to survive.

Ernesto Cardenal is a priest and a poet. I want to share two of his poems.

In respect of riches, then, just or unjust,
of goods be they ill-gotten or well-gotten:
                    All riches are unjust.
All goods,
    ill-gotten,
if not by you, by others.
Your title deeds may be in order.   But
did you buy your land from its true owner?
And he from its true owner?   And the latter . . . ?
Though your title go back to the grant of a king
                    was
the land ever the king's?
Has no one ever been deprived of it?
And the money you receive legitimately now
from client or Bank or National Funds
        or from the U.S. Treasury,
was it ill-gotten at no point?   Yet
do not think that in the Perfect Communist State
Christ's parables will have lost relevance
Or Luke 16:9 have lost validity
        and riches be no longer UNJUST
or that you will no longer have a duty to distribute riches![5]

                    . . .
Maybe we'll get married this year,
my love, and we'll have a little house.
And maybe my book'll get published,
or we'll both go abroad.
Maybe Somoza will fall, my love.[6]

Today Ernesto Cardenal is Nicaragua's Minister of Culture.
Until 1979 he was a leading figure in the broad-based revolu-
tionary coalition formed toward one end: to bring down
Somoza, the dictator whose family had acquired and hoarded
power with the active support of the United States. Cardenal is a
gentle-spirited Christian priest who wrote, "To practice religion
is to make revolution."

Camilo Torres was a priest in Colombia. He wrote:

I have ceased to say Mass [in order] to practice love for people in
temporal, economic and social spheres. When the people have
nothing against me, when they have carried out the revolution,
then I will return to offering Mass, God willing. I think that in this

way I follow Christ's injunction, ". . . leave thy gift upon the altar and go first to be reconciled to thy brothers [and sisters]."[7]

Referring to the Catholic Church in Latin America, Torres maintained, "In my view the hierarchy of priorities should be reversed: love, the teaching of doctrine and finally [formal] worship."[8] Increasingly active politically in Colombia, believing that revolutionary action is Christian, a priestly struggle, Torres was driven finally to think that only a violent revolution would put food in the mouths of the hungry: "Only armed rebellion is left. The people are desperate and ready to stake their lives so that the next generation of Colombians may not be slaves."[9] In 1966, Camilo Torres, priest-guerrilla, was ambushed and killed by Colombian forces.

Cardenal and Torres are two of the better-known representatives, even symbols, of the movement among Latin American people—poor and oppressed people—toward liberation from economic, cultural, and political oppression. The movement is broad based—including poor people and nonpoor people who are in solidarity with the poor; theists and atheists; Christians (Catholic and Protestant) and non-Christians; Marxists and non-Marxist participants; and people in all Latin American countries: from communist Cuba, to recently liberated Nicaragua, to strife-torn El Salvador, to neofascist military establishments in Chile and Guatemala. It is a revolutionary movement founded on and motivated by a shared commitment to break the yokes of oppression so that the hungry can eat and the sick can be healed on a continent in which two thirds of the population is physically undernourished, sometimes to the point of starvation, and over one half the population suffers from deficiency diseases that kill them long before heart attacks or cancer.

The revolution in Latin America seeks to change the structures of society which, with financial and military backing of the United States and other Western capitalist countries, are perpetuated on the economic (capitalist) tenet that for the rich to get richer, the poor must get poorer; that, in fact, the upward mobility of the rich (including most if not all of us here) is dependent on the resignation of the poor to their poverty. In short, the Latin American revolution is rooted in informed analysis of social reality: namely, that the ruling classes and families in Latin America, together with us—their economic and political allies in North America and Europe—feed ourselves, clothe our bodies, run our cars, buy our houses, invest our money, enjoy our work and leisure time, elect our politicians, and worship our god over the dead bodies of increasing numbers of human beings throughout the world. And whereas the revolution in Latin America is, in every intelligible way, a secular, humanistic, materialistic revolution being planned in secret places and carried out with guns and grenades, increasing numbers of Christian revolutionaries are articulating the rationale and ultimate meaning of this revolution in what has become known in recent years as the theology of liberation, or liberation theology.

Liberation Theology

Most Latin Americans are poor. They have no land. They have little food. Some have none. Many are sick, weak, and dying. There are others in Latin America who have suffered injustice specifically because they have cast their lots with the poor. Among these are Christian women and men who have worked with the poor, lived with the poor, learned from the poor, organized with the poor, and who are currently putting into words some of what they are learning from the poor. They are attempting to articulate these lessons theologically—that is, to express the ultimate, final, and most important meaning of the human struggle for liberation from hunger and oppression. To express the theological meaning of the revolution is to name its source, God, and its goal, justice. Liberation theologians believe that the revolution in which they participate is of ultimate and highest value. They are committed to the liberative task and have sought and found that power which they believe to be God in the course of their commitment. One such theologian is Gustavo Gutiérrez, a priest in Peru, whose 1971 book, *Teologia de la liberacion (A Theology of Liberation)*, is widely regarded as the first and most comprehensive statement of liberation theology.

I will now set forth briefly Gustavo Gutiérrez's theological position, suggesting ways in which he is in continuity and discontinuity with the liberal theological traditions most of us share.

Gutiérrez's theology reflects his conviction that "when the wretched of the earth awake, their first challenge is not to religion but to the social, economic, and political order oppressing them and to the ideology supporting it."[10] Gutiérrez articulates a new theology of humanity—that is to say, a theology that takes human life as seriously as it does divine life. This liberation theology is rooted in the populist movements for economic and political liberation among the poor. Theology is "the second act"; commitment to revolution, the first. Gutiérrez is liberal in his rejection of the Augustinian-Lutheran doctrine of the "two Kingdoms," believing rather that "history is the locale where God reveals the mystery of [God's] person"[11] and that "without liberating historical events, there would be no growth of the Kingdom."[12] Gutiérrez's wholly good God is in the world, a God whose advocacy of the poor is apparent in both Jesus' life and the Old Testament.

Like most liberal theologians, Gutiérrez emphasizes the creativity, rather than the fall, of humanity. He faults traditional Western (Augustinian) theology for "a curious omission of the liberating and protagonistic role of humanity, . . . coparticipant in our own salvation."[13] The operations of God and those of "natural" humanity—beings uncorrupted by unjust social structures—are the same operations in history, which is to say that a *human* act of love and justice *is* an act of God in history. Eschatologically, God *and* humanity have the final word, a word of love and justice.

What is new in Gutiérrez's theology, or what distinguishes it from earlier theologies of humanity such as Schleiermacher's, is (1) that Gutiérrez is interested in classes rather than individuals as his primary theological resource; and (2) that he equates natural, or uncorrupted, humanity with "the poor," a materialistic distinction, contending on the basis of a scriptural hermeneutic that "the poor person for the gospel is the neighbor par excellence."[14] This departure from liberal theology is significant in that it serves in a fundamental way to signify a shift from the individual's preoccupation with her own faults to a thoroughgoing analysis of social, economic, and political structures in which "sin is not considered as an individual, private, or merely interior reality." Rather, for Gutiérrez and Latin American liberation theology, "sin is regarded as a social, historical fact, the absence of brotherhood [and sisterhood] and love in relationships . . . , the breach of friendship with God and with other [people], and *therefore*, an interior, personal fracture."[15]

In other words, the "interior" personal brokenness that we experience is steeped in an absence of sisterhood/brotherhood—not vice-versa. Thus, for Gutiérrez, passivity in the face of social oppression, whether the passivity of rich or poor, is sinful and is responsible for the evil of injustice in history.

Humanity, specifically poor humanity, becomes responsible for co-participation with God in redemption from evil. God is with humanity on the earth. Gutiérrez writes, "It is not enough to say that love of God is inseparable from the love of one's neighbor. It must be added that love for God is unavoidably expressed *through* love of one's neighbor"[16]; "Conversion to [God] implies conversion to the neighbor."[17] Moreover, "the neighbor is not an occasion, an instrument for becoming closer to God. We are dealing with a real love of [human beings] for [their] own sake, and not 'for the love of God.' "[18]

This is, emphatically, a theology grounded in the human experience of being human—a theology that can be legitimated only in and by its effects in praxis or the circular movement between practice and reflection. It is a theology that begins with the poor, those whose "epistemological privilege" is to know God, and who become the spokespersons for all humanity. Gutiérrez's methodology applies Marxist social and economic analysis to a biblical hermeneutic founded on the faith claim that God is love. Gutiérrez's biblical hermeneutic is amplified by Juan Luis Segundo's "hermeneutic of suspicion," a way of looking at reality, including the Bible, for whatever is loving and just and for whatever is not; and viewing with strong suspicion any act in society, or any interpretation of biblical texts, that does not contribute to justice in human life.

"To live love is to say yes to God."[19] To live love is to be responsible for justice in society. "Christ is *not* a private individual. The bond which links [Christ] to all [humanity] gives [Christ] a unique historical role."[20] Christ reveals God in history as the love that binds humanity to humanity, person to person. "When justice does not exist, God is not known; [God] is absent."[21]

Thus, for Gutiérrez, God is love, God is wholly good, God is active in history through the poor and oppressed, whose task it is to construct a utopia in history, which is not to be understood as synonymous with the reign promised by God at the eschaton, but which is rather humanity's responsibility in the building of this realm.[22]

Gutiérrez works on the assumption that evil—the injustice fastened in social structures (including our churches)—can and must be undone by humanity and God in partnership, which is to say "in Christ."

Nowhere does Gutiérrez question the existence or the goodness of God. What he does question is God's omnipotence, thereby marking his most radical departure from traditional theologies. He joins Bonhoeffer in suggesting that religion, as opposed to gospel, is bound to the concept of an omnipotent deity, a God who maintains control over creation. With Bonhoeffer, he concurs, "The God of Christians living in a world come of age—meaning a world without God—must share God's suffering."[23]

Gutiérrez and the liberation theology he represents present a constructive and dynamic corrective to the liberal theological tradition of "development"—that is, of God's grace enabling humanity gradually to grow up, "evolving" more and more into the likeness of God. Gutiérrez rejects social, economic, and anthropological developmentalism or evolution, and maintains rather that we must be revolutionary—proactive agents of our own redemption in cooperation with a God who casts down the mighty from their thrones. Liberation theology's momentum is engendered by class struggle and the "privilege" of the poor to find meaning and take heart in their own struggle for liberation from material oppression, a liberation that they themselves can and must effect.

This theology is steeped in a political realism that is infused by faith in a just God. It is thoroughly a theology "from below," in which God's goodness, love, and justice can be experienced and envisioned in the context of God's powerlessness. This is especially true inasmuch as God is believed to be not only identified with the poor, but also close to poor humanity in history—a God both "like" and "with" humanity, both good and powerless in the world, the nature of whose being is to revolt.

This is, in a glimpse, what liberation theology is all about, as I read it: a new theology of humanity, thoroughly Christian in terms of its hermeneutics and symbology, and most importantly the commitment to love of neighbor as self.

Since 90 percent of Latin America's 230 million people are Roman Catholic and most liberation theologians are themselves Catholic—often priests and nuns—the institutional church has not been silent on the subject of liberation theology. It is not possible here to explore in detail or depth the Catholic Church's official responses through its episcopal bodies. But, in summary, I can suggest to you that the response has been abundant with mixed messages. From 1968, when the Latin American bishops met in Medellin, Colombia, to January 1979, when they reconvened in Puebla, Mexico, attention at the episcopal level (both in Rome and Latin America) has been serious and generally cautious. There are a few outstanding liberation theologians among the bishops, such as Dom Helder Camara of Brazil. But for the most part, the popes and bishops have urged gradualism and have been unwilling to side with either capitalism or socialism as acceptable Christian ideologies. Pope John Paul II is, it seems to me, fairly representative of the episcopal attitude: on one hand, he acknowledges the incompatibility of systemic poverty with the charity and teachings of Christ; on the other hand, he has reminded priests and nuns that the religious vocation is— and must remain—transcendent of the systems of material oppression *and* liberation. In short, the Pope is aware that the *problem* is a human one, involving social structures, but he does not recognize that the *solution* is no less human, a responsibility involving social struggle, which necessitates human activity in—not above—the struggle.

So What?

There is a thoroughgoing connection between Latin America and North America, "them" and "us." Most if not all of us here today must count ourselves among the rich—probably not the super-rich, but relative to the poor, the very rich. Regardless of personal fault, we live our lives as a dominating class. Our privilege (even the privilege of being here today) is dependent on the work, the poverty, and the deaths of others, both in Latin America and in the United States. But the etiology and consequences of this social malaise do not have to be located as far away as Argentina, El Salvador, Washington, Roxbury, or Cambridge's city hall. In fact, to locate the problem elsewhere and to shake our heads in grievous concern is forever to deny the problem precisely at the place and time in which we can effect social change, thereby participating in the liberation of humanity—the place being our own lives, the time being now.

Theologically we cannot rightly contrast the so-called larger justice issues with the so-called smaller ones in terms of value—especially when this exercise in contrast is usually an attempt to avoid the smaller ones—those that affect folks like you and me here and now where we live and work together. Issues of Latin American poverty or South African apartheid are easy enough for us to care about—usually at some distance or at least with some guarantee that the ways in which we lead our lives as teachers, students, priests, scholars, ministers, lovers, friends, spouses, daughters, sons, and parents will not be too radically altered in the processes of our caring for others. But the most important challenge of liberation theology to us is that we take serious stock of our own values and priorities, choices and activities, relationships, investments, and commitments, in a realization that what we do here, where we are, is—unavoidably and inextricably—related to what they do there, so much so that what we do here to one another *is* what we do there to them.

Let us be more specific. There are hierarchies of domination and dependence—that is, of injustice—in our seminaries, in our churches and families, which are linked structurally (economically, politically, psychologically, theologically) to the structures of domination and dependence in Latin America. I am referring to our own existent tensions, animosities, wounds, fears, and alienation—between men and women, white and black and brown, straight and gay/lesbian, clergy and laity, richer and less rich, those who make decisions and those who live by them, those who define and those who are defined in terms of values, capacities, and rights.

Yes—we need to consider, analyze, and take very seriously the points of systemic connection between Nelson Rockefeller's official warning to the U.S. government in 1969 of the "troublesome" socialistic tendencies of the church in Latin America and the U.S. involvement in the downfall of Chile's Marxist President Allende in 1973. We need also to consider the relation between John Paul II's condemnation of Hans Küng for venturing beyond the bounds of Catholic orthodoxy and the dictator of Guatemala Lucas Garcia's attack on Jesuit activists for (quoting the pope) "causing confusion among the Christian people and anxiety to the church as well as the Pope."[24]

We must consider also the relation between the worship of a father god and the deep-seated male-on-female domination that is an indispensable screw in the bolt that secures multinational operations that rape humanity and the earth at home and abroad. We can go farther and examine the linkage between the idolatry of nuclear family, assumptions about the headship and profitable value of men, the ongoing promotion of Nestle's un-nourishing baby formula to people in the Third World, and the fact that women and children constitute 83 percent of the welfare rolls in the United States and are usually the first to die of malnutrition at home and abroad. It is called "triage," and it is legitimated by the notion of a male deity in whose image is all that is truly worth saving.

There is mounting resistance in the United States to the so-called smaller issues of women's ordination, the right of women to safe medical abortions, and the lesbian and gay challenge to the "natural" order of both creation and society. The resistance to these movements signals the extent to which men—celibate men and family men—will *not* be moved to relinquish their powers of domination and control in their homes, churches, and businesses. And, moreover, it signals the extent to which women, who have been fed men's definitions of both divinity and humanity, have internalized our oppression and are only slowly learning to fight for our lives.

For our sake as well as that of the rest of humanity, we need to realize that it is more often than not the *same* economic interests, the *same* governmental interests, the *same* ecclesiastical interests, and the *same* special interest groups that line up *against* the revolutions in Latin America and Zimbabwe, *against* aid to the cities, *against* welfare and day care and provisions for safe medical abortions, *against* gay/lesbian liberation and women's ordination, *against* prisoners in Attica and New Mexico, Joan Little, Angela Davis, black power, Native American grievances, and "communism," and *against* most if not all ecclesiastical change. It is usually these same people who are *for* nuclear power and war—not because they like these things, but rather because it is in their financial and/or status interests to keep the power over life and death in the hands of a very few principalities. These are the people who tend to stand firm in their opposition to the relinquishment of any hard-earned privilege— by men, white men, rich white men, rich white private-enterprising men who see themselves as God's special people on the earth.

We need to look very carefully at the relation between the enslavement of the Latin American poor and the fact that people of darker skin have been historically the slaves of the rest of humanity—not only Indians in Brazil and the United States, but also black people throughout the world, and brown and red and yellow and even darker white people. Hitler's vision was no anomaly. It was a grotesque and enormous enactment of a racist assumption that has undergirded the church's missionary efforts as well as the larger society's investment in the manifest destiny of all that is light, white, clean, pure, bright, and perfect. We may recognize this as a common, if perverse, description of a Father God in whose lofty image humanity is said to have been created: a light, white, clean, pure, and perfect "humanity" (read: man).

There seems to me no way that we can begin to hear Latin American liberation theology on its own terms, its scathing indictment of the structures of domination and control, without asking ourselves hard questions about how we live our lives. We are among the rich. Most of us are white. A few are black or brown or red. Most of you are men. Some of us are women. All of us are sexual beings. Many of us are gay/lesbian or sexually active outside of marriage. Yet all of us are encouraged to be silent: to cease from making any connections in any public ways between love and justice and sexuality and the economy and politics and structures of domination and dependence that are embedded in our theological traditions.

But it is *our* business, the business of *our* church, to consider, analyze, speak up about, and act on precisely these matters. We contrive indifference or ignorance at the expense of our souls, and perhaps of our sanity and our bodies as well, and also at the expense of the poor in the world. I am not attempting to be dramatic. I am attempting to name reality as it is set before us by liberation theology: the reality of *our* praxis, *our* priorities, *our* values, *our* choices, the ways in which we live *our* lives. It is not enough to be "liberal" or "interested" or "open" or "knowledgeable"—not in the middle of revolution, a revolution that is with us whether we like it or not. For the revolution in Latin America is, in the final analysis, no more "theirs" than "ours." The dangers and the opportunities are no less great for "us" than for "them."

· 14 ·

Redefining Power*

In a world of superpowers—nuclear power, political power, powers of coercion, violence, and oppression, plastic power, media power, and genetic power—the word power is likely to evoke among us images of brawn, guns, and fierce struggle, and feelings of anger, fear, and helplessness. We know all too well what Paul refers to as the "principalities and powers" that loom ominously above us and among us, tempting and threatening us, menacing us, luring us, much as they did Jesus, to sell our souls for what may appear to be larger pieces of various pies: property, prestige, status, approval, security, reward, money. As a byword for control over our own lives and perhaps also the lives of others, and as a synonym for "machismo" (the ability to instill awe-full fear in others), "power" has become synonymous with possession. In a given situation, we either have it or we do not. The government has power; the people do not. The rich have power; the poor do not. Armed soldiers have power; hostages and unarmed citizens do not.

Pick up the newspaper and glance through it. Political candi-

---

*This essay is taken from a sermon given at Dartmouth College, Hanover, NH, April 1980.

dates, economists, sportscasters, and fashion editors call upon us to do whatever we can to enhance the power of our country, our dollar, our teams, our bodies, and our sex appeal. We learn as we live that to be a person—happy, worthy, gratified—is to possess a power that is, by definition, ours and no one else's. Either we are the best, with the most power, the strongest ability to command whatever it is we seek, or we are to some extent failures. And this is true whether we are speaking of the United States, our own value systems, or the beauty and appeal of our bodies. To possess power is to be on top—of someone else. To have power is to be able to look down on others. It is to be above the common folk—to flex the muscles of our brains, bodies, or ideologies—and to win. It is the stuff that political campaigns, as well as all religious and ethical systems that teach the way to Absolute Truth, are made of. Everybody wants power (you and I no less than others), and at the same time most Christians "confess" regularly that we have "done those things we ought not to have done" by stepping on the lives and dignity of one another and of our sisters and brothers around the world. Like sex, power is something we want—and feel guilty about when we get it.

Christians always talk about the power of God as being more powerful than the power of humankind and the world itself. Christians also talk about the power of God as giving us "a peace which passeth all understanding." But what we who are Christian have difficulty believing (and it is a faith issue) is that the power of God is powerful in the world only when we ourselves have been inspired by it, have been filled with its spirit, and have made it our own while we are alive on the earth. God's power is ours—to the extent that we choose to make this tender power in-carnate in history.

And the woman who was bleeding heavily had heard reports about Jesus and came up behind him in the crowd and touched his garments (see Mark 5:25, 27). What is it that moves any of us to reach out for help? To seek something from someone else? Why does any of us who is hurting go to a doctor? Or a teacher? Or a friend? Or a therapist? Or a colleague? What help do we seek? What power do we seek? If we are seeking to be healed—to be made whole, to be strengthened, to gain confidence, to be assured, to be encouraged—what power do we seek? Are we seeking some assurance that there is someone else—someone out there—be it Jesus, the doctor, or the supervisor, the president, the priest, or the one with authority— someone else who possesses a power that he, or she, may use to help us? Or are we seeking something deeper, something lasting, some radical re-encouragement to claim a power that is ours? In our answers to these questions may hang the balance between our life and death—as human beings on the earth.

At stake here is not the authority and credibility of our leaders—our professors and congresspeople, our president and politicians, our scientists and role models. At stake is not our belief in the divinity of Jesus or the extraordinary power of the One, or Ones, whom we adore or worship. At stake is our own—and the rest of humanity's—capacity and commitment to live as responsible, creative people of God on earth, people whose common vocation is to share and celebrate the power of God among us: the power of God, which is the power of our relational bonding; a persistent power that makes "justice roll down like waters" and against which "principalities and false powers" do not prevail at any level of our lives, as individuals, friends, partners, spouses, lovers, colleagues, or as communities and collective groupings.

And the woman who touched Jesus' garments "felt in her body that she was healed of her disease. And Jesus, perceiving in himself that power had gone forth from him, turned about in the crowd [Mark 5:29–30]." A flow of power, a reciprocal situation, in which both persons are affected by what is happening between them: Jesus is vulnerable to touch, relation, the healing process, not as "the one who heals," but as one who *participates* in the healing. Here, as elsewhere, Jesus says to the person who has initiated this transaction, "Go in peace. Your faith has made you well." Jesus does *not* say to those who come to him, "*I* have healed you." Or even, "*God* has healed you." But rather, "Your *faith* has healed you." Which is to say that you have played a part in what has happened. You yourself have participated in the making of yourself whole, well.

The power that goes forth from Jesus, the power released by the woman's reaching and touching in faith, is a power quite unlike the principalities and powers within/between/among us that seek control and domination over our own lives and the lives of others. The power that goes forth from Jesus has nothing to do with wealth, status, orthodoxy, or conformity to established patterns of thought or behavior or feeling in society. The power that goes forth from Jesus is *dunamis*—raw, spontaneous, unmediated power—which breaks down established roles of control and possession and sets the stage for a new experience of power, as reciprocal.

Faith is believing not in Jesus, but rather in the power that goes forth from him: the power of God, which is, by its nature (the nature of God) shared—never a "possession" of Jesus, you, me, the United States, the Christian church, or the Ayatollah Khomeini. The power of Jesus, which is the power of God and the power of all persons with faith in this power, is a shared power—moving, given, received, passed on, celebrated, held in common as ours, not mine alone or his alone or hers alone. God's power does not belong to Jesus. It belongs to us, to the extent that we pass it on.

There are two common perversions of this power that can destroy us individually, as a church and as a society. The first perversion of power is as the hero. Sheldon Kopp warns, "If you have a hero, look again; you have diminished yourself in some way."[1] Whenever we project our shared power/God's power onto someone else—as something s/he possesses—be it a spouse, a lover, a teacher, a guru, an author, a public figure—we thereby relinquish our participation and cooperation with that person and others in bringing our power to life—to our shared life together. We give up something of our own souls, or the essence of who we are as human (relational) beings on the earth. Simply by having been created, we are empowered by our Creator to join in the creative enterprises, to "re-create the universe" (Elie Wiesel), to join hands in common venture with God and one another. Simply because we *are*.

To the extent that we seek heroes to do it for us—someone else to incarnate the power, set the standards, lead the struggles, pace the celebrations—we give up our birthrights to pick up our beds and walk into the world, the next room, the next class, the next meeting, and claim our own power to do something—simply because we believe that we must. A hero is an uncreative relational construct, someone we set above us, out of our reach; someone who may move us but who is himself/ herself not moved. A person who takes herself seriously as a person of God—empowered and empowering—is the mover and the moved, the changer and the changed (Cris Williamson), a giver and a recipient of gifts.

Certain presidential candidates today are manipulating our desire for heroes, rather than calling us to join hands in the creation of a just society. Moreover, they evoke our self-interest and our love of possessions rather than our vocation to love our neighbors as ourselves. If the first perversion of power is our inclination to make heroes out of others and to abdicate our own creative power to them, the second is its flip side (although frequently the two manifest themselves together in our lives).

The second perversion of power is narcissism. We have probably heard enough about the "me generation" by now to have quit listening to what folks have to say about it. That has been true of me at least. Yet listen we should, because those of us who were growing during the sixties and seventies (whether we were children, teens, or older) could not help brushing up against both the positive and the negative edges of the cultural phenomenon characterized by the obsession with "my needs." You know what I mean: "I can't make up my mind until I discover what my needs are." "I can't do this because my needs aren't getting met." "I need to tell you how I feel, and so I'm going to—whether or not you want me to." Now, it is not all bad. Because the power that we share in relation to one another and the rest of humanity is enhanced by authentic self-love, or appreciation and respect for who each of us is, uniquely and individually. It is a fact. I simply cannot be really with you— mutually open to who you are—unless I realize my own value and worth as a person who means something to you and others.

I love myself. But there is a moral difference between my loving myself as I do you and my positioning myself at the center of all that matters, as if my needs really are more valuable than yours—as if my needs for anything (compassion, approval, money, promotion, freedom to speak my mind, whatever) really do take some strange precedence over yours and those of others. The seeds of emotional and physical violence are planted deep within this narcissistic impulse. Moreover, the seeds of our social malaise—we who are North Americans (especially middle- and upper-strata North Americans, most of us white, most of you men)—are lodged firmly in the soil of a cultural narcissism that teaches us that "every man lives for himself" and that sharing power—and I mean positive, good power—with blacks, Native Americans, women, the poor, gays, "others," is to relinquish what it means to be a man: to have power.

Few of us know what to make of our current foreign policy. Consider Iran. It is apparent to me that, however we might view the taking of hostages and the madness of the Ayatollah, the Iranian grievances expressed toward our country for its ongoing role in support of the shah, his business interests, and his money, are legitimate complaints that cut to the heart of our own sociocultural narcissism—a preoccupation with "our needs"—which is all but endemic in American society and too often in the Christian church. The moral question is not whether we are more or less "moral" than Iranians, Shi'ite Muslims, Russians, whomever. The question is whether we are a nation with moral foreign and domestic concerns. Or are we, as a nation, so taken with ourselves that we do not actually care about others? Do we or do we not regard with respect, a high degree of appreciation, the rest of the people of the world? The moral question for us is whether we view all other nations as allies or enemies on the basis of our economic profit and military control, or whether we perceive ourselves as a cooperative nation, whose economic interests and well-being must be shared widely and generously. I am no statesperson or expert on foreign affairs. And I do not claim to be a professional politician. I am a sister in the faith, who shares with you a moral obligation to address the issue of power, a political issue. With you, I am a citizen of the nation, a person of the world, a sister/co-participant with others in the making or breaking of the earth. I am obligated to preach that our narcissism as a nation, together with our endless search for heroes to get us out of the messes we get ourselves into, is a moral outrage that flies in the face of both humanity and God. There *is* another way: a way more fully human and more fully divine.

Jesus taught it and lived it. Paul preached it and prayed it. Other figures in history have seen it, lived it, and died for it: to be filled with the power of God, the power that is humanity's by nothing more than faith in the power of our common bonding on common ground. Leap. Take an imaginative step into the experience of the power that goes forth from us, each and all of us, when we stand vulnerable to being touched by humanity, open to seeking the ground on which we can stand together not as competitors for grades or lovers, salaries or promotions, but rather as sisters and brothers, co-operative and co-creative, moving together toward and into a Promised Land that Moses saw, Jesus heralded, and Sojourner Truth and Harriet Tubman and Martin Luther King and Alice Paul and Harvey Milk and Oscar Romero lived and died for.

There is no one among us who is not on this journey—equally and forever, whether or not we claim to be—women and men, white and black and brown and red and yellow, U.S. citizens and others, sick and well, confused and clear, straight and gay/lesbian. We are in a common world. The moral question for us is whether or not we will claim our shared power, whether or not we will choose to share the power that is good, creative, and redemptive when it is ours together—and nothing less than evil when we "possess it" as ours and ours alone.

Till Now We Had Not Touched Our Strength[1]

In the diary as the wind   began to tear
at the tents over us   I wrote:
We know now we have always been in danger
down in our separateness
and now up there together   but till now
we had not touched our strength

In the diary torn from my fingers I had written:
What does love mean
What does it mean   "to survive"
A cable of blue fire ropes our bodies
burning together in the snow   We will not live
to settle for less   We have dreamed of this
all of our lives[2]

Often the real theologians are the poets, those who speak out of
and in god by allowing an intense expression of human experi-
ence to take a form that we can share. Adrienne Rich's "Phan-
tasia" is written as though through the mind of a Russian
woman, "the leader of a women's climbing team, all of whom
died in a storm on Lenin Peak," in August 1974.[3] Rich's experi-
ence of what is valuable in human life finds words in this poem

that convey the power of human bonding in trust and adventure and shared efforts and common vision; the power of the human body in physical bonding, stretching, reaching, touching; the power of women's love and respect for women, power even in dying.

We touch this strength, our power, who we are in the world, when we are most fully in touch with one another and with the world. There is no doubt in my mind that, in so doing, we are participants in ongoing incarnation, bringing god to life in the world. For god is nothing other than the eternally creative source of our relational power, our common strength, a god whose movement is to empower, bringing us into our own together, a god whose name in history is love—provided we mean by "love" not just simply a sentiment or unfocused feeling but rather that which is just, mutually empowering, and co-creative. To profess love for someone, or for humanity itself, or for god, and to do nothing to bring those whom we love to life and power is to lie in the most shameful and cruel way, to make a mockery out of love, justice, humanity, and god.

I want to reflect on strength—to share some of my own ongoing struggles in order to see more clearly what is worthwhile and what is not in our life together, to tell you, insofar as I can, how I am coming to believe that whatever is valuable springs from the rich soil of human power rather than from our misinformed attachments to suffering, helplessness, and weakness. If we direct our attention and faith to the "power in powerlessness" and the "strength in weakness" (which is what such theologians as Bonhoeffer and Jürgen Moltmann suggest), we are misled into a wilderness of assumptions in which our saints *must* be martyrs rather than revolutionaries, dead rather than alive, singled out and set apart rather than *with* us holding all things in common. I want us to dwell on our strength and consider in what sense, when we are dealing with our strength, we are dealing with our sexuality.

In 1979 I was in North Carolina on a special mission: to discuss with my family and a few old friends why I had decided to make a public statement about my sexuality, why I had decided to come out. The difficulties in this mission felt almost insurmountable.

First, as those who know me knew, I had never appreciated the various sexual categories we, as social beings, use, often to contain, restrain, or avoid the depths, heights, and breadth of our sexuality as an expansive, open, relational movement. "Why," my family and friends would ask, "would someone who says that sexuality and relational power are one and the same thing choose to put limits on that relational power?" "Why would you, who have said that you believe that the relationship between an artist and his poetry or a revolutionary and her people are potent sexual relationships, choose to distort your own values by virtually dismissing men from your own realm of relational potency?" (I must note in passing that these same questions are not often put to people who say or show that they are heterosexual.) "Why limit yourself?" "Why tell the world that you're a lesbian and thereby invite others to perceive you as a woman who hates men?" "Why, if you really feel you must discuss your sexuality at all, not speak of yourself as 'bisexual,' or 'sexual,' or even as 'polymorphously perverse'?" These were questions I was hard-pressed to answer, questions with which I have struggled, and still do.

Second, there was the problem of imprudence, a multidimensional quandary steeped in my capacity to be politically inexpedient, insensitive, and callous. What about the other women priests? Did I realize what I might be doing to other women's, if not my own, chances for professional credibility? The "tar-brush effect": lending support to the anxiety-laced contention that *all* women priests and ministers are lesbians because some have said they themselves are. And the timing? After all, it had been only five years since eleven of us had been ordained in a controversial service. What might happen now, to the others as well as to me, if the Episcopal public were given another opportunity to dismiss us all as a bunch of publicity seeking, sick, selfish, sinful women?

I knew at the time that coming out seemed to me to be the best way to lend some integrity to my vocation: as a teacher in a seminary in which, like all schools, many students are struggling fiercely with their sexuality; and as a priest, a member of an order representing human being in its many dimensions of seeking and finding, brokenness and wholeness, coming into one's own in the world and coming out of oneself to the world. The time seemed right, personally and professionally, to claim and articulate to myself and others that I have been discovering something terribly important as a woman in relation to women: those in the world who are most fully my sexual peers, those with whom I am planted in common social soil and beside whom I stand on equal ground in this sexist society. Coming out was, for me, *not* first a statement about *who I sleep with* but rather a statement about *what I value* in human and divine life: learning to walk a common way; a process at once sexual, political, spiritual, economic; a relational journey both individual and collective.

Still, I had serious questions and, at every turn, they were raised by others as well: first, about whether I really believed in what I was doing—namely, taking on a label that means many different things to different people, a mark especially hard to bear for someone whose anthropological and theological antipathy toward sexual categorizing is strong; second, about whether I was contributing to the damaging of other people and, if so, whether I was prepared to take responsibility for what I was doing. The answers were fuzzy. The processes of clarifying them have been made more complex and more important than I might have imagined at the time by two simultaneous experiences: (1) the writing of a dissertation on "mutual relation," a process in which I was continually having to stretch my mind and faith beyond proof into dimly lit forests of intimation and suggestion simply on the basis of what we see through a glass darkly; and (2) my love for someone, a commitment to a particular relationship that moves slowly and unevenly into places of trust and mutuality and has been an occasion as much for questions as for answers about what it means to love, to do what is just, to live well in relation to those closest to us.

Hence, I found myself simultaneously coming out as a lesbian and coming into doubts about my understanding of sexuality, the effects of my sexuality on others, my capacity to think or write clearly about anything (a classic misgiving among graduate students), and my ability to cherish relationship, as well as about the fallout of my action onto the lives of my family, students, sisters, friends, and lover. There have been days and nights, from week to week and month to month, in which I have felt propped at the farthest edge of sanity, kept from toppling by the barest of shining threads binding my heart and bringing me into a circle of friendship with those who sing, speak, preach about a strength which is *ours*, even in those moments beset by feelings of weakness, confusion, and craziness.

Our strength is the power that we touch together, not alone. It is power not as we ordinarily define "power" in the world—a power that cannot be possessed or owned by a lone soul, a hero, any one of us. For it is not a possession, an achievement, a goal, or a gift from anyone else. Our strength is not bought, sold, or cultivated simply in the privacy of our prayers or in our therapeutic chambers. It cannot be fabricated or contrived. Our strength does not transcend or trivialize our weakness. It is not the opposite of vulnerability, but rather is its fulfillment. Our strength is the power of being human, through which we realize that we are in relation to others—quite literally, an experience of knowing ourselves as *only* in relation. We may live alone. We may need and crave solitude. But it is in relation that we live, and need, and desire; relation to the ground on which we stand, the fruits of the earth that we enjoy, she or he whom we embrace, our friends and our enemies; in relation to rich and poor, to peoples of same and different colors and beliefs and ways of constructing reality.

To touch our strength is not, in the first instance, to have a mystical experience of universal unity, but rather to look and see what is right before our eyes, and to see that we are together in this life. It is to see that we are in common—even in our alienations, apartness, and differences.

My strength which is our strength begins in the soil of my vulnerability—that is, when I do not deny myself or you, as I often do, in playing games of how "strong and together" I am. Vulnerability is an openness to our common places, places of confusion as well as clarity. It is the willingness and ability to be seen as well as to see, to be touched as well as to touch. Vulnerability is the giving up of control, the turning of oneself over to the common life, not to be absorbed, stepped on, or negated, but rather to experience ourselves as co-creators of the world we want and believe in. The image is of her, or him, who is standing with both feet on the ground, with one arm reaching out, making love/making justice, in touch with others, and the other arm relaxed, hand open—waiting?—holding a book, a beer, a ball, a cracker, a flower, a hoe, a hammer? It is not an either/or. In touch with others, we are most likely to discover the roots of true autonomy.

But vulnerability in itself is not enough, whether in personal relationships or political systems. Our strength is our vulnerability's fulfillment. Without vulnerability, we are only pretenders, macho/manipulative women and men who come on cool, impressive, and impassive. Unless we are vulnerable, with hearts and minds and arms open to sharing ourselves on an assumption that we hold much in common, we will never know our strength, because we will never touch that power available only in relation. But it is possible to drown in vulnerability. It happens all the time. It is easy to get lost in the maze of pleas and cries and human possibilities and choices. Too many choices. Too much openness. Too little focus. When we open our eyes and really see what is at hand—people trying to touch, lesbians beaten up by boys in bars, people trampled to death at Oscar Romero's funeral, blacks ripped apart in Miami and Boston—it is easy to make a truce with indignation (Al Carmines) and begin to feel at home with our pain-in-our-vulnerability. We become attached to bleeding hearts and moist eyes, because among ourselves we get high mileage out of being sensitive, deep-feeling, vulnerable people. This will not do.

Our strength is our commitment to *do something* about what we have experienced, to celebrate the just and change the unjust; it is our commitment to act on the basis of what we have seen and come to know about humanity—our own humanity and that of others, a humanity that is ours. Our strength is our commitment to *live* our values.

The time since I have come out publicly has been a time of being driven toward our strength. I tend to act and write ahead of myself, nudging and tugging at my consciousness, urging myself into new behavior. I came out before I was "ready" to come out simply because it seemed to be the least morally cluttered way to live my life. I was not "ready" for what would happen—specifically, for the enormity of the anxiety this process has stirred within and around me in the world church. But if it is true that we act our way into thinking, I would never have been ready.

Had I waited until I was settled and stable in my relationships, ideological constructs, theological reasons; until I knew the full answer to the question, "Why are you doing this?"; until I was absolutely sure of myself and others; until my family understood fully; until my relationship with my special friend felt secure; until I knew exactly what to expect, I would have come out (if at all) as an impassive, controlled and controlling, invulnerable woman, cemented rather than grounded, unable to be bent, taken, or hurt, and out of touch with our strength.

I want to say something about the relation between strength and suffering. Suffering has long been hailed as a religious virtue, "the way of the cross," self-denial, sacrifice, humiliation. We can see it, feel it, find it everywhere. We mold our heroes out of blood and tears. Christianity, both Catholic and Protestant, has been a religion that glorifies suffering and death; a resurrection cult in which visible physical pain and death is "justified" by invisible spiritual comfort and life. The problem here—and it is a critical one in which sexuality is very much at issue—is that we have learned, generation upon generation, to take pleasure in pain—that is, to respect our distress and appreciate our bruises as signs of our blessedness. (Blessed are the poor, the despised, those who are mocked, betrayed, denied, spat upon, beaten, and crucified.) A battered spouse is a victim of a battering spouse but also, I think, of a pervasive mentality in which battering is related to justification or "setting things right." Sadomasochism is testimony to the same cult of battering, pain, and suffering. And not only the sadomasochism of leather and chains, bondage and discipline, slave and master, but also the sadomasochism many of us experience in the connections between sexual coerciveness/overpowering and genital titillation and pleasure, or simply in our attachments to the very people who treat us worst.

Consider the violence unharnessed not only in bars and bedrooms, living rooms and kitchens, but also in our sanctuaries and government, in which justice, life, liberty, and the pursuit of happiness are assumed to be available largely in systems of domination and submission, control and condescension, paternalism and obedience! Who are these gods that we worship? What are we doing to ourselves and one another? What are we doing to the world?

In its nonperverted, most radical dimensions, sexuality is our socio/psychophysical drive toward right, mutual relation. It is loving. It is just. It is co-creative. Sexuality is, I believe, our impulse to seek and find what we, and all creation, *need* in relation, both to one another and to the source of all creative power, that which is god. Sexuality is a protest against structures of alienation. It is a NO! to humiliation; a NO! to the denial of the human—created and creative—yearning for reciprocal, mutually empowering connections. As such, sexuality is the wellspring of vitality in *all* relationships, *all* creativity, *all* productivity. To be out of touch with our sexuality is to be literally cut off—physically, emotionally, spiritually, politically—from our remarkable and potent capacity to co-create, co-redeem, and co-bless the world. It is to be out of touch with our strength, cut off from the movement of god in the world; out of sync with the source and resource of what it means to make love, not only in bed, but also on the streets of New York or in conversations in the Poconos.

Our sexuality does not seek suffering, but rather its release. It does not glorify pain and death, but rather creates pleasure, life, birth, and rebirth. Our sexuality does not construct systems, ideologies, religions, relationships of domination and control, cruelty, compliance, and competition, but rather presses on toward cooperation between and among human beings as well as between humanity and that source of power we call god.

Given the weight of "holy things" we have been carrying for generations and centuries, it might be irritating for me to suggest an equation between sexuality and the Holy Spirit, but I am tempted to do so, if only to provoke recognition of the utterly all-pervasive movement of sexuality in creativity. It is the power, the yearning, the hunger, the drive, the YES to the breaking down of the walls that separate person from person, creature from creature, creature from creator; and to the making of the connections between and among us in which we find our *common good*. Thus, sexuality pushes in socialistic directions, in which the drive to satisfy the hunger for food, for freedom, for friends, for dignity, for tangible and visible relationships of caring, supersedes the "rewards" promised to obedient children of state, church, society, or the mores of social organization.

Our experiences of sexuality offer us a reading of our strength and vulnerability. If sexuality is the experience of our strength, then sexuality is rooted in vulnerability. Strong, vulnerable people do not rape, batter, beat, and destroy one another. Rape is an act of violence, indeed of sexual perversion, as are all acts of violence. (Perverted: turned completely around from itself.) Invulnerable, impassive persons (and we are they more than we care to admit) who boast of "strength" are those best equipped and most likely to assault humanity on the streets, on the battlefield, or behind the button. We who are afraid of our strength are those most likely to submit to violence—emotionally, institutionally, and physically. Our fear of our strength may be our undoing. And our learning to stand and speak up for ourselves may well be our salvation. "We have dreamed of this all of our lives" (Adrienne Rich). Will we settle for less?

· 16 ·

God or Mammon?*

"Make friends for yourselves by means of unrighteous mammon, so that when it fails they may receive you into the eternal habitations [Luke 16:9]." There is only one way I can read Jesus' bid to his friends to go and be dishonest wheeler-dealers, and that is as terse, sardonic jest. Jesus' ability to mock fraudulent relationships constructed upon greed may suggest the extent to which Jesus held lust for power as anathema, an outrageously immoral way of being in the world, worthy only of bitterly sarcastic attention.

The stories that surround this Lucan passage in its context leave no question about Jesus' unqualified contempt for the business of climbing after worldly riches; and the lesson from Amos (as indeed the whole book of this justice-obsessed prophet) underscores the wrath of God as directed against those who put profit before people. "Surely I will never forget any of their deeds. Shall not the land tremble on this account, and every one mourn who dwells in it . . . ? [Amos 8:7–8]."

We need to consider seriously what God is saying to us as

*This essay is taken from a homily on Luke 16:9 delivered at St. John's Chapel at the Episcopal Divinity School, Cambridge, MA, September 23, 1980.

well as to the people of the Northern Kingdom in Amos's time or to the disciples and multitudes of folks in Jesus' time: We cannot serve two masters. We cannot serve God and mammon, the power of love itself and money, the wellspring of all that is worthwhile and our upward mobility. We cannot serve two masters.

It is remarkable how quickly most of us find ways of exempting ourselves and others from this rather clear gospel imperative to give up our attachments to worldly possessions if we intend to love and serve God. The parable of the rich young ruler, the story of the rich man and Lazarus, the strange analogy between a rich person's entry into heaven and a camel's passage through the eye of a needle. . . . Most of us are quick to assume that it does not mean that rich people cannot serve God, and that it does not mean that God does not love the rich. We assume, do we not, that it is a matter of priority, of how those who have worldly wealth use this wealth, *their* wealth. And it is usually "their" wealth, because most of us here do not think of ourselves as rich—students having to work at various jobs, teachers managing to squeeze by, staff with even fewer benefits, and so forth. With some exceptions perhaps, we hardly consider ourselves rich—until we hear, really hear, that two thirds of the world's people, human beings, live in, or at the edge of, hunger, malnutrition, starvation, and death every day of their lives. This may suggest to us that we are rich by virtue of what we take for granted—that few of us may expect to lose our lives, or those of our loved ones, due to starvation tonight or tomorrow or next year. To be rich: what does this mean to us, for us, and to God, whose word seems to be clear—we cannot serve both our God and our own sense of security here on the earth?

Yes, those of us who see ourselves as "progressive"—theologically or politically "left"—may try to beg off: not only are we not "the rich," neither are the Rockefellers nor the Mellons "the rich" anymore. We understand that "richness" has shifted beyond the grasp of plain old human folk and has its own complexity and impersonality in the structures of multinationals and other networks of global economic intrigue. It is true that we are all victims of an economic enterprise founded on a motive of profit at the expense of all but the top 3 or 4 percent of humanity. Politically and economically, it is true that we are not "the rich," not "the powerful," not the high priests of mammon.

But I want to suggest that theologically—in relation to a God whom we meet most intimately in the humanity of our sisters and brothers on the earth—we are not only among the rich, but we are moreover absolutely responsible for this situation and for its solution. God is precisely that voice, that spirit, that intuition or compulsion which pushes us into a realization that we cannot both love God in the world and attempt to pass the buck, plead our own helplessness, or pity ourselves because we experience ourselves as victims of structures we do not understand. We cannot love both God and mammon. We cannot love the God whom we meet in our brothers and sisters and take psychic or spiritual refuge in our senses of being helpless pawns of "the system."

The biblical allusions to mammon, money, riches, wealth, treasures of this world, refer quite literally to material gain. Our mammon is what we work hard to get, what we possess, the things in life that make us feel important—nice clothes, good jobs, ordination, some status in the pecking order, the kinds of things we want, and want more of. Mammon. But the power of Jesus' intuition and faith cut even more deeply to the core of mammon. Yes, mammon is our possessions, our various security blankets; and mammon is also the near impossibility of not getting stuck there, the enormous difficulty of letting go of what we own, precisely because we consider ourselves so powerless and unlovable without it. We hang on to what we have and we strive for more and more because we have learned to believe that it is the only way to live life in the world, the only way to cope with our senses of being victimized by the rich, the powerful, the government, the church, the bishop, the one on top. To give up our attachments to mammon is to give up what reasonable chance we think we have to live as self-respecting, happy people in the world. Jesus knew, it seems clear to me, that mammon is not only our material security, our upward mobility, or efforts to "make it" in terms of power, privilege, and prestige, but is also our radically deep neediness for these things, a neediness rooted in our individual and collective senses of being powerless, helpless, victims. When Jesus underscores the difficulty of breaking our attachment to mammon, he is simply naming reality. It is no easier for us to give up our love of mammon than it is for a nail that has been driven deeply into a board to be simply lifted out, or for a tree that has been rooted in the earth to be plucked up. So deep is our neediness—for security, for a sense of self-esteem, for a feeling that we matter. And so shallow is our faith in ourselves as people of a God whose power is ours in the world.

We cannot love both God and mammon because we cannot *live* both with a God who is alive in our neighbors and with our own senses of helplessness, powerlessness, and fear when it comes to doing anything with or on behalf of suffering people. The vocation of *all* Christians is to be "converted to the poor," to choose the option of siding with/being with the poor. Indeed, God is on the side of the poor—not the rich. As Jesus suggested, mammon and God are irreconcilable. Those of us in the world who are among the rich (as we most certainly are), have a choice to make—either God or mammon, either a willingness to suffer—bear up—the power of love in this world or a lingering attachment to our own yearnings for power, privilege, and prestige, whatever forms they may take, however subtle they may be. We cannot love both God and mammon because what it means to be people of an incarnate God—a people in whose lives God comes to life—is that we come to believe in our own participation in the power of God. People who love God are not helpless pawns at the mercy of the rich, the powerful, business, government, Church. People who love God are people empowered by one another (God with us) to share and enjoy a life that is common, a journey taken together in a world that is hungry for justice.

There is no good point in feeling guilty. Our guilt feelings can serve only our mammon—our senses of powerlessness, apathy, and neediness for security. Rather than wringing our hands or beating our breasts, we have a common vocation: to open our eyes to the presence of God who is with us, every one of us and all of us together, and to realize that God's power, God's spirit, God's movement is our power, our spirit, our movement; and that as we believe this, affirm this, and infuse our values, our relationships, our work, and our goals with this radically incarnate faith and power, our own attachment to mammon will indeed be torn from its roots. We may discover that as mammon falls and God rises, this world (our own life-styles, relationships, homes and parishes, schools and churches, governments and businesses) will be more fully human—and more fully divine as well; stronger, tender, creative, and just; a place to be in which there is no rich and no poor, a common-wealth of God, both with us now (if we so choose) and coming (with our help). God help us, as we do ourselves.

· 17 ·

Liberating the Body*

As reprehensible as I believe the so-called right-wing religious movement is today—misdirected, misinformed, mistaken in terms of fundamental values—these people, our sisters and brothers, are on to something that seems to me so often to elude most of the rest of us, in both our respective denominations and churches, whether they be Episcopal or Unitarian, and in our special interest or constituency groups—women's rights, gay and lesbian groups, black groups, urban groups, and so forth. Especially in the recent past I have been struck, sometimes almost dumbstruck, by how fully these Christian folk whose conventions oppose the Equal Rights Amendment, gay rights, provisions for safe, legal abortions, and liberation movements throughout the world—whether in the Philippines, El Salvador, or the Middle East—have been grasped by a fervor, a zeal, that appears to me to be biblical and which they believe, of course, is thoroughly biblical. These people believe they are inspired to teach, preach, vote, and legislate in the name, and by the power, of God. They are committed to a reconstruction of this world in

---

*This address was given at the Arlington Street (Unitarian) Church, Boston, MA, November 16, 1980.

the image of their God, these Bible-believing sisters and brothers who have felt under attack by principalities and powers and whose passion has been sparked in a mounting resistance to what they believe is evil, a swell of commitment to what they believe is God.

This is not the first time religious people have risen up with passion, zeal, and confidence. Listen to the words of Paul in Corinthians: "We are afflicted in every way, but not crushed; perplexed, but not driven to despair; persecuted, but not forsaken; struck down, but not destroyed. . . . For this slight momentary affliction is preparing for us an eternal weight of glory beyond all comparison [2 Cor. 4:8–9, 17]." It seems to me that we need to pause and realize that this kind of passion, this determination, and this expectation today characterize the Right to Life movement—*not* the Episcopal Church, and I doubt that they characterize the Unitarian Church. This zeal—I am not speaking here of the substance, I am speaking of an attitude—this zeal abounds in the reemergence of the Ku Klux Klan, *not* in our mainline churches and task forces. This energized effort to restore the society in the name of God is mobilized around promises on the parts of preachers and politicians to save the family, save the children, save the country, save the soul, rather than around the promises of Episcopal, Presbyterian, Baptist, Catholic, Unitarian, or Jewish leaders that we will not now, or at any time, make peace with any oppression for any reason, anywhere, anytime.

What these right-wing Christians have discovered—something thoroughly Christian, something implicit and explicit in the ministry of Jesus of Nazareth as well as his friends and colleagues—is a passion in and a commitment to a faith that infuses the social and political order. Pat Robertson, Jerry Falwell, Henry Hyde, and Mildred Jefferson have seemed to realize that their religious beliefs *are* political beliefs and that the things they believe—that homosexuality is evil, that abortion is murder, that women are meant to be subordinate, and that capitalism is God's own economy—are things worth fighting for, things worth stirring people up over, things worth spending money on, things worth electing a president over.

The passions of the litanies that echoed in the convention

hall during the 1980 Republican convention in Detroit bore an eerie and strange resemblance to those of the psalmists, the prophets—resemblance not in content, but rather in a level of commitment, energy, and determination. And so these right-wing conventions of Christians, whether in Detroit, Dallas, San Diego, Atlanta, or Boston, are inspired in at least one way that most of the rest of us are not. They are absolutely and un-equivocally *committed*, politically as well as theologically, to what they believe to be the way and the will of God.

Now, we could enumerate the various points of serious dis-agreement we hold with these sisters and brothers who believe that most Unitarians, and even most Episcopalians, are held fast in the claws of Satan. But this is not what I want to do.

I want to talk about *us*. About what it means for us to gather as God's people. First I want to say something about the body, about the sanctity and the value of the body, which I believe to be the ground of all holiness. And then I want to say something about passion, which I believe will always characterize inspira-tion.

In September 1979, at the Episcopal Church's Integrity Con-vention (organization for lesbian/gay Episcopalians and friends), I suggested that the women's movement and the gay movement are fundamentally the same movement, and that this movement constitutes a serious threat to the religious and social order of our time.[1] The challenge is even more serious, and more basic, when our interest in eliminating sexism and homophobia goes hand in hand with an interest in eliminating all forms of repression and discrimination on the basis of race, class, ethnicity, age, handicap, or whatever. This becomes clearer to me as I ponder with others the extent to which *all* evil, that is, the malicious violation of creation itself—human beings, plants, animals, air, water—seems rooted in our failure to know and to take seriously the holiness of the body.

Most of us *say* this, of course: that the body is holy. After all, it is the handiwork of God. But I wonder how many of us really believe this. Few, I think—at least among Christians, who usu-ally follow up our affirmations of body with qualifications about how much *more* important the soul is, or the spirit, or things unseen.

The grass-roots theology springing up in Latin American countries today, rising out of the struggle of the poor for food and survival, instructs us that the body is to be taken with ultimate seriousness. There is nothing higher, nothing more holy. It is nonsense, it is wrong, to contrast God with the body. Be it the individual human body, or the body of humanity itself, or indeed, the body of all that was created: the creation. My body is not a shell into which and out of which God moves, leaving me either godly or ungodly. The body of humanity is not a network of flesh and blood and bones that is either visited by or not visited by God, leaving humanity itself either godly or ungodly. If God is worth our bother and if the life of our brother Jesus means anything worth our knowing, it is that the body is godly, the body is holy, without qualification. Our hands are God's hands in the world. Our hearts are God's heart in the world. God pulsating. God beating. God yearning and open and growing in history. Our suffering and our tears are God's pain and trauma in history. Our laughter and our pleasure are God's own joy in history. Our work and our commitments are God's activity in this world. Our sexualities, our expressions of sexuality, our lovemaking in this world, is God's own expressiveness, God's own lovemaking, in history. When a human being reaches out to comfort, to touch, to bridge the gap separating each of us from everyone else, God comes to life in that act of reaching, of touching, of bridging. The act is love and God is love. And when we love, we god. And I use the word god here intentionally as a verb. If we are as fully human as we are able to be, and Jesus suggested we *are* able to be, then we are godders, we god—human beings/created bodies bringing God to life again, and again. Serving God in the act of serving humanity. Loving God in the act of loving humanity and one another. To point to a spiritual realm "up there" and a physical world "down here" is blasphemy, a destructive assault against both humanity and divinity. Because God is here to be fed, healed, encouraged, given shelter, befriended, accepted in the person of the neighbor or not at all.

Granted, we encounter a puzzling confusion between the holy value of who each of us is as a body on one hand, each of us needing badly to realize and celebrate the wonder that she or he is, and a preoccupation with the self on the other. Therapy, spirituality, charismatic religion, women's and gay/lesbian movements have heightened our capacities to claim our worth and power. This can be, and usually is, a very good thing. Its positive effects are often self-evident. Women and men are able to cast off sex-role expectations and other false expectations that prevent our knowledge of ourselves. We are meant and called to be more creative, more honest, more joyful, and more caring human beings when we do this than when we see ourselves largely through the eyes of others—parents, employers, doctors, lovers, gurus, those to whom we give social and ecclesiastical authority. Yes, there is a moral imperative to love ourselves, to be tender with ourselves, to comfort and enjoy ourselves, our bodies—to grow in self-esteem, to take pleasure in who we are, delighted to realize that our bodies are members of God's body in the world. And in tending our own needs and yearnings, we are tending God's.

But this same self-centeredness/centeredness of self that is vital to our constructive faith can be perverted. And this happens in the very instant we forget that *all* bodies are holy and as important as our own. And that, therefore, *you* must be as holy to me as *I* am to myself. Constructive faith is grounded in relation between a God who is good, a God who is love, a God who is justice, and the people of God who bring this God to life on earth. God does not stand alone beyond relation.

Unitarians may well look upon the doctrine of the Trinity with deep bemusement. If so, it is a confusion shared by most Trinitarian Christians, if we are honest. The Trinity is a much overworked, underthought and often glib doctrine. But I am coming, through my own Trinitarian roots, to believe that there is an important impulse behind the doctrine. An important dimension of human intuition. An intuition of ultimacy in relation. An intuition of a God who is "internally" relational. The Trinity is a patriarchal and sexist image about which, I must hasten to add, something will have to be done if self-affirming women are to continue as members of any traditional Christian body. For those who do not know, the Trinity is a homophilial/homoerotic image of relations between *males* (father/son). But my point is not right now the unequivocally sexist imagery. The point is the love relation, the intimate friendship, as that which is ultimate, most valuable, as that which is God. God is imaged as in the relation between those who speak, touch, reach, walk, weep, and act. God is nothing except in relation. Behind this badly reified, stagnant doctrine is the intuition that nothing has been, nothing is, and nothing will ever be unrelated.

And in the image of God so too are humanity and creation in relation. We, no one of us, are important in and of ourselves. Life cannot be lived in front of a mirror unless it is to be lived in a distorted, ultimately evil way. No one of us can live creatively or responsibly apart from the needs of the rest of the human body. Each of us as a body is a member of a larger body—the human body, human family, humanity itself—alongside and with other creatures, the "four-leggeds" and the "wingeds" who join us, the "two-leggeds," at the banquet of life. My body is significant not because I have unique or special needs, desires, or goals. My body is valuable because this flesh and blood and mind and heart and spirit represent the flesh and blood and dreams of every woman and man that has ever lived on this earth. Everybody is as valuable to the creation and to the creator as any other body has ever been.

Granted, we are not taught to believe this, and we must realize the extent to which we are not taught to accept it. Presidents seem more valuable than peasants. Generals seem more valuable than foot soldiers. Chairmen of the board seem more important than welfare mothers. The rich seem more valuable than the poor. Episcopal bishops seem more valuable and more important than gay/lesbian seminarians.

But constructive faith corrects this distorted vision by driving us toward the realization of a God who was active among a two-bit bunch of first-century nobodies. God was potent in the lives of these folks, Jesus and the others. Jesus and his friends, other outcasts, lived and taught a very simple life of faith, of expectation, and of love of neighbor and self. They bore witness to the power of love as the only necessary common ground among people who desire to experience themselves as valuable and worthwhile. These Jesus-people seemed to realize the value of the human body, the whole human body, as the cornerstone of constructive faith. They were/we are called to live for the body, in the body, as one of its member bodies, to stand and act as centered selves, cultivated in appreciation of our value, our power and glory in solidarity with all others whose power and glory and dignity and worth we are willing to struggle for.

We do not live above others. If we love others, we cannot hand things down to them, expecting that they will choose what we will choose, or live the way we will live. Rather, our commitment is that all persons can discover and attain whatever they need and want to live and grow in relation to still others. One of the reasons lesbians and gay men seem to pose such a threat when we acknowledge who we are is that the very word sexual implies body—and not just our own bodies, those of us who are gay or lesbian, but also the bodies of those who fear and despise homosexuality/sexuality itself. These are people who, like us all, have learned well to denigrate and renounce our bodies in embarrassment and trivialization and shame. Those of us who are gay and lesbian will learn better how to cope with homophobia, how to defeat it, when we realize that it is not simply something that others have toward us, but rather that homophobia is rooted in a fear of the body—the individual body and the collective body. A body that we share, a fear that we share.

How many folks do not fear the body's changes, the mysteries of our cells and pulses, the fleetingness of bodily pleasure, the unpredictability of bodily pain, accident, loss, and death? How many of us do not fear losing control over our own bodies, or being introduced to new and seemingly alien feelings, functions, fantasies in our bodies? How many of us do not fear bodies that seem to be quite unlike us? Bodies maddened, bodies starved, bodies stretched in strange-looking ways? Bodies speaking goals and dreams and languages that sound to us like babble? Angry bodies, bleeding bodies, bodies yearning for justice? Iranian bodies, Guatemalan bodies, Palestinian bodies, Salvadoran bodies, Ugandan bodies, Native American bodies, and Appalachian bodies? Bodies that we neither understand nor appreciate well as members of our own human body? How many of us do not fear bodies we must distance from our own in order to feel that we are in control of at least one body in this world?

The moment we see ourselves in others and realize that, in

reaching for and touching some bodies, we ourselves are reached and touched, we encounter the ultimate meaning, the divinity, if you will, of being human, of being *some body*. We love, we god, we let go of our need to control any body, including ourselves. Our control gives way to the movement of God. And our fear is increasingly swallowed up in our faith.

Now, passion. This characteristic of faith, and it would seem today especially of born-again faith and right-wing religions, merits a few words. Listen to what the author of Isaiah 55 (1, 12–13) says.

> Ho, every one who thirsts,
>   come to the waters;
> and [the one] who has no money,
>   come, buy and eat! . . .
> You shall go out in joy,
>   and be led forth in peace;
> the mountains and the hills before you
>   shall break forth into singing,
>   and all the trees of the field shall
>   clap their hands.
> Instead of the thorn shall come up the cypress;
>   instead of the brier shall come up the myrtle;
> and it shall be to the Lord for a memorial,
>   for an everlasting sign which shall not be
>   cut off.

Why is it that liberal religious people do not insist that yes, indeed, by God and for the sake of humanity, we have seen an everlasting sign which shall not be cut off? Either we have not seen the sign, in which case we should ask ourselves what, if anything, it really does mean to be people of God. Or we have seen signs somewhere, hidden however deeply in the recesses of what we dare admit. And we are so often reluctant to say so with passion—to insist, to stake our reputation, our interests, our possessions, and maybe even our lives upon what we have seen: the value, the power, the centrality, the holiness, indeed, the divinity of the human body, the whole body with its many members, breathing, pulsating, yearning, speaking—the body of humanity. We have seen each and all of us as God's hands and heart and spirit on earth.

We have seen signs which shall not be cut off. The branches shall not be cut off from the vine. Our power will not be diminished or rendered ineffective. The sacrament of life shall not be withheld—the body, the blood, the sensuality of God's presence on earth. God is here/now. She is no absent deity, no God away in God's heaven, but rather the power of *actual* love among us. This is our God incarnate. Our God in flesh. Our God with us, among us, between us. God our sister. God our mother. God our father. God our brother. God our friend. God our lover. The sign is the power of human love. God's own lovemaking in history. That which strives for justice. That which strives toward mutuality. The creation of relations and governments in which no body is denied. No body betrayed. No body put down. No body cast out. No body crucified on the basis of greed, fear, or malice.

Either we have seen this sign—the power of human love for human bodies—or we have not. If we have not, it is because we do not want to. It is because we choose to deny ourselves the power of God. It is because we choose to grovel in the restlessness of our own failures rather than to look and see what is right before our eyes: bodies of people, indeed the body of creation, groaning in search of family, in search of relationships in which bodies can rest, in which bodies are at home.

In 1980, I attended the Theology of the Americas Conference in Detroit. This gathering of six hundred North Americans, Latin Americans, Africans, Asians, and a few Europeans wrestled for six days with what it means to do a theology of liberation. This was, on the whole, not a gathering of liberal Christians who pass resolutions on world hunger, sexuality, and peace. This gathering, I know, would have scandalized the Episcopal Church, just as it would have scandalized the various conventions of fundamentalist activists. But I left Detroit realizing that it probably would have scandalized the fundamentalists *less* than it would have scandalized the Episcopalians. Because, like the fundamentalists, the liberation theologians gathered in Detroit were filled with zeal, commitment to values that were spiritual and political. Like the fundamentalists, many of whom had been gathered in Detroit two weeks earlier at the GOP convention, we shared our dismay about the state of the world and about United States society in particular. Like the fundamentalists, we deplored the ineffectual liberalism of many of the major denominations we ourselves represent and need to accept responsibility for. Like the fundamentalists, we stated a corporate belief that the economic, sexual, racial, and other social and political problems besetting our society are basic theological problems, basic religious issues—and that it is most certainly the business of faith to do something in society about whatever we believe.

It is precisely, primarily, and specifically the business of the church to act on its faith. There is no other reason for the church. To pretend that there is, to belabor images of a spiritual realm that is worth more attention than the present world, is to blaspheme against both God and humanity. Racism is a spiritual and a theological problem. Sexism is a spiritual, theological problem. Classism and ageism and homophobia are spiritual, theological problems. And none of these problems will be solved unless people of faith commit ourselves unconditionally and absolutely to the undoing of injustice within and without the church. There can be no greater priority for us, it seems to me, than an uncompromising allegiance to the re-creation of a church, a society, and a world in which black, brown, yellow, red, and white women and men stand on common ground, holding all things in common, encouraged to make love/make justice in relationships where there is commitment to mutual well-being, growth, and choice; a world in which color, gender, sexual preference, nationality, and age are simply not issues in terms of human worth and value; a world built not on the bodies of the poor, but a common-wealth in the most literal, nonimperialistic sense of what that word might mean. Holding our wealth in common. The common-wealth of God.

Finally, acknowledging, as I believe we must, and bowing, as I believe we must, before the mystery and the wonder of all that is created, we go, aware of our own limitations and boundaries, beginning with those of our own skins. We go with one another, according ourselves and one another a tenderness and a compassion that will become a resource of our courage and our power. We go, comforted/strengthened by God, who is nothing other than the power of love in history, the power for right-relation in history, the power of justice in this world. We go, believing that either we will re-create the world, or we will destroy it. We go now, responsible for what happens in this world. We move as a body seeking a common-wealth that we will break down with our indifference or build up with our loves.

A Eucharistic Prayer[1]

May God be with you.

And also with you.

Open your hearts.

We open them to God and one another.

Let us give thanks to God.

It is right to give God thanks and praise.

It is right, and a good and joyful thing, to stand open in the presence of God and one another as thankful people, lifting our voices in chorus, with those who have gone before us, and with men and women throughout the world today, singing,

ALL:
Holy, holy, holy God,
God of power and might,
Heaven and earth are full of your glory,
Hosanna in the highest!
Blessed is the one who comes in the name of God!
Hosanna in the highest!

Wise and gracious God, Creator of all good things, Redeemer of this broken world, you who bless your people and the earth itself, Holy is your name.

You are the source of love in the world, the wellspring of justice in history, the resource of peace on earth. Holy is your name.

We pray to you,
God of our fathers and mothers; God of the judges, prophets, and priests of Israel; God of the Old Covenant and of the New Covenant; God of Mary and Jesus; God of the church. Holy is your name.

Elohim, you are God. You lead your people out of bondage into freedom. Holy is your name.

Following Jesus, we call you *abba*, for you love us. Guiding us, you are insistent, patient, protective, encouraging, comforting. Holy is your name.

God our father, your will be done, on earth as in heaven. We thank you for giving us the bread we need. Holy is your name.

You hold us in your strong arms like a mother with her newborn infant. You have raised your children from generation to generation, planting seeds, harvesting grain, baking fresh bread, preparing meals, feeding your people, holding us up when we are too weak to stand on our own, teaching us how to walk and empowering us to go forth in the world as your daughters and sons. Holy is your name.

God our mother, you are the matrix of our power, our tenderness, and our courage. We forget too often that you are God. Holy is your name.

We know that your names are as numerous and varied as your people, to whom you reveal yourself in different ways so that we may be your co-creative, imaginative lovers in a world abundant with redemptive images.

We see you in the sun and the moon, the rain and the wind, coming with power.

We see you in the liberation of humanity from injustice and oppression. We see you, coming with power.

We see you in our friends and lovers, our spouses and children. We know your passion, your intensity, your commitment to right-relation. We experience you, coming with power.

We see you in the bodies of hungry people, broken people, tortured people, and a tortured earth. We tremble, and we believe that you are coming with power.

We believe in you, we love you, we expect you to be with us, because we remember the power you revealed to us in the life of Jesus, our brother and Christ.

ALL:
We remember that on the night before he was executed by those who feared both him and you, he ate a Passover meal with his friends, in celebration of your liberation of people from bondage. Remembering your power, he took bread, and blessed it, and broke it, and gave it to his friends, and said, "Take. Eat. This is my body, which will be broken for you. Whenever you eat it, remember me."

After supper, he took the wine, blessed it, and gave it to them, and said, "Drink this. This is my blood which will be shed for you, and for others, for the forgiveness of sins, to heal and empower you. Whenever you drink it, remember me."

Remembering Jesus and the power of your love revealed through him, we ask you, Father and Mother and Friend of all, to bless this bread and this wine, making it for us the Body and Blood of Jesus the Christ. Bless us, also, that we may be for you living members of Christ's presence in the world, people who are in love with you and your creation. All this we ask in your holy name, that with Christ and in Christ and by the power of your Holy Spirit, we may live forever as your people, O gentle God of power and grace.

PART IV

Going Well . . . Beyond Liberalism

There is nothing sweet here
and nothing bitter
tonight   today
only the pungent odor
of salty faith
rooted   watered   opening
turning and turning
opening and rooted
we are making
revolutions

· 19 ·

Limits of Liberalism:
Feminism in Moral Crisis*

You shall love God, and you shall love your neighbor as yourself. This is the fundamental law of both Jewish and Christian faith, and it is on the basis of this extraordinary law that I take my stand. I want to thank those of you who planned this symposium for inviting me to participate. I want to acknowledge also, with appreciation and affection, my sisters meeting today in the Boston area in a Consultation on Feminist Ethics. These women supported my decision to be absent from the Consultation in order to be with you, and they have encouraged me on my way. I will be returning to these friends this afternoon. Finally, I want to acknowledge a certain debt to Phyllis Schlafly, who—with others like Jesse Helms, Jerry Falwell, and others

---

*This essay is adapted from the Antoinette Brown lecture given at Vanderbilt Divinity School, Nashville, TN, and from an elaboration of this lecture in the symposium Religion, Politics and the New American Morality, Hobart-William Smith College, Geneva, NY. Both lectures were delivered in spring 1981. The participants in the symposium at Hobart-William Smith College included Phyllis Schlafly, spokeswoman against the Equal Rights Amendment. Schlafly spoke first and was responded to by the author.

before them like Robert Welch and Joseph McCarthy—has done much to clarify for me the radical moral character of Christian faith. It is about the morality of feminism that I wish to speak.

First, I should tell you a little about myself. I am an Episcopal priest, a believer in God's empowering love among the people of the earth. I was born and raised in North Carolina (turf that I share with Senator Helms). I am the eldest child of gracious, caring parents, who are alive today and committed now as ever to the God in whom they believe; to the world and its people whom they respect as sisters and brothers; and to their own children—my brother, my sister, and me—who, despite significant differences among us, remain a closely bonded family. I attended public schools through high school; was active in both church and school activities; loved my church, my school, my country; received all sorts of little awards from about the second grade on—for good citizenship, sportsmanship, churchmanship, service, and grades. I was in many ways the ideal daughter, a so-called all-American girl. I attended Randolph-Macon Woman's College in Lynchburg, VA (a town associated with the Rev. Mr. Falwell, whom I once heard preach on how Christians should stay out of politics, a position with which I disagreed then and now). During my college years I made my debut, worked with the YWCA, majored in religion, and became increasingly aware of the ways in which my white skin, my female sex, and my upper-middle socioeconomic background had contributed to making me who I was and am. Following college in 1967, I enrolled at Union Theological Seminary in New York City, a liberal Protestant school, well known in this century as the teaching base of such persons as Reinhold Niebuhr and Paul Tillich but more importantly as the faith and commitment base of many thousands of Christian women and men whose ministries have been rooted in the struggle for social justice in the name of a God whose way of being in history is just.

It was in the spring of 1971, while working toward my master's degree at Union, that I was "born again," compelled by the power of the Holy Spirit to open my eyes wide to the movement of God in my own life and in the lives of people throughout human history who have been inspired, sparked, and awakened to God's will that *all* women and men on this earth be created truly equal—that is to say, come into a world in which food, shelter, warmth, education, work, play, and creature-comforts are rights—givens—rather than privileges to be earned. The vehicle of my spiritual transformation was the women's movement, in which, with other women, I began to see clearly for the first time the extent of my participation in a socioeconomic, political, and religious system constructed upon certain assumptions not only about women and men, but also about domination and submission, or the assumed rights of one group of persons (men, white people, the United States, wealthy people) to dominate and control others. Coming on the heels of the civil rights and antiwar movements, the women's liberation effort called me into the heart of the Christian faith I had professed from childhood, and, for the first time, I looked straight into the eyes of my sisters and brothers and met there the compelling eyes of God: God of Jesus and Mary, God of Abraham and Sarah, God of Hagar the slave woman and of Joan of Lorraine and Harriet Tubman and Martin Luther King, liberators of their people. Washed, cleansed, and made new by the power of God, many of my sisters and I, knowing full well the extent of our own brokenness and participation in sins of lovelessness, selfishness, and arrogance, made a common commitment to spend the rest of our lives in efforts to build a world both more fully human and fully divine, in which all God's people are empowered by one another, and the God who works through us all, to live with dignity, nourishment, the right to make life-affecting choices, and the responsibility to make them for the common good.

And so, I speak to you as a feminist, a participant in the movement among women and men toward the equalization of our human rights in a just, or moral, world. I speak to you as a Christian, a person who works among, and chooses to identify herself as a member of, the tradition of people who have found positive meaning in the life and teachings of Jesus of Nazareth. Unlike most feminists and most Christians, I speak to you also as a lesbian, a woman whose strongest matrix of encouragement and empowerment has been within and among communities of women and whose primary commitment of love and partnership is with another woman. I tell you this because I think I should be as candid as I can be with you about my own deep wellspring of human love and support. I do not mean to belittle heterosexuality. But it is not my vocation—not the way in which I personally can make the most creative contribution to society.

I speak to you as a priest, a person charged specifically to represent something about both the human and the divine being we all share. Most importantly, I speak to you as a sister, a person like you, a person like Phyllis Schlafly, a person here on the earth for one fundamental purpose: to grow more and more in the love of God, a love/a justice that is ours to share as sisters and brothers. My experience of God and of human being is "mine" only in the sense that I, like everyone else, stand always in a relational intersection between myself and the many other selves, both past and present, whose lives touch my own. What I read and hear about El Salvador, for example, becomes part of my experience of the world and, as such, another thread I can use in weaving a tapestry of meaning that is both mine and yours insofar as our experiences of El Salvador converge in common experience. My tapestry of meaning is theological in that it is a way of imaging God, or that which is, from a moral perspective, of highest value in human life; not in the first instance a power beyond human experience or an ideal to which we aspire, but rather a power among us, which we share.

As you might well assume, Phyllis Schlafly and I represent two radically different and incompatible moral perspectives. We are in fundamental disagreement about what is good and what is evil in the world. You could hardly have found two women whose images of a just society would be more fully at odds. And yet, Phyllis Schlafly and I are alike in one important respect: we are both white women in a racist society who have benefited from the economic privileges and options available to those whom the society allows to be upwardly mobile. We are well-educated women who have made choices—to marry, or not; to leave our homes and loved ones in order to give speeches; in short, to live the lives we want to live. The options available to Phyllis Schlafly and to me are precisely the options that should be available to all women and men of all races and classes. And yet they are not. Ask any welfare mother. Any battered woman. Any bag lady.

Rather than attempt to respond to Phyllis Schlafly, I want to speak directly to those persons here who are feminists—both women and men. We have much to do and much to share with each other in order to be effective agents of love, which from a moral perspective is a synonym for justice, whether in one to one, or group to group, relationships.

Feminism in Moral Crisis

Feminism is in crisis, that much we know—and not only feminism, but also the moral character of this and many nations. The manfully waged war against human rights—whether targeted specifically against women, gay men and lesbians, black people, poor people of all colors, Jews, Arabs, the people of Latin America, the Philippines, or South Africa—is an assault on the shared right, the common right, of human beings to make choices among various options available to them. That this war against human rights is waged by persons who speak charismatically of freedom (seldom of justice), and most often of their own freedom (seldom of anyone else's), should alert us to the perverse spirituality—immorality—running rampant in our land and through its high places of government. Greed and self-righteousness have become the golden calf before which all who "love God, country, and family" are expected to bow. And the calf is cemented in a deep and well-cultivated fear of equalization, the fear of "being common" in a world in which all women and men actually would be created equal—that is, would come into a world in which human access to food, shelter, education, work, and play is assured, a given—rather than a privilege, a reward, something to be earned. Central to my thesis is that it is moral—good, just, of highest value—that all persons have access to life-sustaining resources; moreover, that feminism is grounded in this affirmation.

Believing as I do that a "crisis" is a "dangerous opportunity," my purpose is to probe feminism in order to demystify it. As feminists, our effectiveness rests on the extent to which we understand and trust our experience and our visions. We can do neither as long as we internalize the perceptions of reality that have been shaped historically for us by those whose interests fly in our faces: for example, those currently in power in this nation and in many, if not most, of our churches, schools, and media. As Nelle Morton, one of our strong and beautiful foremothers, has charged us: We must learn to "experience our experience," which is to learn (because we have not been taught it) to experience, recognize, name, and take seriously what is true for us: what we experience as good, what we experience as evil, what we will adore, and what we will despise. Our crisis as feminists may be rooted in our ambivalence about our capacity to re-create the world, that which Peggy Ann Way, pastor and theologian at Vanderbilt, has called our "authority of possibility."[1]

That feminism is in a serious political crisis is obvious. The Equal Rights Amendment (ERA) is in trouble. Abortion rights are being whittled away. Life affecting options available to women of color and white women, working women and single women, lesbians and straight women, women with and without children, elderly women and especially poor women, are in jeopardy. What we who are feminists do about this political crisis may well depend on whether or not we realize the extent to which feminism is in moral crisis. Not only "religious" feminism, such as that we have brought into our Christian and Jewish and other religious traditions, but rather all feminism, secular and religious.

The Moral Tension

The feminist movement is energized by the moral concern that all persons, male and female, be empowered to choose among options available to us. The U.S. feminist effort, from its official inception at the Seneca Falls Convention in 1848, has been toward the establishment of a social order in which women as well as men are empowered, by law and custom, to make choices among various options: to work, whether in the home or in some other work place; to bear children; to own property, whether married or single; to marry or remain single, without penalty; to raise children in an environment in which food, shelter, education, and reasonable comforts are rights rather than privileges; to maintain one's identity (as symbolized by one's name), whether married or single. Where there are life affecting options, there is also the issue of morality, inasmuch as significant decision-making involves the discerning of value—of what is good and what is evil, or of what is better and what is worse, for oneself in relation to the common good. The feminist movement is a moral movement in two profoundly inextricable, but distinct, senses.

First, the feminist movement is motivated by an explicit commitment to women's moral right to choose among options made available to us. This commitment, evidenced by our efforts on behalf of the ERA, abortion rights, and women's ordination, is rooted in the eighteenth-century liberal ideal of "liberty, equality, and fraternity." Our commitment to women's moral right to choose makes explicit our positive valuation of women's absolute right to the same choices as men, within the same arena of options.

Second, the feminist movement, when assessed from a thoroughgoing moral perspective, also bears an implicit commitment to women's responsibility to make moral choices even though we must demand a spectrum of options and the same opportunity as men to make mistakes and wrong decisions. I am not suggesting that women have a *greater* responsibility than men to make moral choices, nor that women have any natural or given capacity to make choices that are more moral than those made by men. I am suggesting that none of us—women or men—can extricate our rights from our responsibilities, our own freedom from the common good, the Enlightenment focus on individual liberties from the utopian vision of universal justice. To attempt to do so, to bifurcate our efforts for rights and privileges equal to those of the men at the top from our commitment to a social order in which there are no men—or women—at the top of a pyramid, is to lose sight of the vision of our common-being, our common-wealth, which Jesus himself called "the kingdom of God."

Because feminism is a moral movement, motivated by commitment to the common good, we are bound to see our commitment to common-wealth through to its actualization in justice for all, rather than for only a few women priests, a few tenured women, a few women politicians, a few women artists, and always a few Queen Bees, who are most often white women, financially secure women, able to be conciliatory with the men at the top.

Let me give three examples of the critical tension between our moral right to choose among various options and our responsibility to make moral choices.

First, the movement for the ordination of women continues to be, in all denominations, a moral struggle on behalf of women's rights. This effort is steeped in the positive valuation of woman's equality with man. At the same time, Christian feminists have options that involve significant moral issues, including—in those places where women have the option to pursue ordination—the choice of whether or not to be ordained. What may be a moral choice for some women may be an immoral choice for other women. These choices—whether or not to be in the church, whether or not to seek ordination—demand a discerning of what is better or worse for both the individual woman and others: the choices a woman priest or minister must make, for example, about in what ways, if any, to continue to be part of a tradition that devalues not only women, sexuality, and the laity, but also the human body in both its individual and collective senses. Feminist Christians must determine together how we can be most responsible in helping ourselves, one another, and other church-people both accept the full humanity of women (as represented, for example, by women priests) and, at the same time, become more critical with us of the ways in which, for example, a nontransformed priesthood—whether peopled by men or women—continues to be a patronizing office that represents the arrogance and set-apartness of a male deity whose image is wholly other than that of female, earth, body, sex, death, relationality, and human vulnerability. What this means for Christian feminists is that we must understand our struggle for women's equal rights as a significant movement within a broader struggle for a world-church that is truly "beyond God the Father" (Mary Daly).

A second issue in which we can detect tension between our

right to choose and our responsibility to make the right choice is the draft, the business of requiring young people to be trained to make war. Certainly women have no more or less right or responsibility than men to choose in what ways to "serve," or not to "serve," this country. If young people are to be drafted, a feminist perspective must insist that women as well as men be given this responsibility, which carries with it a right to say yes or no or under what conditions they will "serve." The draft symbolizes the merger of right and responsibility, which are always hand in hand. Feminists who argue for the drafting of women—or for women's moral right to a fair share of the war load with men—need also to consider what it may mean for women and men to make a moral choice when faced with the draft. Questions of what is moral, of what is right, must be asked, such as under what if any circumstances killing is justifiable, of whether the United States is likely to be involved in a "just war," or of whether the draft is itself moral.

Third, the dialectic between our moral right to choose and our right to make a moral choice is manifest in current efforts to ensure that women will now and always have the option of safe, legal abortions, rather than be either butchered or forced to bear children they do not want and cannot have.[2] The pro-choice movement reflects the positive value women have discovered in our lives and bodies and in the right to make choices that will affect not only us but also our partners, families, commitments, work, other children, and society itself. The pro-choice movement is exactly that: pro choice, pro women's choice, pro women's right and responsibility to make a difficult choice that affects no one else as deeply as the woman herself. At the same time, women seeking abortions, and we who support the pro-choice position, need to be aware of the serious moral character of the decision to have, or not to have, an abortion. The moral challenge here is for us to be able to struggle fiercely for women's right to have options about child-bearing and to admit readily the moral complexity of abortion to which most women who have had abortions bear witness. To be pro choice in an informed and positive way involves the recognition that the antiabortion movement mounted by the new right represents a higher valuation of fetal life than of women's lives. Consider the following news item of March 20, 1981:

In action long sought by antiabortionists, the Reagan Administration has proposed that federal funds be used to finance abortions only when the woman's life is in danger—but no longer when rape or incest is involved. *Even when a woman's life is in danger, states would not have to spend public money for abortions if they chose not to,* according to the Administration's proposals.[3]

To be pro choice in this political climate is to share a profoundly moral commitment rooted in the religious belief in the value and sanctity of women as well as in the value of options and responsible choice. A woman's responsibility to make a moral choice, one she believes will benefit herself in relation to the common good, is a responsibility absolutely dependent on the availability of options and her right to choose among them. Feminists do not have to argue that having an abortion is "like cutting your hair," or even that having an abortion is not the taking of life, in order to protest forcefully that because women are actual persons, alive in the world, our rights to significant options must necessarily take both moral and legal precedence over the "rights" of that which is unborn and, therefore, not of the same social value as the woman who bears it.

Today more than ever before in this country, we need to understand that a female fascist is no less morally culpable than a male fascist, and that feminism is, at heart, a movement against the greed and self-righteousness of the fascist's first allegiance to herself and those whom she believes are created in her own racial, social, economic, political, sexual, national, or religious image. Dorothee Sölle has characterized contemporary U.S. society as "christo-fascist," a society bent in the name of a false Christ upon a monolithic—nonpluralistic, intolerant, arrogant, and genocidal—image of what is moral, valuable, beautiful, and worthy of life.[4] If Sölle is correct, and I believe she is, our task as feminists is no less than that of mounting passionately a campaign against fascism, not only on our own behalf, but always on our own behalf, inasmuch as we understand the common good to be our own, and vice-versa: a common good that is a personal good, our liberation from common bondage to a dominant-submissive social relation in which the one on top—whether male or female, white or black—always represents white male wealth.

Zillah Eisenstein suggests that "liberal feminism," which is manifest most explicitly in the movement for equal rights, is potentially subversive to the status quo.[5] Whether feminism will actually bring about fundamental social change is dependent on whether feminists experience and understand the failure of the Enlightenment's liberal idealism to effect justice, true equality of opportunity, for all people rather than simply for the upper white socioeconomic strata of society. According to Eisenstein,

> Liberal feminism involves more than simply achieving the bourgeois male rights earlier denied women, although it includes this. Liberal feminism is not feminism added onto liberalism. Rather, there is a real difference between liberalism and liberal feminism in that *feminism requires a recognition, however implicit and undefined, of the sexual-class identification of women as women.*[6]

Eisenstein's thesis is that the liberalism of such persons as John Locke, Jean Jacques Rousseau, and John Stuart Mill is at core patriarchal, premised on the separation of public and private spheres of social relations and on the rights of individuals to move upward from private to public sector and to continue rising in the ranks of public life. Liberalism does not account adequately for the class structures of society and the extent to which individuals are not simply free to rise and fall as we choose.

This same liberalism has been implicit in the works of feminists, from Mary Wollstonecraft, in the late eighteenth century, to such contemporary feminists as Betty Friedan. Eisenstein does not attempt to categorize simplistically individual feminists as liberal or radical, but rather takes care to demonstrate how past and present feminism in this country is both a liberal and a radical ideology. Feminism is liberal in that it is—and must be—a movement for equal rights in a society founded upon ideals of liberty and justice for all individuals, regardless of how far short it may fall in terms of racial, sexual, or economic inequity. Feminism is radical in that it threatens to bring down the sexual class system that provides the underpinning of social structures which have little to do with the rights and abilities of individuals, and everything to do with segregation by sex, race, and class.

Eisenstein's political analysis of feminism informs a moral perspective. The movement for the moral right of women to choose—to be ordained, to have an abortion—is both a liberal movement for universal human rights and a radical movement toward the overhauling of structures cemented in sex roles and sexual class segregation. Our capacity to realize the morality of what is at stake in our options and our choices—including the choice to press for equal rights—draws us into the arena of radical politics; that is, into an opportunity to participate in the re-shaping of social values and the re-making of social policy in such a way that the social order is actually transformed for the common good. The danger is that we will miss this opportunity by failing to take seriously the radicality of the feminist movement's commitment to actual equality for *all* women of *all* races and classes. Such radical equality would involve the revolutionizing of the social and economic order of this country. Opponents of the feminist movement often tend to see this more clearly than we do. From their perspective, feminism is a curse, because it signals a challenge to "the American (socioeconomic) Way." But from my perspective—precisely because this challenge *is* implicit in feminism—our movement is a bearer of blessing to this land.

Let me be clear: the feminist moral vision is not simply that there be an equal number of female bishops or of women generals or that women have abortions—although we must insist that these possibilities be legally ours. Our vision is that the church, the military, and the procreative option/lack of option (e.g., marital structures, birth control practices—including sterilization abuse practices, and health care for women and children, support systems and lack thereof) be transformed in such a way that women are actually empowered to have, and to make, life affecting choices.

Feminist Moral Theology

Let us move farther into the morality of the feminist commitment to the common personal good. We articulate a number of interrelated goals. Among them is the struggle for equal rights, which is, in fact, a struggle for access to our share of social power. Another of our goals is to be whole persons. A third is to grow more and more into an appreciation of our bodies. Drawing on our commitment to these goals in process, I want to examine our struggle for power, our efforts to be whole, and our love of our bodies, as these experiences may reveal something of what and where God is in our lives. These theological reflections are meant to elucidate more fully the substance and significance of what is actually moral in our life together.

Our struggle for power. Morally as well as politically, the requisite for making choices is power. Politically, power means options: the option to do what will benefit the common and personal good and the option to fight for the right to do it. Political power and moral power are not easy or likely correspondents in social structures of domination and control, such as most ecclesial and civil governments.

Our fundamental commitment is to moral power. Our moral vision is not, finally, that women have institutional power—that we be bishops, generals, or senators—but rather that we come into a power that is ours despite the political structures of our lives, a power that cannot be undone by electorate, promise, threat, or force. But we cannot lose ourselves in a romanticization of what actually constitutes life in the world. It is not that institutional power is irrelevant to women's lives, but rather that it is not our end-goal. Wherever women have no institutional power, women have no justice. But for a few, or even many, women to have power within an institution does not ensure that others—women or men—will be treated justly. As we know well, might does not make right, although Reagan, Haig, Schweiker, Helms, and Schlafly would have us believe that it does.

Feminists, like others in history—most often those located beneath the decision-making places in the social order—have discovered power in consciousness-raising, protests, political activism, common work, collaborative study, and in our friendships and love for one another. This coming into our common personal power continues to be a basic resource of our insistence, our indignation, and, in the face of injustice, our hope for ourselves and our sisters. We have come into our power in relation, our power not in isolation or apart from one another and the world, but rather an energy between and among us that enables and compels us to involve ourselves in the ongoing struggle for human well-being, our own and that of others.

Through the feminist movement, I have come to experience, recognize, and name our power in relation as God, that which we may image as mother or father, sister or lover, friend or brother, a still small voice or a clap of thunder. God's transcendence is experienced in the constancy of God's "crossing over" between and among us. God is not mine, but rather ours; and not only ours, but also theirs; and not even simply theirs, but moreover is the power in relation between and among plants and dogs and whales and mountains and cities and stars. Divinity drives us, yearns for us, moves in us and by us and with us in the coming to know and love ourselves as persons fundamentally in relation, not alone.

From the moral point of view, our power in relation compels us to be careful of others, to love our neighbors as ourselves. It is only in relation to these others that we are in God. What may sound to the naked ear like a rehash of liberal theology is both that and more. The problem with liberal theology, like liberal politics, is its emphasis on the individual's self-possession rather than on our power in relation.[7] Political and theological liberals beckon us to consider the primary and ultimate value in individual freedom, individual rights, and individual choices. God loves every one and every one should love her neighbor as herself. This theological assumption was the bedrock of our civil religion and of our national politics until the 1980 elections, in which the electorate replaced liberalism's impotence with a barely disguised fascist attack on both individual human rights and the common good.

Theologically, the emphasis on the individual is misleading, even false. It is naive and misplaced. It does not do justice to either the human or the divine way of being in the world. Morally, theological liberalism is bankrupt. It does not work. It does not encourage the shaping of a just social order. It evokes bleeding hearts and charitable sentiments, and, in our failure to actualize the common good, it paves the way for the Moral Majority.

Although feminist theology is liberal in its beckoning us to dance to the songs of the people of the earth rather than to the spiritual sounds of a heavenly kingdom, feminist theology is not liberal theology that happens to be done by women. The radical implications of feminist theology are rooted in our experiences of our power in relation.

Consider the teaching that we should love our neighbor: The theological truth of the matter is that I love my poor sister not simply because I *should* love the poor, but more basically because it is only together, in our relation, that my poor sister and I *can* come to love each other. Where there is no effort toward mutuality, there is no love. This means that Christians cannot love people whom we do not respect. We cannot love those whom we do not invite to be with us as sisters and brothers. We may pity them; we may treat them charitably; but we cannot love them. Love is born in the hunger for reciprocity, a desire and capacity to receive as well as give, to learn as well as teach.

Only together, in mutual relation, is there any common personal power, any love, any actual God. I have no power to give on my own. Love is not something I can do without you. God is ours to share, to give into and receive from, to experience together or not at all. The difference between liberal charity and radical love is that, while the former is condescending, the latter is mutual. The god of the liberals is a deity who looks down and takes benevolent pity, who gives to the needy but has no needs himself. Ours is a God who reaches and is reached, touches and is touched, empowers and is empowered.

The moral choice, or the making of a decision for the common good, may well be different for different people in different situations, but it is motivated always by our power in relation: the power in a woman's relation to her friends, her lover, her children, her community, her spouse, her sense of commitment to certain values, her pledge of allegiance to justice for herself in relation to others. The moral choice may be made on the basis of prayer, meditation, reflection; silence, conversation, study; analyses of the various options and possible outcomes insofar as they can be anticipated. Sometimes the choice is made spontaneously, sometimes with great enthusiasm, sometimes with sadness. But it is always made in relation.

Our efforts to be whole/healed. The feminist movement has stressed woman's personhood, our fullness of being, our autonomy apart from man. This is a critical affirmation in that, legally as well as theologically, woman has been viewed traditionally as an extension of man: Adam's rib, and Adam's property as well. Both at the very personal level of relation (as in a particular marriage) and at the structural level of society (as in the institution of marriage as cornerstone of our economic and social building), women today are still relegated to less than full citizenship legally and to less than full human status theologically.

Mary Daly lays bare the outrageous ways in which women have been deprived of our names and our naming, our senses of sanity and self-esteem, our appreciation of our bodies and our work; and how women have been feared, trivialized, spiritualized, despised, persecuted, mutilated, burned, and put to death emotionally, spiritually, intellectually, and physically, all in the name of God the Father. Daly demonstrates convincingly how the church has functioned historically to define women as less than fully human and, hence, as undeserving of the right to make choices affecting our own lives. In effect, Daly lifts the veil from woman's mutilated self. She proposes that, if we are to be healed—to realize our wholeness and, in so doing, to come into our power (which I have called God, our power in relation)—we must separate ourselves from the patriarchal, "phallocratic Enemy."[8] Daly acknowledges that the Enemy is not only men, but also the "internalized God-father"—women's internalization of our own oppression—which seduces women to oppose our own liberation, whether in public, political debates such as among women like Phyllis Schlafly who oppose the Equal Rights Amendment; or in more mundane but equally devastating ways, such as in our tendencies to trivialize our feelings, ideas, and activities as "unimportant," "confused," or "wrong."

We live in a patriarchal world in which men define both God and humanity. We are given our fathers' names when we are born and, most of us, our husbands' names when we marry. To the extent that we are trying to do our own naming of what is truly human and truly divine, we meet obstacles from right to left, among friends and foes, at every turn. Christian feminists cope constantly with obstacles: We hear the source of our power in relation named "Father," "Lord," and "King." We are asked to pray for the "Kingdom" of God. We know that churchmen meet regularly to discuss women's ordination, abortion, sexuality. We attend meetings of predominantly male clergy or of seminary faculty who make decisions about what should be required (normative) in Christian life and education. We converse with male colleagues about "why 'the women' are upset" and with women about why they feel a little crazy when their babies are baptized "in the name of the Father, Son, and Holy Spirit." We counsel students sick with homophobia and we listen to women tell us that their marriage contract has become their death warrant. We are met daily by theological and ecclesiastical assumptions writ large in men's language about men's experience of God and humanity, men and women, spirit and flesh, reason and feelings, life and death, right and wrong, health and sickness, propriety and perversion. In short, Christian feminists are adrift in a sea of symbols, assumptions, and expectations about *our* lives, relationships, values, and God that have been formed by men, and in a most fundamental way are *not ours* at all.

Daly is right. We need to get to know ourselves rather than to continue simply to absorb men's "knowledge" of us, which is our common and perverted experience. We need to learn to trust ourselves, to act for ourselves, to experience the wholeness of ourselves apart from men's opinions of us; indeed, to act and be on our own—separately from men, the extent and character of our separatism being determined by women ourselves. We may choose to be in all-female groups, attend women's schools or women's cultural events, work with women in business, have a female lover, or live in a feminist community. All these seem to me creative options, depending on the motives, expectations, and goals of the women who choose them. Somehow we must get clear, get our hearts and heads uncluttered, break the bonds of the historically cultivated misogyny we have internalized so thoroughly that we are unable to know or love ourselves apart from men's definitions, opinions, and approval of who we are. We must find ways together of healing and being healed, we who are feminists: woman-identified ways, in which we learn to do our own naming of ourselves, our humanity, and our God.

And while it is untrue that all feminists are or must be lesbians, every feminist, at some time or another, will be perceived as a lesbian and will be vilified as such to the extent that she is perceived to be whole—that is, as a woman whose fullness of personhood (choices, values, and actions) are not contingent on either man's "grace" or man's opinions. The lesbian has symbolized historically the woman who does not need men to make her a full person. As such, to most men and male-identified women, the lesbian represents the wholeness, personhood, and integrity that *all* feminists seek, whether lesbian or straight, celibate or sexually active. In other words, in a sexist/heterosexist society, the lesbian represents the autonomous, free-spirited woman—and thus she is feared and despised. None of us, lesbians or other women should forget this.

I do, however, take strong issue with Daly's insistence that all women must be "separatist"—via lesbianism or any other route—in order to be whole. I disagree with her, first, because she does not take into account the pluralism among women, most of whom *cannot choose* to separate themselves from men because their own lives, or those of their children, are dependent on their support from, or work with, men. Daly's solution to the problem of woman's mutilated self presupposes that women are able to choose to leave the world of patriarchy and move into an Otherworld. This seems to me a classist, racist, and hence not a moral solution insofar as Daly attempts to universalize it, which she does. The fact is, poor women, most of whom are women of color, do not have the option—cannot make the choice—to take their leave from the world of men.

I object also to Daly's presupposition that a full and radical separatism from patriarchy is possible—for any woman, even well-educated, financially secure women. I have noted already that I agree with Daly that separatism is a viable moral choice for women. But to assume that any of us—female, black, whatever—can actually live outside the sexism or racism of the social structures in our world is naive. The best we can do is learn to recognize the sexism—including what we have internalized—and break its stranglehold. We cannot simply ignore it, or pretend that we have left it behind, without fooling ourselves.

The problem with Daly's solution is rooted in her philosophy. Her highest value is not of this world. There is, for Daly, no power in human social relation in the patriarchal world. Her Goddess/Truth/Gyn/Ecological Be-ing is no less an Otherworldly deity, cut off from human struggle and yearning, than the Father God she holds in such contempt. The structures within which Daly's Spinsters Spin are no less elitist, racist, classist, separatist, and contemptuous of "the other" (men and male-defined women) than the theological and ecclesiastical structures of the transparently sexist Thomist philosophy in which she herself was schooled. Mary Daly's philosophy bears witness to the folly of the illusion that any of us can simply up and leave the patriarchal structures that surround and fill us. The most we can do is recognize them, name them, struggle against them in the day-to-day concreteness of our lives together, and do whatever we can, with whatever talents we have, to see to it that, as history is written, the sexism burrowed deep in our institutions, attitudes, values, and actions will be broken and undone and that women will increasingly know and love ourselves as whole human beings.

Our love of our bodies. The characteristic that renders feminism unique among the various movements for human liberation is our emphasis on the body, woman's body in particular. Historically, men—male theologians, doctors, scientists, educators, theorists, fathers, husbands, and celibate clerics—have viewed woman as body: specifically as the embodiment of sexuality and related feelings. Women have been deemed significant only insofar as our bodies have been useful for sex, child-bearing, and, by functional extension, for the mothering of both men and God. To the extent that women have been intelligent conversationalists; talented in art, athletics, or business; or interesting partners to men, such women have been viewed by men, and often by ourselves as well, as "exceptional women"—not like the others. Many a woman has been told that she "thinks like a man." Women who do heavy labor are branded pejoratively as "masculine." Girls who enjoy contact sports are called "tomboys." In each instance, the woman or girl is perceived as somehow different from "real" or "normal" women. Through male eyes, we have been imaged as "soft." Our bodies, our feelings and juices, have been prized as trophies, trivialized in their one-dimensionality. Where we have refused to be demeaned and have chosen rather to assert ourselves as many dimensional shapers of our own lives, we have been held in base contempt. The story of Lilith's expulsion from the garden because she re-fusd to obey Adam and Yahweh reflects the primitive patriarchal assumption about the worth—and the fate—of any woman who dares to defy the male expectation of what a "good woman" is.

Taking seriously the degree to which men have seen us and treated us as mindless bodies and refusing at the same time to accept men's negative valuation of our bodies, feminists are committed to a celebration of our bodies, rooted in our bodily experience of our power in relation. Beverly Wildung Harrison writes:

> If we begin, as feminists must, with "our bodies, ourselves," we recognize that all our knowledge, including our moral knowledge, is body-mediated knowledge. All knowledge is rooted in our sensuality. We know and value the world, *if* we know and value it, through our ability to touch, to hear, to see. *Perception* is fundamental to *conception*. Ideas are dependent on our sensuality. Feeling is the basic bodily ingredient which mediates our connectedness to the world. When we cannot feel, we literally lose our connection to the world. All power, including intellectual power, is rooted in feeling. If feeling is damaged or cut off, our power to image the world is destroyed and our relationality is impaired. But it is not merely the power to *conceive* the world which is lost. Our power to value the world and act into it gives way as well. If we are not perceptive in discerning our feelings, or if we do not know what we feel, we cannot be effective moral agents.[9]

The power of Harrison's point should not be missed: Without awareness and appreciation of our bodies, in which our feelings spark our thoughts and our actions, we are impotent, disempowered, disembodied, disfigured characters, who know no relation to anything and who, therefore, have no experience of God in-carnate. Theologically, our emphasis on body is a radically incarnational affirmation: to be fully human—bodies alive with feeling, bodies related to bodies near and far, bodies empowered in relation—is to participate in the movement of divinity. It is between and among ourselves that God is incarnate, empowering us together to create, redeem, and bless the world.

Jesus' power in relation, that which he knew as his *Abba*, was manifest in and through Jesus' flesh and blood, as he chose to touch, address, and relate to others. It was in relation that Jesus had power. And it was in and through his body that he experienced his power in relation: his *Abba*, our God, our sister and lover, friend and brother, that which compels us to pick up our beds and walk.

Alison Cheek suggests that current debates in the churches around the issue of homosexuality lead to a central question: Are bodies good? What Cheek means is this: If our bodies are *not* good and can be morally contrasted with spirit, then, as Augustine contended, our bodies do indeed represent the *massa damnata* and the sinful concupiscence in which they were conceived. If our bodies are *not* good, then not only should we despise our sexual feelings and deny strong feelings in general, but moreover we need not be concerned about feeding our bodies and caring for our bodies/ourselves, because our physicality has no value in and of itself. Our bodies and the physical world are merely temporary places of turmoil for our spirits, which must surely yearn for their disembodiment in the City of God.

If, however, our bodies are good, not simply the reservoir of a spirit with which we may contrast them, but rather are good in themselves, then we are pressed morally to reassess traditional Christian thought about both the body and its historical synonyms—woman, sexuality, death. If bodies have positive moral value—high spiritual worth—then what of the body's senses: touch, smell, taste? What of the body's pleasures—gastronomical, sensory, sexual? What may be the moral value in the mutual experience of bodily enjoyment, sexual enjoyment, if bodies are good? If bodies are good—worthy of care and pleasure—good in relation—then the church's attention needs to be directed toward the encouragement of responsible loving, empowering, mutual sexual relations rather than toward the discouragement of touch and pleasure between consenting adults.

All liberation theology reveals a bias for the spirituality *in* physicality, the spirit *in* flesh, the God *in* humanity, rather than a spirituality that lifts us out of our bodies and points us toward heaven rather than earth. Among feminists, this celebration of the physical is essential to every choice we make. For as woman has been equated with body and earth and feelings and death, and as all these experiences have been equated with evil (that which is anti-God, antispirit), feminism makes an explicit and unequivocal commitment to the liberation of the body from disrepute, the liberation of sexuality from contempt and embarrassment, the liberation of feelings from trivialization, and the liberation of death and dying from shame and denial.

Conclusion

I have attempted to explore feminism from a moral perspective as a movement both liberal in its commitment to women's rights and radical insofar as this commitment implies a re-creation of the social order, the creation of a common-wealth in which justice is for *all*.

Our right to make choices is morally inextricable from our responsibility to make these choices for the common good, which is the personal good, because each person is empowered in relation. Our personal and common power is in relation, only in relation, always in relation. This power in relation is God, by which we are compelled to involve ourselves in the ongoing struggle for human well-being.

Our well-being, like that of all earth creatures, is not determined by a disembodied spirituality, but rather by the food, shelter, respect, dignity, and love we are able to give and receive as persons in relation to all living things. As living bodies, we are good—of high moral value—as are all persons. It is in relation to one another, all of us, that each of us is empowered to help build, experience, and celebrate the common personal good we call justice (right-relation), in which such penultimate pleasures as liberty and the pursuit of happiness may be possible not only for us, but for all. This is a vision of feminist morality.

The Covenant: A Meditation
on Jewish and Christian Roots*

And Jesus returned in the power of the Spirit into Galilee, and a
report concerning him went out through all the surrounding coun-
try. And Jesus taught in their synagogues, being glorified by all.

And Jesus came to Nazareth . . . and went to the synagogue . . .
on the sabbath day. And Jesus stood up to read; and there was
given to him the book of the prophet Isaiah. Jesus opened the book
and found the place where it was written,

> "The Spirit of God is upon me,
> because God has anointed me to
>   preach good news to the poor.
> God has sent me to proclaim release
>   to the captives
> and recovering of sight to the blind,
> to set at liberty those who are
>   oppressed,
> to proclaim the acceptable year of God."

And Jesus closed the book, and gave it back to the attendant,
and sat down; and the eyes of all in the synagogue were fixed on

---

*This essay is based on a homily delivered at St. John's Chapel, Episcopal Divin-
ity, School, Cambridge, MA, February 1, 1981.

him. And Jesus began to say to them, "This text is being fulfilled today even as you listen."

—Luke 4:14–21, paraphrased

And Ezra the priest brought the law to both men and women and all who could hear with understanding. . . . And Ezra blessed God and all the people answered, "Amen, Amen," lifting up their hands. . . . And Nehemiah, who was the governor, and Ezra the priest and scribe, and the Levites who taught the people said to all the people, "This day is holy to God; do not mourn or weep." For all the people wept when they heard the words of the law. Then Ezra said to them, "Go your way, eat the fat and drink sweet wine and send portions to those for whom nothing is prepared; for this day is holy to God; and do not be grieved, for the joy of God is your strength."

—Nehemiah 8:2, 6, 9–10, paraphrased

A theme that binds together today's readings is one of ongoing fulfillment, the constancy of the co-creative movement of God and God's people from bondage to liberation, from discouragement to expectation.

It is important that we read today from both the Old and New Testaments, because we Christians too often look upon our "new" covenant as the true and final fulfillment of God's ways, and upon the "old" covenant between God and Israel as precursor to our completion, or fulfillment, in Christ. This also is a typical, even normative, Christian attitude toward the faith/ ethical claims made by non-Christians: Their way may be fine and good, but our way is, finally, *the* way to blessing and true health of spirit, because only in, by, and through Jesus Christ is God's realm finally brought into being. We hear it said that "the best" of the others—"good" Jews, Muslims, Buddhists, and atheists, or unchurched or postchurched "graduates" of Christianity are in fact Christian—and just do not know it! This patronizing of the rest of humankind is steeped in the same misunderstanding in which the arrogance of Western imperialism is grounded: a misconception about power—God's power and our own.

Believing ourselves, mistakenly, to be impotent—without power—in the tasks of liberation, of making justice and true love in the world, we seek something other than human, greater than human, something in-human/super-human/something we call God—to do for us and the world what we are, in fact, empowered to do for ourselves and others—simply because we are human. By virtue of being human, a creature, we are empowered by God, our creator, to go forth in the world and, with God, to co-create right-relation among ourselves. We misunderstand the ownership of good, creative power. We do not believe we have it. We project it onto "God," making it unattainable, something out of the realm of simple human being. We call "God" good and ourselves sinful; "God" omnipotent, ourselves weak and powerless. We praise "God," love "God," and are not too sure about humanity—the ultimate and final worth of human being in all its physicality, with all its material needs. It is much easier to love "God" than to invest ourselves caringly in the needs and pains and smelliness and hostilities of hungry, angry, or alienated people. It is easy to love "God" and despise humanity.

We misunderstand power—our own and God's—because we have trouble trusting that humanity is neither God nor un-God; neither omnipotent nor without power in the world; able neither to be identified nor contrasted with God. Rather, we are cooperative agents in creation and redemption; co-participants with God in bringing righteousness into the world, into our homes, classrooms, parishes, and elsewhere in society. We have power, simply because we are human—born with a right, a capacity, and a call to claim and share and use and love the power that frees captives and gives the blind new sight and sets at liberty the oppressed. To claim and use this power in our own times and places is to love God. It is to participate in the fulfillment of God's realm. It is to understand that our power *is* God's power when we bring good news to the poor, liberation to the downtrodden, justice to the oppressed, and hope to the needy.

And Jesus said, "Today this scripture has been fulfilled in your hearing [Luke 4:21]." Here is the beginning—of Jesus' Galilean ministry. Similarly, as Ezra read the Law to the people gathered at the Water Gate, he too was beginning something—launching a period of newly emerging identification among the people of themselves as a holy nation, Israel, God's state, a theocracy established on the Law.

The fulfillment of which Jesus speaks in Luke—proclaiming the inbreaking of liberation, the "good news"—is the same, ongoing fulfillment that God and God's people have always accomplished *together*. It is the same fulfillment that Ezra proclaims, urging the people not to be sad but rather to be joyful and give thanks for the extraordinary and active relation between God and God's people who together do justice in the world. When Jesus speaks of the fulfillment of God's realm on earth, he is speaking of the same accomplishment as the psalmist ("God raises the poor from the dust") and the same fulfillment about which Paul preaches consistently and passionately under the rubric of "Christ Jesus." Christ is God's activity in conjunction, partnership, friendship with humanity: human and divine being in a single act. We see in Jesus that this is the way it has been all along.

The fulfillment—the end of the tale—is actually an ongoing process—before the worlds began, unto the end of time. It did not begin with Jesus of Nazareth. The fulfillment of God's realm—what the psalmist, Ezra, Jesus, and Paul all taught and preached—is the constancy of empowerment of God's people by God *and* the ongoing empowerment of God by God's people to break the yokes of oppression wherever they exist. God is with us, and we are with God, and together we can re-create the world still, by reaching to touch one another and our sisters and brothers, both human and other creatures. This "news" is old—and it is good. And it is hard to believe, because it means that we must believe not only in God, but also in one another and ourselves. We must believe that we can do what we must because God is with us and because we are with one another. O God, we believe. Help thou our unbelief.

· 21 ·

Gay Pride Day*

We are here this morning to celebrate our liberation. Not that we have made it. Not that we are in the Promised Land. Not that we do not have a long, long way to go. But rather that, like our forebears in Israel, and later in the hills of Galilee, and even today in El Salvador and South Africa and in the United States, we are gathered to declare our belief in justice. We know that wherever two or three are gathered together to work and pray for justice for women, for black and Hispanic and Native American people, for the poor, for lesbians and gay men, the Spirit of God is alive and well. And so, we are gathered to celebrate a shared commitment to justice—not only for ourselves and gay men and lesbians, but always for ourselves. We are here to sing, preach, teach, organize, work, and play for justice, knowing well that justice—or mutually empowering relationship between and among human beings—is and always has been God's way, God's will, God's desire, and God's own movement among us.

The liberation journey is not a place to be. It is ongoing,

---

*This address was given at a religious service in celebration of Gay Pride Day at Arlington Street Church, Boston, MA, June 20, 1981.

unending; it is a way of life, not simply a part of life. By God and with God and in God (a god who is our shared and common power in relation to one another and to all that lives and breathes), *we* are not only the liberat*ed*—we are the liberat*ors*. Journeying in history alongside Miriam and Moses and Deborah and Judith and Isaiah and Jeremiah and Jesus and Mary and so many others; with witches and faggots tied together and burned whose flames engulfed four centuries; with black saints and prophets, leaders of their people and of us all—Harriet Tubman, Malcolm X, Fannie Lou Hamer, Martin Luther King; with these sisters and brothers, we are the liberated—and we are the liberators.

The celebration journey is an endless and irrepressible way of living; and, brothers and sisters, it is ours. To be liberated liberators—this is our call, our mission, our vocation—faithful in spirit both to the Jewish understanding of the covenant relation between God and God's people, a liberation-covenant, a faith journey; and to the Christian understanding of God's power incarnate, embodied, in-fleshed between and among all persons who are true lovers of humanity.

We are in for a long haul. History instructs us that as soon as small gains are made, reaction sets in; we move and are moved—socially, politically, theologically, otherwise—in dissonant tension with counterforces. Right now in this country, the reaction is fierce against gay men and lesbians, against all women, against blacks and racial/ethnic people, against the poor. Those of us who expect fast, dramatic progress in our liberation efforts must expect also to spend our lives in serious disappointment, plummeted ever deeper into depression or rage, apathy or co-optation, despair or burn-out. Liberation is not an achievement. It is not a victory. It is not something we can measure or compute. It is not a state of being—carefree, happy, mindless, or foolish. It is not a place to be reached and settled into.

The early Israelites very wisely had a strong sense of the value of *time*—holy time—liberation time. Forty years, centuries, wandering. The holiness was in the journey through time. It would behoove both Jews and Christians today to take very seriously the power and holiness of the liberation *journey in time* as our resource of God's power. If indeed the journey is our home, we need to learn and celebrate the journeying.

We cannot wait to celebrate our arrival—until we have made enough money, won enough political victories, found enough security in work or relationships, gained enough acceptance in sexist/heterosexist society. We cannot wait to sing our songs and dance our dances and make our love and write our poems and join our hands to raise them high, until we have made it to the Promised Land in which there will be no more tears, no more cruelty, no more bigotry, no more hatred. The time is now—in the journeying. Now—to play. Now—to rest. Now—to begin to realize that now is the time to begin to see deeply the value of small changes and of whatever moments of love and truth-telling and delight we do share.

Feminists in this country have a saying: The personal is political. And we mean it: everything is related. There is actually *no* private-public split in our lives, however desperately we may want to insist that there is. No tiny happening between two people is unrelated to what is happening in Washington, and vice-versa. Our lives are being affected in significant, troubling ways by every piece of legislation now being hammered out on Capitol Hill and Beacon Hill. We have one hell of a lot of organizing to do in order to undo the damage being done: to block the monster at the door in the shape of "pro-life" and "family protection" legislation, which—whether or not we realize it—will gobble up all homosexual rights just as surely as it will women's rights and the rights of all persons who are not living in conformity with the standards sought by a bunch of white, straight, rich Christian men and their handfuls of closeted homosexual flunkies, Total Women, black Boy Fridays, and others who are too blind to see that they dig their own graves with every "Yes, Sir" to The Man.

These are troubling times. And yet—if the liberation journey is our home, we are able to see that just as we must learn to fight effectively against these brothers and sisters who say they love God and who show they hate humanity, we must also learn to take delight in, and celebrate, the vision we have seen, the power we are sharing, and the justice we are making, even in the smallest places, between and among ourselves. We cannot work well, over the long haul, unless we are able to rest and play—together and in solitude. Our effectiveness as teachers, priests, organizers, community leaders, students, artists, parents, friends is enhanced by our pleasure in ourselves and each other and the extent to which we are able to be tender and playful with each other. And our gentleness and joy becomes a sign not only of what the world may see as gay/lesbian liberation—a political movement—but moreover of our lives together and the ways we use our time alone.

The journey is our home—forever, a way of working hard, playing hard, committed to making love, which is always making justice—right-relation—in the world, a commitment made simultaneously to one another, to the world, and to God, our wellspring of right-relation, our resource of love, in the world.

We are both the liberated and the liberators. Like a young species, a new being, we are learning actually to see ourselves and others and to love ourselves and others in new and empowering ways. We are no less afraid, but we are perhaps more courageous in our fear; less willing to equivocate our values and dreams, to bow ourselves before golden calves/false promises/ greed and money/empty commitments/cheap thrills/dehumanizing expectations/disembodied spirituality (the idols are many). In this process of liberation we find that we are coming to life (re-born, if you will) and are among those whom God is calling, here and now, to be liberators—to share a vision, to join hands with others—in the city, in the country, in the world—and to realize our work as common work. This is exactly what the Hebraic covenant was all about and what Jesus was talking about when he stated his own moral norm: love of God that is inseparable from love of neighbor as self.

We cannot fool ourselves (or we do so at our own peril) that somebody else is going to liberate us: somebody in Washington, some employer, or lover, or friend, or army, or God, or Christ. That is not what liberation is all about. We need to realize the inseparability of *our* efforts and *our* commitments and *our* lives from the activity, and love, and life of God who lives and moves through us, and with us, and in us, and among us.

We are in it together, folks. Not just you and me. Not just our sisters and brothers struggling for justice in El Salvador. Not just our peace-loving friends who refuse to shake hands with the demons of nuclear madness. But rather *all* human beings who love humanity and the earth first and profit second. We stand on common ground—the earth and God, our source and resource of love—active, moving, creative in the world—*if* we allow it; *if* we release this God among us.

God needs us. Our commitment. Our hearts. Our touching and our pleasures. Our bodies, including our common sense, our intelligence, our friendships, our love. God is our liberator, the wellspring of all that we do on behalf of humankind and of the earth. And, just as surely, we ourselves are the liberators of God. Not somebody else, older, wiser, sharper, more astute; *we* are those upon whom our God depends in the ongoing creation, liberation, and blessing of the world. There is no faithful way off the hook. And, as we grow in wisdom, God with us, we begin to see that not only is this a holy way, but also an immensely creative, sensual, relational, lovemaking way of commitment, truth-telling, play, and work, a way of touching and being touched to the core.

When I consider the future of the world—what is going to happen to us all, whether we shall live or die, I think of a little story:[1] Once there was a wise old woman, a witch, who lived in a small village. The children of the village were puzzled by her— her wisdom, her gentleness, her strength, and her magic. One day several of the children decided to fool the old woman. They believed that no one could be as wise as everyone said she was, and they were determined to prove it. So the children found a baby bird and one of the little boys cupped it in his hands and said to his playmates, "We'll ask her whether the bird I have in my hands is dead or alive. If she says it's dead, I'll open my hands and let it fly away. If she says it's alive, I'll crush it in my hands and she'll see that it's dead." And the children went to the old witch and presented her with this puzzle. "Old woman," the little boy asked, "this bird in my hands—is it dead or alive?" The old woman became very still, studied the boy's hands, and then looked carefully into his eyes. "It's in your hands," she said. And so it is.

· 22 ·

Sexual Fidelity*

I want to make four theological affirmations upon which everything else I say—about God, humanity, sexuality—are based.

1. Christians must take humanity—humanness—our own and that of everyone else—very seriously, as a precious and holy wonder.

2. Our love of humanity is our love of God; and our love of God is our love of humanity. Simply that.

3. Love is concrete—a matter of feeding and being fed; of touching and being touched; of making justice in the world.

4. Fidelity—faith, faithfulness—is a matter of making a commitment to love, rather than simply drifting into "love" or being run over by it.

I will elaborate a little on each of these affirmations and then

---

*This address was presented at the Integrity Convention (organization for gay/lesbian Episcopalians and friends) in Santa Monica, CA, August 22, 1981. The theme of sexual fidelity emerged out of Heyward's work with gay/lesbian groups in which questions about monogamy had frequently been raised. In this presentation, the author attempts to articulate what she believes to be the appropriate theological/moral context for any consideration of questions about monogamy as an ethical issue—namely, an exploration of what it means to be faithful—whether sexually, politically, spiritually, etc.

discuss briefly the meaning of fidelity in this context; finally, I will spend some time talking about lesbian/gay sexuality from a faith perspective. Let me say here at the outset that I do *not* understand sexual fidelity as synonymous with monogamy; and, moreover, that from a moral perspective, decisions about monogamy can be made responsibly only insofar as we have struggled to know what may be involved in being a faithful friend or lover.

Loving Humanity

As you know, Christians tend to undervalue humanity—by positing humanity, human being, as less good than divinity, divine being, or God. The problem is not in our belief in an altogether good—morally good (just, merciful, loving)—God. The problem lies in our tendency to polarize, and thereby make dualistic, human and divine life, ourselves and God. This is not first or primarily a philosophical problem, but rather an experiential dilemma that begins in our life experiences of guilt, shame, anxiety, and fear. Ashamed of ourselves, we turn to "God" as our hope. "Not worthy to gather up the crumbs," we find solace in our belief that God, in "His" infinite mercy, will nonetheless feed us. Philosophically, we inherit symbols and ways of naming this predicament most notably from the Platonists, and especially from the later Augustine. What is missing from this theological and anthropological construction is the pastoral encouragement to experience and name ourselves as God-bearers, people by whom and in whom, through whom and among whom, goodness is made manifest. Another way of articulating this is that we, as Christians, have been required historically to give God the praise for all good that we do and to blame ourselves for all evil that we do. And while there may be a seed of truth in this orthodox assumption, the claim is largely both pastorally and morally mistaken.

It may be that our hope as the human race, the people of God, is rooted in our ability to understand ourselves as people worthy of both praise and blame and *able to choose* to do good or evil, to go with God or against God's justice and mercy. At the heart of this challenge today is my prayerful plea that we may grow more and more in an experience and understanding of ourselves as people in whose human lives, bodies, commitments, and faith God may come to life. This can happen only to the extent that we cherish and celebrate humanity, our own and that of others, as no less holy and worthy of praise and caretaking than God.

My second affirmation follows closely. It is wrong—morally out of sync with the life of Jesus—to speak of "God" or of "faith in God" (which is held traditionally to be the basis of all fidelity in human life) unless we love humanity and creation. Love of brothers and sisters as self is the arena in which speaking of God makes sense; the place in which we begin to realize that this loving of humanity and of our other creature-partners on the earth constitutes and is the substance of our love of God.

Love of God is utterly inseparable from the love of humanity. Love of God does not take precedence over love of humanity, in terms of either time or importance. Those who speak of "God" but who hate humanity; those who give us commandments, but who take food and money from the poor; those who love to "worship," but who despise "secular humanists" for caring too much about human beings; those who read the Bible and other holy books (Book of Common Prayer, Missal, Talmud, whatever), but who do not love their neighbors as themselves are hypocrites and blasphemers against both God and humanity. To love God *is* to love humanity.

The third point is that love, like truth and beauty, is concrete. Love is not fundamentally a sweet feeling; not, at heart, a matter of sentiment, attachment, or being "drawn toward." Love is active, effective, a matter of making reciprocal and mutually beneficial relation with one's friends and enemies. Love creates righteousness, or justice, here on earth. To make love is to make justice. As advocates and activists for justice know, loving involves struggle, resistance, risk. People working today on behalf of women, blacks, lesbians and gay men, the aging, the poor in this country and elsewhere know that making justice is not a warm, fuzzy experience. I think also that sexual lovers and good friends know that the most compelling relationships demand hard work, patience, and a willingness to endure tensions and anxiety in creating mutually empowering bonds.

For this reason loving involves *commitment.* We are not automatic lovers of self, others, world, or God. Love does not just happen. We are not love machines, puppets on the strings of a deity called "love." Love is a choice—not simply, or necessarily, a rational choice, but rather a willingness to be present to others without pretense or guile. Love is a conversion to humanity—a willingness to participate with others in the healing of a broken world and broken lives. Love is the choice to experience life as a member of the human family, a partner in the dance of life, rather than as an alien in the world or as a deity above the world, aloof and apart from human flesh.

We might well wonder why anyone would choose *not* to love. You know as well as I that folks have been working on that question for generations; scientifically, since Freud; theologically, for millennia. The answer is mythologized in Genesis as the story of the fall, a matter, we are told, of a naturally good, naturally loving humanity's willful choice to disobey God, the source of love itself, and therefore to become "unnatural," or from a theological perspective "sinful." But I think Paul Tillich may be an honest spokesperson for us at this juncture when he suggests that human sin is part and parcel of being human, simply that. Tillich says that we "fall into creation"; our very existence, our life as human being, is "fallen." I believe this is true; moreover, that in our birth we are empowered by God (our relational power) to choose to love or not to love, time and again, consciously and even unconsciously, forever.

Please note that I do *not* say that we choose whether or not we are loved. We do not choose to be loved, and this is a critical moral distinction. For we are not responsible for the un-love that comes our way. We are not responsible for the injustice that is done to us. We are not responsible for others' failures to love us, themselves, or others. In other words, the victim of injustice is not to be blamed, and please hear this well. For this blaming of the victim is a moral outrage—the assumption that women "bring it on ourselves" by being angry; that gays and lesbians "ask for it" by flaunting our sexualities; that black people "get what they deserve," and so forth. No! God empowers us to choose to love or not; and therefore, we are responsible for the love we do and for that which we do not do, for whether in fact we bear God in and to the world.

To really love . . . To love with passion—a willingness to "bear up" the pains and joys of making justice . . . To choose to love is to make a commitment, to be converted either from an aversion or a refusal to love or from the more commonplace experience of just sliding by, slipping away, drifting along. To make a commitment to love is to be faithful.

Faith

Fides, or faith, has been defined historically in very different ways. There is the "developmental" faith, characteristic of the maturing person who is growing in knowledge of both self and God. (Irenaeus championed this line of reason, which in modern times has resurfaced in liberal Protestantism and in the "human potential" movement.) Then there is the "self-denial" faith, which, for Augustine, was a matter of letting go of one's self and allowing one's will to be overcome by or subsumed in the Holy Spirit. Self-denial faith stands in bold contrast to the notion of self-development. Augustine's teachings on faith became fundamentals in the predominant schools of Catholic orthodoxy and were reaffirmed by the reformers who taught that faith was a positive response to God's personal call, a response of giving oneself over to God, letting oneself be made new. Whereas most so-called orthodox, as well as fundamentalist, Christians have held historically that faith in God necessarily takes precedence over love of humanity and most so-called liberal Christians have believed that love of humanity is the necessary result of faith in God, there have been no well-received Christian voices that have suggested that Christian faith is, at its heart, necessarily and primarily, a passionate commitment to sisters and brothers, and that this commitment is more fundamental than any credo or doctrine.

Even the most liberal Christians, people such as Paul Tillich and Hans Küng, have maintained that faith in God is the beginning and end of wisdom, love, justice. I do not think it is simply a matter of semantics (as if semantics were a simple matter) to suggest that it makes a great difference whether we believe in God first or in humanity and creation as the only wellspring, or resource, or embodiment of God we can know, love, go with, and live into.

Faith in humanity and creation is immensely critical today, as in perhaps no other time, because here in the United States we have come into a period in which people have lost faith in humanity (both our own and that of others) and have instead turned our hearts toward that which is "above" us, something that knows what is best for us to guide and protect us, something or someone whom we can image as a benevolent father— be his name Ronald Reagan, Jerry Falwell, John Paul II, or Jesus Christ.

Faith in this patronizing "God" is being sold and bought in the marketplace and is the underpinning of the thus-far spectacularly successful efforts of the ambassadors of this "God" to turn away from "the common folk" toward those who have been blessed abundantly by this false deity; to turn away from human rights and hungry stomachs toward the defense of the hard-earned privileges of the blessed; successful efforts to turn away from humanity ("humanism," "human rights," civil rights, women rights, gay/lesbian rights, wars on human poverty) and to turn instead toward "God."

For a dime and a disavowal of the ungodly, folks today can buy faith in "God" and the things of "God"—country and family; national security and male headship; prayer, patriotism, and passive women. The prepackaged political contents of faith in a "God" in whose image mockery is made of that way of being which is most fully, most splendidly, human in our commitments to sharing, solidarity, and going with one another rather than going above, climbing over, racing ahead of, or beating one another down in order to get there first.

To be faithful is to seal a declaration of bonding with brothers, sisters, and other creatures. From a Christian or Jewish perspective, it is also an affirmation of a positive relationship with a God whom we believe to be the wellspring of our love. Thus, the faith of which I speak as a Christian is simultaneously a humanistic manifesto and a theological confession. I am certainly aware that there are many non-Christians who would agree with most if not all of what I am saying—many Jews, humanists, practitioners of Wicca, many atheists. From these people I have learned much. Similarly, there are many Christians who would disagree with me. I do not pretend to speak on behalf of "the true" Christian faith. We have too much of this presumptuousness already—whether from the Moral Majority, the Vatican, or Episcopal ecclesiastics. Rather, I am speaking of something that is important to me, and I speak as a Christian, a feminist, a lesbian, and a priest.

I would like to suggest a definition of faith that moves us beyond, or at least away from, both orthodoxy (which tends to lure us away from humanism) and liberalism (which tends to rationalize away our passion and commitments). *Faith is our commitment to participate, with and by the power of God, in the ongoing creation, liberation, and blessing of the world.*

Faithful people are committed people, people with a purpose, a vision, an intention. It may be as simple as meditating on a rose, or as complex as attempting to solve the problem of world hunger. Commitment involves a dedication of oneself—one's energies, resources, talents—whether for a long or short while. It is a very different thing from floating along, bumping into experiences that feel like "love."

Faithful people are participants. None of us is here alone. The commitment of faith is an acknowledgment of the collective character of human being. There is no such thing as one's "private" faith. Faith is no more a private affair than our work in the world. Yes, solitude is vital and good. But solitude and finding "a room of one's own" is always in relation to others, the community, the family, our friends, our work, the entire created order.

Faithful people are empowered by God, going with God, godding. Whether or not we name "God," whether or not we are even aware of God, much less able to celebrate God, all creative participation in the making of love in the world is inspired by God. As Christians, it is our business not only to go with God, to love as God's people, to bear God up in the world, but also to name God, to worship and celebrate God. But it is also our business as the church to see that we do not speak so loudly of "God" that we drown out the names and voices of our neighbors or get so enamored of "holy things" that our feet leave the earth we share with the rest of humanity and creation. It is time for Christians to celebrate humanity and, in so doing, to bring God to life.

Faithful people are co-creators. We have tended for a long time to undervalue ourselves as creators—with God and with one another. To create is to make new. To create is to give life. Whether or not this world of ours has a future is up to us. Either we claim and deploy our co-creative energies or we most surely will perish.

Faithful people are liberators of creation, which is the arena of all that lives. As we are shamefully, painfully aware, the creation is groaning. Lovelessness is rampant. If the work and play of creation is to make new, then the work and play of liberation is to redeem or salvage the old—that which is with us now, that which has been violated, broken, or lost. Creation involves willful imaging, leaping ahead, conceiving. Liberation requires re-membering, re-gathering, and healing.

By God's power, faithful people bless the world. Creative, liberating people bless the world—giving themselves, receiving the gifts of others, giving and receiving justice, mercy, kindness, candor; making this fragile earth, our island home, a more delightful place to share, blessing it with beauty, tenderness, strength, integrity, the many fruits of various talents and abundant grace. To bless is not only to give, it is to receive—a bearing of witness to mutuality. To bless is to share, and to really share. To distribute good things among ourselves is to bring hope into the world. By God's power, faithful people are a blessing and a hope.

Sexual Fidelity

If faith is a commitment to participate with and by the power of God in the creation, liberation, and blessing of the world, what then may it mean to be *sexually* faithful? I need to say again that I am speaking as a lesbian as well as a feminist and Christian woman. I need to say this in order to underscore the *particularity* in which all moral theology is rooted. I am not speaking of an "issue" that is "out there"—an interesting idea to ponder and discuss. I am speaking as a person with particular life experiences and interests, with certain biases and prejudices, with specific insights. I am speaking to a special group of people gathered around a common concern. To do sexual ethics here, to explore sexual fidelity with you, is to do so from a gay (in my case, lesbian) perspective, trusting that it is in the particularity of personal experience and interest that whatever may be common among us may be recognized and named.

If, as I have suggested, creation, liberation, and blessing is— at heart—a matter of making, saving, and celebrating right-relation or justice, then to be sexually faithful is to experience and express ourselves relationally in such a way that both we and others are empowered, and empowering, as co-creators, liberators, and bearers of blessing to one another and to the world. To be faithful lovers is to touch and be touched—whether physically or otherwise—with a depth and quality of tenderness that actually helps create life where there is death, comfort where there is despair. To be faithful in our sexualities is to live a commitment to mutual, reciprocal relations between and among ourselves in which no one owns, possesses, dominates, or controls the other but rather in which the lover participates with the beloved in living together in a home, a society, and/or a world in which each gives and receives. Sexual fidelity presupposes, I believe, that our sexual organs (like our other organs, limbs, cells) are part of the whole of who each of us is, and, as such, share the responsibility and delight of making right-relation, the opportunity to make love.

I want now to examine briefly several characteristics of gay/ lesbian sexuality—or the lesbian/gay experience (insofar as we have a common one) as they might clarify some resources for our faith. Only in taking serious stock of who we are can we come better to appreciate the value and power of our faith as homosexuals in a homophobic society. What is the common ground on which we, as lesbians and gay men, stand today (setting aside for the moment the discussion of the separate ground on which men and women stand, to which I will return shortly)?

There seem to me to be at least three experiences common to lesbians and gay men in our society at this time: (1) our experience as victim; (2) our experience of the negative value of sex roles; and (3) our experience of the importance of our bodies.

1. Our sexualities constitute grounds, in social custom and law as well as by religious sanction, for our exclusion from a variety of rights and privileges: employment, legal aid, adoption of children, ordination, blessing of our relationships, etc. This experience as victim of scapegoating and of various forms of exclusion, denial, and cruelty suggests that our faith will reflect some pain, some alienation and, as we grow stronger (and more faithful, I believe), some anger in a commitment to loosen the bonds of oppression, to break the yoke of victimization, to refuse any longer to accept any other than the Promised Land as our home. Our experience of victimization stands us alongside many other victims in this world: racial and ethnic people here in the United States and elsewhere; Jews throughout the world and dispossessed Palestinians/Arabs in the Middle East; the poor of Latin America, as well as of our own cities and countrysides; women throughout the world—of all social classes and colors, of all ages and religions, but especially poor women and women of color, whose jeopardy is always double because women of all colors, all people of color, and all poor people are deemed, by holders of social power, to be lesser members of the human family. If our commitment is to love our sisters and brothers, and if we are as in touch as we ought to be with the seriousness of our own victimization, then our concrete faith as lesbians and gay men will reflect (1) awareness of our common situation as victim; (2) commitment to making right this situation, to creating justice; and (3) solidarity with other victims of injustice, oppression, and discrimination. I must add that there is no moral justification for a gay man or lesbian to participate intentionally—or in unexamined ways—in the perpetuation of sexism, racism, anti-Semitism, economic exploitation, or U.S. imperialism. To the extent that we do, we are participating in the victimization of others and, in ways we may not fully understand, in our own ongoing victimization.

God is on the side of the victim in any relational transaction. This is the God of the Jews, the God of Jesus and of Jesus' followers, the one and only true God, source and resource of all co-creative power in relation among all persons and all living things. This God is the wellspring of all that is moral, all that is beautiful. This God is from the beginning, and will be forever, on the side of the suffering and the poor. God is not neutral. God is not bipartisan. God is not "value free." God does not bless, sanctify, and glory in suffering. God is neither sadist nor masochist. God empowers us toward our release from suffering.

Traditionally, this inspired release has been called salvation or redemption. Many speak of it today as liberation. God is our liberator from victimization. God is the source of revolutionary love. God is the power that moves toward the creation of mutual relation in a just world; God is loving itself. The making of love in the world is the making of justice, whether in one-to-one or group-to-group relations: justice, in which both or all parties give and receive, share and share alike, in ways empowering to both the lover and the beloved. To the extent that anyone, or any group of people (such as homosexuals) are victims of injustice, *God is with us precisely in our efforts to call into being a more just society; a more loving church; a more empowering, creative faith, as resource and reflection of a wiser, saner, and more responsible sexual ethic.*

2. In addition to our experience of victimization and our commitment to its undoing, a second experience that gay men and lesbians share, I believe, is our sense (if only in intimation) that sex roles weaken, rather than strengthen, our power in relation—our capacities to be lovers of one another, others in the world, and hence of God. In making this claim, I am venturing out on a limb that some of you, and certainly many people elsewhere, both gay and straight, might wish to chop out from under me. But I believe this is critical if we intend to probe the possibilities of strong faith. What I mean is this: Sex roles—the designation of what men do (or should do) and of what women do (or should do) simply on the basis of gender—are prescribed for us as social norms or standards by which we are expected to live as women and men. Where I climb out on a limb is in articulating my conviction that gay men and lesbians are among those people in society who have known, probably very deeply,

for a long time that these sex-role expectations are confining, uncreative, debilitating.

Both heterosexuality *and* homosexuality—as "conditions," or as psychosocial categories—are rooted in sex-role stereotyping. To the question of why anyone is heterosexual, or the more common question among heterosexuals of why anyone is homosexual, I would offer, somewhat speculatively, the response that people become heterosexual to the extent that they are able and/or willing to conform to the sex roles prescribed for women and men in our society. Furthermore, that the healthiest heterosexual relationships are those in which the man and woman are able and willing to stretch these prescribed sex roles to fit themselves in ways that enhance their individual and corporate creative power. I would also suggest, along the same line, that people become homosexual to the extent that we are unable and/or unwilling to fit into sex roles given to women and men in our society; and that the healthiest, most creative homosexual relationships are those in which the women or the men do not then simply duplicate, or act out, the very sex roles we have rejected—at the core of our being, if not by choice—as ill-fitting and disempowering.

I realize the presumptuousness of any attempt to say definitively why anyone is gay or straight, and I do so very tentatively. But I have come to believe that our gayness (lesbianism if we are women) may be, in some sense, a creative response to the presumptuousness of religious and social teachings about the correctness, normality, or holiness of what men "should" do and of what women "should" do. If what I am saying bears any truth, then it may be true also that gay men and lesbians—living our lives at the edge of intimation of the sham of sex roles—can be potent visionaries and prophets in the area not only of genital morality, but moreover of the whole arena of human relationships and morality in general, so thoroughgoing and all pervasive are sex roles in society in the functioning and organization of society.

I have heard it pondered why there are so many homosexuals—men and women—in the ministry of Christian churches, especially in those churches, like mine, of strong sacramental tradition. Maybe it has something to do with the human creative impulse to search beyond external givens (such as sex roles) for the more dynamic, enigmatic, and creative character of whatever is truly valuable and life-giving. At its best, sacramentality is the search beyond what seems to be (sex differences, race differences, etc.). At its best, sexuality is too. We may be forebears, unable in our own time to realize ourselves as witness-bearers to an emerging social order (now barely visible in tiny ways) in which God and humanity, divine love and human love, may be experienced, shared, and celebrated together by persons who live together in a society in which neither spiritual ecstasy nor sexual orgasm is bound up in power plays about who is on top, who is stronger, who is more seductive, whose will is to be done. This is a utopian vision, a vision of something already present, yet not fulfilled. It is also a faithful vision and one which, I believe, gay men and lesbians can share. Many of us already do.

3. I have suggested that our faith may be cultivated in our commitments to move beyond victimization and beyond sex roles. A third common resource of our faith, and the last I will mention here, is our awareness that our bodies are important. This is significant in the emergence of *incarnational* faith. Let me say emphatically that "incarnational" is not necessarily "Christian." While the incarnation is a central doctrine in Christian thought, Christianity has, historically, promulgated a much less fully incarnational theology—theology of embodiment, of God's presence and activity in and among human beings and all creation—than some other religions, such as Judaism and Wicca.

Now, I must tell you what I do not mean by incarnation and the importance of body. As a lesbian, I must admit my anxiety about the body cults/body worship I see every day in television commercials, magazines, films, and store windows. The sexist and heterosexist cult of body worship is a multibillion-dollar-per-annum enterprise, and it is also a people-eating machine that devours the flesh and spirits of girls and women, boys and men—to the tune of God knows how much money in medical bills, diet books and pills, figure salons, cosmetics, clothes, nervous breakdowns, and therapy bills. I cannot say any more for the gay male "meat racks" and what I hear about the gay male cult of body worship. This has its counterpart among lesbians, but it is a much smaller, less conspicuous counterpart, because *as a class, women have been acculturated to understand our bodies as ourselves.* This may be a place at which women and men, lesbians and gay men, part company. Many women experience exactly what all women have been taught about ourselves by men—church fathers, social and political legislators, the men who rule the world: namely that we *are* our bodies. We have been taught that we are full of feeling, emotional power and tenderness; needing and wanting to touch and be touched physically and emotionally; able to love and make serious relationships; nurturers and caretakers; and "naturally" good mothers and child-raisers. So we have been taught. We have learned that we do not divorce our physical needs from our emotional needs, because our bodies are ourselves. Woman is body. This has been the message.

I will not attempt to belabor the negative and damaging dimensions of this lesson except to point out that as far as women are concerned, the most damning dimension to us is that, as a class, men (and through their eyes, we too) have undervalued women's power: our intellectual, conceptual, artistic, relational, emotional, and physical power. Men—the movers and shakers of social, political, economic, and ecclesiastical power—have undervalued, even denied, the power of body, their own juices, their own neediness, their own yearnings to touch and be touched, as the source of all intellectual, conceptual, moral, emotional, and spiritual power. By lopping off the body from real power, value, creativity, and spirit, and by projecting the body in its enigmatic mystery and neediness onto women, and by equating body with woman / feelings / lust / out-of-controlness / scary places / evil / death, men have split themselves in two. On the one hand, there is the rational, creative, reasonable, constructive, and spiritual self. On the other, there is the irrational, emotional, chaotic, needy body—which, like a woman, can be hung on the meat rack, admired, and fucked, without affecting in any way the daily life, work, and character of the rational, spiritual, hard-working, all-American man whose sense of *himself* bears no relation to his sense of his *body*.

If I am being too hard on men, you will have to bear in mind that I am a woman and that the scenes I hear about, read about, and even see from time to time acted out between gay men remind me all too closely of the scenes that *all* women are expected to play in relation to *all* men—to the extent that all of us, women and men alike, are playing our parts well. To that extent, I take the cult of body worship in gay male culture, just as in straight male culture, as a structure of sexist/heterosexist oppression.

For all the damaging effect of men's equation of woman with body, there has been also a positive consequence, and this is in the realization by many women that, indeed, our bodies *are* our selves. Women's bodies are women's selves. Men's bodies are men's selves. And it is as bodies that we share creative power: intellectual, moral, emotional, spiritual power. As physical beings—pulsating, sweating, bleeding, thinking, feeling, eating, touching, moving, sensing—we come to know ourselves, and one another, and we come into a power that moves among us, between us, within us, inspiring, encouraging us toward the realization of what may be best for all of us, of what we truly value when we take seriously our yearning for relationship in which we are both the lover and the loved. Mutual relation. Just relation. Relation on earth between and among human beings and other creatures—all of us living bodies. Relation that *is* God's incarnation—the making in-carnate, em-bodying, of our power in relation; the making incarnate of love.

Gay men, as well as lesbians, have a particular opportunity, I believe, to embrace this incarnational faith, because—like all women—gay men have been cast in the role of being "body lovers," specifically as being lovers of men's bodies, which religion and society have held as perverse (since so-called real men do not *have*, much less *love*, bodies—body being the definition of woman). For a woman to embrace another woman's body is at best silly and futile, at worst tragic or sick—provided, of course, that women-loving-women/lesbians remain *publicly* under the control of men or male-defined institutions (such as the church). But for a man to touch and love another man's body is intolerable within the sociotheological walls of an ideology constructed on the definition of a man as a disembodied, rational mind/spirit that is ever in control and always "above" body. Thus as a sociopolitical institution, male homosexuality—far more than lesbianism, because women's power is not taken seriously— threatens to bring down the sacred canopy of an economic, sexual, and racial order founded on the assumption that the "real man" is a disembodied, dispassionate agency of control— over his own wretched body (which he must deny if he is to be spiritual); and over his private "members" and possessions— including women and children—who, if we are "truly blessed," become "members" of "His Spiritual Body." Gay men who experience, and choose to celebrate, the value of their bodies and those of other men have a remarkable opportunity to join in the reshaping of a radically incarnational faith.

In summary, I have spoken of love of humanity as love of God; and of faith, or fidelity, as our commitment to making love/ making justice here on the earth among our brothers and sisters. Passionate faith, angry, expectant and promising faith . . . Sexually, I have suggested that we, as lesbians and gay men, have some particular resources for faithfulness: our experience as victims of injustice; our knowledge of the sham of sex roles; and our elusive and bittersweet awareness of the moral power and value of our bodies. We badly need one another, in community, if any of us is to learn more and more about what it means to be faithful lovers. We need one another's accountability, challenge, and upholding.

· 23 ·

Judgment*

Ah, [my God]! Behold, I do not know how to speak, for I am only a youth.

—Jeremiah 1:6

Never have these words of the prophet rung with a more resounding toll than today: our sensibilities are shattered, our sensitivities blocked for the sake of sanity as the news flashes: assassinations and executions, for which the victims are said to have asked for it; hunger, for which the poor are held responsible; gang rape, in which the woman is assumed to have wanted it; bombs designed to destroy only human flesh, but not tanks or concrete edifices; an economy bolstered by the expectation that our drive to own, hoard, control, and hand out is basic and vital to both our "human nature" and the well-being of society, as it was in the beginning, is now, and will be forever.

It seems to me no wonder that liberal Christian people, in seminaries and parishes, are beating fast retreat into the realm of liberal "spirituality," in which faith is secured in a discovery of

---

*This essay is taken from a sermon delivered at the Sixth Anniversary Celebration, Integrity/New York, St. Luke's in the Field Church, New York City, October 20, 1981.

"the kingdom of God within" (for liberal Protestants) or the mystical Body of the Universal Christ (for liberal Catholics). In both instances, liberal faith is steeped in the conviction that social justice is a happy byproduct of religious piety, a derivative of wholistic consciousness or universality of the faithful. As someone involved in both seminary life and the feminist and gay/lesbian movements, I can testify to the movement among good liberal folks both "inward" into deeper self/god-consciousness and "outward" into prepossessing attentiveness to spiritual form and symbology.

It is a simple enough matter to attach ourselves to the notion that either our self-awareness or our adoration of a mystical unity of Christ's body is the basis of God's work of redemption/liberation. It is easy enough to address eloquently the problems of injustice from the perspective of one who lives in the confidence of discernment: able to understand and articulate theological corollaries between one's peace of mind and the peace of the world as being different but related manifestations of the peace of God.

But the ability to speak out of either the peace of one's own togetherness or the assurance of one's membership in an unseen and intangible Body is a characteristic alien to the Hebrew prophet. "I don't know how to speak—I'm only a youth," says Jeremiah. Small comfort to have reminded Jeremiah that youth is not a matter of age but rather of maturity, or that out of the mouths of babes comes the wisdom that will inherit the realm of God. No! The soulful lament of the prophet is that s/he is asked to speak God's Word in and to a world crumbling at his/her feet: a social fabric woven with threads of greed and violence; a community to which s/he belongs, in which the prophet lives and works, has been taught and has grown; a historic situation that has helped shape the personal consciousness and faith system of the prophet himself, in the case of Jeremiah. The prophet is not in a position to stand back and make pronouncements—to speak with objective distance of neutral dispassion, to remain bipartisan or patronizingly to take on the task of teaching maturity to people hell-bent on destroying themselves, at least in part because they do not understand.

The prophet does not understand the "nature and destiny of

humankind" or why we act as we do. The prophet is not charged to bring religion to infidels, to speak as a "religious" person/true believer to pagans, humanists, or secularists who lack the necessary "symbol-system" for liberation. The prophet is called neither to maturity nor to understanding of an academic nature nor to greater religious formality, but rather to speak God's harsh word of judgment, repentance, and conversion to and among people who are his, or her, own people. The words that take prophetic voice call the prophet's own world, the prophet's own life and values and investments, into question, for the prophet is a participant in the very society s/he addresses. What Jeremiah experiences as his inadequacy is what we all do: uncertainty about who we are to be speaking; fear that we do not know what we are talking about; anxiety that we have an incomplete knowledge of the facts; a sense of our political incompetence; the realization of our immaturity, our undeveloped self-awareness, our lack of "worthiness" to speak with authority about good and evil.

What in the name of God can *we* say about racism, sexism, homophobia, classism, militarism, or consumerism that someone else with more "expertise" or a stronger sense of "realism" cannot refute, dilute, or lay to waste on grounds of greater competence or better credentials? We write to the secretary of defense about the neutron bomb (as I did) and a letter comes back saying, "I'm surprised that so many Americans don't have the facts . . ." Who, after all, is going to listen to us, take us seriously? And how in the world do we (to echo Bonhoeffer) even speak of "God" in a "world come of age," a world in which to profess both religious faith and a primary commitment to justice, or human being, is as often as not met with raised brows or expressionless faces?

Nothing could be clearer to me than that my prophetic credentials are null and void insofar as I harbor them in the merits of my own personal growth or in the forms and symbols of Christian tradition. This is not to say that personal maturity and religious credo are negative forces or that they have no place in our lives and in God's ongoing struggle for justice in history. Rather, I want to try to put these inward experiences and their formal expressions in a perspective of liberation, a praxis of prophecy, a vocation of passing *judgment with compassion.*

We must understand well that there is nothing precious about the church or the Body of Christ that is unrelated to justice, or the moral act of love, in the world. There is nothing healthy about a high degree of self-awareness that is unrelated to justice, or right-relation between self and others, in the society. There is nothing spiritual about a "spirituality" that wears blinders to our complicity in, and responsibility to do something about, the perpetuation of these structures of injustice that do not allow three fourths of our sisters and brothers in the world the leisurely refreshment in which may stir meditations on the peace of God or the beauty of the human soul.

If our spirituality or our faith, our corporate or our private prayer, lifts us *up above* the realm of class, sexual, and racial struggle for justice, then whatever we are doing, we are not at prayer; whatever we are giving, it is not love; whatever we are receiving, it is not grace. In which case, there is nothing to say— no word to speak—nothing that is of God. Our words, as heard by most of humanity, are at best incredible if what we are saying does not call radically into question our own lives as well as the actions and attitudes of our politicians and decision-makers within and without the church.

The prophetic word is patently false if we speak it without appropriating the extent to which our own values, investments, uses of time and money, our symbols and faith, are related—in simultaneously spiritual and material ways—to the life-and-death situations of four billion people in the world, *most* of whom are hungry, *most* of whom are women, *most* of whom by far are black, brown, yellow, and *most* of whom are in one way or another "deviant" from the white-upwardly-mobile-male-constructed-and-male-dominated-Western-European norm of what it means to be "acceptable": achievement oriented, profit motivated, in control of women and other creatures who are "naturally" out of control—except when possessed. To be such a man is "naturally" to be a heterosexual man. To be such a woman is "naturally" to be submissive to and under the control of the man. The poor are "naturally" dependent on the rich.

Black people are "naturally" indebted to the economic and intellectual achievements of white architects of social consciousness. These ways of being are "natural" in the "real world" and no spirituality or liberal attempt to be either transcendent of this bitterness or neutral about it is grounded in *actual* relationship to an *actual* creator and liberator.

And so prophetic speech is always offensive. No one wants to give it voice; no one wants to hear it: it cuts the ground of security from under us, always. It is speech that makes a demand, a judgment, and it is nonnegotiable: *No more! Enough!*

Jeremiah speaks: "Execute justice in the morning, and deliver from the hand of the oppressor [Jer. 21:12]." No more injustice!

Jesus speaks: "The captives will go free." No more bondage!

Sojourner Truth speaks: "I toiled and slaved, and none but Jesus heard me; and ain't I a woman?" No more slavery!

Martin Luther King speaks: "I have a dream today!" No more racism!

Oscar Romero speaks: "In the name of God, I ask you, I implore you, I demand that you stop the oppression!" No more rulership of rich over poor!

The voices of women and gays/lesbians: No more! Enough! Stop the oppression. Stop it now. Stop the lies. Stop the hypocrisy. We will not be silenced, not even by force, not even by violence, for our commitment is strong, and we are everywhere!

Oh, this is "utopian," they tell us. "Pipe dreams," we hear. But of what value is nonvisionary, nonutopian faith? Of what use is a dream? The prophetic voice calls us to create the future now, beginning now, every now, always now, a *kairos*, the moment in which we must say, "Enough: No more!"

The prophetic voice is *not* our liberal Christian voice, our voice of reason, sophistication, knowledge, or credentials. It is the speech of compassionate, inspired women and men, black and white, Christian and Jewish and Arab, the speech of Wicca (wise women today and before), of gay men and lesbians, of secular humanists, and of evangelical Christians whose first allegiance is to justice, the moral act of love, here on earth as God's manifestation of God's own way of being—incarnate, in history, active, here now, tearing down and building up, uprooting and planting; an inclusive, direct voice that warns us that our precious securities, our objects of affection or adoration (including religious affections), may have to take back seat to justice/right-relation.

It is enormously difficult to take seriously the radicality of prophetic speech as that which immerses us in an experience of judgment on, and compassion for, a situation in which we ourselves are called into question. But I submit that this judgment of, and compassion for, the world—*our* world, *our* homes, *our* lives—is the heart of the gospel/the harvest, for which laborers are few. The prophet teaches not only *to* the people, but *as* a person; not only about what is happening out there, but also about what is happening here—between and among us, as well as to and in each of ourselves—as we who speak and listen, we who share prophetic vocation, are called into question.

We are called into question because our lives are linked fundamentally with/in the deep-seated structures of injustice that trouble us: sexism, racism, economic injustice. And so we speak judgment and we speak compassion—toward others, toward ourselves, and perhaps toward God as well. We speak God's judgment and God's compassion to the extent that we give voice to God in the world. We cannot speak God's judgment without compassion; and, contrary to what most liberal Christians have been taught, we cannot speak compassion without judgment.

A mistaken notion free-floats among many of us that we Christians can choose between prophetic and pastoral ministries; and, of course, a good many Christians toss in a third option: sacramental ministry. As if each gets to opt for what he or she is most comfortable doing. Those who do not like social or political struggle become good pastors and counselors. Those who prefer the nameless, faceless currents of social change to individual people become prophets, and those who prefer "God" to both people and society become sacramentalists. Admittedly, this is exaggerated for effect, but I believe most of us can hear echoes of our own voices begging to be spared: "But that's not my thing; that's not my strong suit; that's not what I'm called to do." Paul's teachings on the one Spirit and many gifts and on the one Body with many members are cited some-times as biblical sanction for this separate but equal call to differ-ent ministries among members of the church. The fallacy here is that any one of us is spared the disturbance of being called to relate to individuals (whether or not we like them), *and* to par-ticipate in the ongoing struggle for justice (whether or not we want to), *and* in so doing, to make God's presence heard, seen, touched, and tasted in the world. The prophetic call is to judg-ment *and* compassion; it is an invitation to participate in the struggle for justice and to live with an open heart to one's neigh-bor and oneself.

The root meaning of passion or suffering—*passio*—is to bear, to withstand, to hold up. We are called, collectively, to bear up God in the world. To withstand/"stand with" is to be in solidar-ity with God, to bear up God in the world, to go with God in our comings and goings. This vocation involves pain, as Jeremiah, Jesus, and all bearers of God have known—but not only pain. To be passionate lovers of human beings, the earth, and other earth creatures; to love passionately the God who is Godself the re-source of this love is to participate in an inspired and mind-bogglingly delightful way of moving collectively in history.

Com-passion is our way of *bearing with* one another in our work and relationships, at home, in the office, in the larger society. Compassion for those to whom we are called to speak judgment is possible only when we realize the radicality—fundamental character—of our bonding with sisters and brothers and the extent to which the world we share is being called into question/judged. The judgment we speak is of and to ourselves as well as "them."

This is not to say that all are equally guilty, or that all are equally responsible for the emergence or perpetuation of specific structures of injustice. Black people are *not* responsible for white supremacy, although many black people share in its continuation because they have appropriated the attitudes and assumptions of white supremacists, an appropriation that often seems necessary to their survival. Women are *not* responsible for male gender superiority, even though many women contribute to its perpetuation because we have learned to believe what men have believed and taught us about ourselves and all women. But to blame the victim—black people for white supremacy, women for male gender superiority, the poor for their poverty, gay men and lesbians for homophobia—is an odious and false charge that serves a single purpose: it lifts the legitimate burden of guilt and responsibility from the backs of those with the social and political power to cease the victimization. Compassion is *not* a feeling, or an attitude, of all people being the same or of all of us being one in some sort of amorphous mutual oppression in which there is actually no victim. To the contrary, honest compassion is possible only where reality is actually named and dealt with. It is the bearing with you—taking you seriously, listening to you and speaking to you in faith that you, too, are a sister or a brother, worthy (because you, too, are an earth creature) of honest attention, engagement, and perhaps confrontation and challenge.

Compassion does not require me to "identify with" you in any sense that would diminish or trivialize our differences. The poor in El Salvador do not have to "walk a mile in the (emotional or attitudinal) shoes" of the oligarchs or military in order to speak judgment with compassion to them. Women and gay people do not have to view the world through the eyes of sexist or homophobic people in order to judge them with compassion. We do not have to be fools to know and judge foolishness. To "identify with" may or may not be a useful psychological ploy because its result can be either constructive, in empathy, or destructive, in a loss of one's own center and identity. Compassion is not simply empathy, much less the loss of self. It is the bearing with *in spite of* radical difference and conflict, on faith that in compassion a seed of justice may be planted in spite of our feelings to the contrary.

Our society suffers a lack of compassion. There is much judgment *without* compassion, which is a mark of false prophecy. At the risk of being simplistic, I would suggest that what sounds like the prophetic voice of reactionary politics (as distinct from the conservative effort to hold fast to what has proven itself, historically, to be valuable) is, in fact, false, and that one sign of this false prophecy is that its rigid spokespersons teach judgment, wrath, and retribution without compassion.

By the same token, many of us who are liberal fall all too often into the opposite trap. A "liberal" is one who embraces values of inclusivity, universality, and the worth of every human person; politically, somewhere to the "left" of center; philosophically and theologically, open to historical criticism and scientific theories of relativity in which serious historical analysis is grounded. Taking seriously the relative and open-ended possibilities of all that is true or good, liberals are reluctant to pass judgment on anything or anyone. Thus, like our reactionary brothers and sisters, we are likely to be falsely prophetic. Liberals often think of ourselves as compassionate—open, reasonable, eager to find common ground on which to stand with those who are different from us. But often we fail to realize that an openness to others is an utterly vacuous posture unless we acknowledge who we are, what we value, what we stand for, and what we do not stand for. We tend to confuse a recognition of the relativity of all that is with a moral acceptance of all that is, as if our intellectual appreciation of reality's complexities demands passive moral response.

If I were to preach to members of the Moral Majority, I would spend most of my time on our need for compassion. But since I am here in this congregation with folks who are liberal (I risk to assume)—at least, in terms of moral theology—I want to emphasize our need to exercise judgment. To be liberal is to be inclusive, open, and tolerant; it is to live in this compassionate way precisely in relation to the judgments we make. To be radically liberal is to understand that our call to judge is sharp and urgent and that this judgment—if it is God's—is formed, tempered, and exercised compassionately.

Compassion is hard. It is not blanket acceptance. It is not "going along with" for the sake of not offending. It is, rather, rooted in realization that judgment is being made. It is the voice of the prophet who says, "No more!" and who knows also the wisdom in Augustine's claim that "we cannot not sin" *(non posse non peccare)*—not in a world in which structures of injustice constitute the foundation upon which we all stand together.

Our world is in bad shape, and we are in it, participants, getting mileage out of the very structures of sin and evil we judge. Driving our cars, eating our food, buying our clothes, taking our vacations—and always at the expense of others. Just as our compassion signals our acceptance of our own humanity with others, our judgment calls into question and draws lines between good and evil in human attitudes, actions, and institutions. We indict our sin and that of others.

The inclination "not to be judgmental" is especially pronounced these days among gay men and lesbians. Because we are the victims of intolerance and exclusivity, we are necessarily wary lest we do to one another what has been done to us. The wisdom in this tolerance is that, by it, we may actually help tear down structures of sexual injustice. But the folly in our tolerance may be that we do not hear, or understand, the prophetic judgment our very lives are passing not only on "those others"—out there in straight, homophobic society—but also on our own lives.

If what we, as lesbians and gay men, are about, at the heart of our liberation, is simply that all people be permitted to have sex with others who consent, regardless of gender, then, indeed, tolerance and inclusive acceptance are necessarily the cornerstone of our sexual ethics (if we see any value in sexual ethics). But if we see that our lives as lesbians and gay men constitute a judgment not only on the rules about who sleeps with whom, but also on the sexual and economic fabric out of which human relations are cut, we are able to hear more exactly the word that our lives speak. And we begin to understand that the prophetic speech of our own lives calls into question not only the rules about where we put our genitals but also about where we put our money, our energies, our values, our actions. Our prophetic judgment is exercised not simply against the presumptuous prerogative of those in Washington to tell us with whom we can make love, but also against the immorality of our own contributions to relationships of ownership and control, domination and submission, whether in our bedrooms, our economic investments, or our intentional or apathetic allegiances to sexism, racism, militarism, anti-Semitism, and other structures of injustice in the world.

It is morally inexcusable (albeit often politically and economically expedient) for gay men and lesbians to be indifferent to the poor in our cities and world. It is morally repugnant for lesbians and gay men to be apathetic toward racism. It is morally unacceptable for homosexuals to continue to feed into, and off of, sexist assumptions, jokes, and behavior, within and without the church. And it is exceedingly dangerous for us to allow *any* structure of sin and evil to go unchecked in the society, because in the end we ourselves will be the victims. Those forces in the world (which, in the advanced capitalist quarters of the earth, take the impersonal shape of militarism and multinational interests, flying under the guise of "free enterprise" and "Christian blessing") are bound to act *against* women's liberation, racial equality, gay/lesbian rights, the demands of the poor, all revolutionary movements, and the integrity of the earth itself.

The prophetic word, God's word, spoken through us, to us, and to others, is a word of strong judgment: Repent! Turn around! The time is at hand! No more of this abuse of human bodies, human blood, human minds, human hearts, human hands, human genitals, human beings at the pleasure of those on top, those with money, those with the power to control. No more! Enough!

The prophet exercises judgment and compassion. The judgment is the calling into question of our lives and those of others. The plumb line of justice is our standard. The compassion is our bearing with one another and others, in faith that we do not go alone, none of us. And so, with and by the power of God, and speaking on God's behalf, prophets are able to proclaim: "Do not be afraid. By God, we are with you. Do not be anxious how you are to speak, or what you are to say; for it is not you who speaks, but the Spirit of God speaking through you . . . and we will bear your witness."

· 24 ·

Must "Jesus Christ" Be a Holy Terror?
—Using Christ as a Weapon Against Jews, Women, Gays, and Just About Everybody Else*

The agenda before us is critical. I am convinced that our future as people on this planet rests on our commitments to reach over the walls that divide us—white women and black women, Jewish women and Christian women, women and men—not by pretending that we do not live different lives and not by attempting to dilute or diminish the structures, practices, and beliefs peculiar to our people; not by seeking false peace, but rather by addressing one another, listening to one another, and committing ourselves—without "losing" ourselves—to a common task, the making of justice in the world. And so I am pleased to be with you, a feminist Christian woman who is

---

*Originally titled "Re-imaging Jesus: Moving Beyond Sexism, Anti-Semitism, and Other Structures of Evil in Christian Theology," this paper was presented at the Feminists of Faith Conference, Hebrew Union College–Jewish Institute of Religion, New York City, November 11, 1981. Heyward's earlier examination of who Jesus was/what Jesus was doing is in *The Redemption of God: A Theology of Mutual Relation* (Washington, DC: University Press of America, 1982).

white, lesbian, a daughter of social and economic privilege, aware even as I speak these words that each signals a serious division—separation from—some other and marks my particularity, the specificity of my life experience, which I must take seriously if I am to engage creatively in any work with those whose life experience is different from my own. I do not envision our goal as "oneness" or "sameness" but rather as right-relation, an operative sisterly bonding marked by mutual respect, trust, and advocacy that can be built only over time in shared realization that this right-relation is key to our survival.

For as far back in my life as I can recall, I have been troubled by certain tenets of Christian theology, which, very early, I was taught were simply "true"—the way it is, period. None of these tenets was more puzzling to me than the church's teaching about Jesus: the Christ, the Messiah, the Lord, the King of Kings, the Son of God who, in early orthodox development, is hailed as God the Son, himself divine, "true God of true God, Begotten not made, of one being with the Father, by whom all things were made; who for us men and our salvation came down from heaven and was incarnate by the Virgin Mary." In A.D. 325 at the Council of Nicea, the question of whether or not Jesus was God the Son, himself divine, was laid to rest among "right-thinking" Christians. For the last 1,700 years, the matter has been all but closed. Attempts to open it evoke historically charges of heresy. And most Christian theologians who have raised questions about this doctrine have attempted fastidiously to keep their questions within the limits of the traditional Greek metaphysic. However seriously theologians may probe the intelligibility, wisdom, or justice of this teaching, most attempt to demonstrate the continuity between their christological reflections and the ancient confessions and formulas of the ecumenical councils of the church.

I believe that the feminist theological agenda pushes us into *discontinuity* with orthodox Christology, beyond even the most adventuresome theological spokespersons of the past and present Christian male collegium. I do not think that historical christological teachings that are rooted in trinitarian philosophy can be accommodated to the critical analysis of feminist Christians.

Feminist Christian women are spiritual sisters of feminist

Jewish women. We are bound together not only in resistance to particularly blatant misogynist practices and teachings of patriarchal religion (such as refusals to ordain women), but also—and here is where Christian theology may meet its most formidable challenge—in our suspicion that women's lives (and the lives of many men as well) are deformed, often destroyed, within a sexist, racist, anti-Semitic social order that is legitimated by what we have learned to accept as essential to our respective traditions. Having said that, I must admit at once that I do not know exactly what Jewish women are taught as the heart of their tradition. I do understand, however, that religion grows in the soil of human society, and the social relations of early Israel, which gave rise to Judaism, were patriarchal. This relationship leads me to ask questions about the character of YHWH—especially in relation to women—and about expectations of the male-female social relation that have been transmitted through Jewish history to the present time. My hunch would be that Jewish women, like their Christian sisters, come out on the bottom—whatever the reforms within Judaism. Is there not something in the major currents of Jewish teaching, as in Christian thought, that is antithetical to the well-being of adult women and free-spirited little girls? I will say no more about Judaism at this point, primarily because this is not the business of a Christian in the praxis of a social order seething now, as for so long, with a patronizing and vicious anti-Semitic impulse.

Christian belief and practice is my business. Christian belief and practice has been frequently antithetical to the well-being of not only all women, but also of all people of color, Jews, Muslims, the poor of the earth, and the earth itself. Which is to say that not only has traditional masculinist Christian thought and behavior denied, denigrated, and trivialized all women but also the vast majority of men in the world. Doctrinally, the problem is a serious one insofar as much damage done by Christians is done "in the name of Jesus Christ" and because faith in Jesus Christ as Lord and Savior is very much at the heart of Christian faith and practice.

The questions with which I have been wrestling for some time are (1) whether there is something fundamentally damaging to most of humankind in the Christian belief in, and commitment to, Jesus Christ as God's only begotten Son, God the Son himself, our only Lord and Savior; and (2) if so, what creative, constructive relation we might have to Jesus, we who are Christians.

• • •

Worship of Jesus: Christolatry

Christian faith and practice is necessarily destructive to most people in the world insofar as it is cemented in the insistence that Jesus Christ is Lord and Savior of all. At this point I am in agreement with Mary Daly's diagnosis of the problem as Christolatry, the worship of Jesus Christ as if he were God.[1] This is a serious stumbling block for women, as Daly contends, because we must constantly look up—for inspiration, leadership, role-modeling, and redemption—to a man. But it is a problem, I think, not only for women (who are, from the perspective of "natural law," "unlike a man") but also for all people who reject this particular man as divine—Jews and others who do not accept Jesus as the Christ, much less as God himself.[2] Alongside Jews and women, the majority of human beings in the world have been in trouble historically—put down, done in, by leaders of Christendom, who, even today, sit close to the seats of power in most Western nations and societies and in multinational structures throughout the world.

"In the name of Christ," Christian leaders justify and bless capitalism, racism, sexism/heterosexism, and anti-Semitism in societies in which to be "one with Christ," "members of His Body," is necessarily to value, and pay homage to, various assumptions held fast and dearly by those in power and cemented in the foundations of social organization: assumptions that "believers" (in Christ) will be blessed, spiritually and often materially as well; assumptions that followers of Christ are willing "servants" of those in power (who lead in the name of Christ); assumptions that "light" (the "purity" and "holiness" that comes through Christ) shines above "dark" (the "tainted" and "unholy," associated with darker skin pigment as well as with female sexuality and bleeding; with Jewish "motives" and business practices; and with whatever or whoever is perceived as pagan, perverse, deformed, possessed by sinister spirits). Christian rulers teach "obedience" as a virtue in itself and exercise their authority in behalf of God, in whose service the nation/institution is active. Christians learn and teach that poverty is a blessing, simply one's lot, or perhaps even a punishment (an odious assumption, apparent in the fundamentalist sectarianism promulgated by those with social power during periods of social turbulence, such as today by the leaders of the Moral Majority). Such assumptions about the value and justice of human submissiveness to Christian leadership, passivity in the face of suffering, and obedience to The Man ("father knows best") are, I submit, political corollaries to a Christocentric faith built upon an image of Jesus Christ who gladly suffered in obedience to his Father; the Christ whom, *from the perspective of privilege*, the poor and dispossessed are encouraged to worship as God (ultimate good) and to imitate as human role model.

This image of Christ is manipulated in the praxis of privilege (by those on the top, representatives of white male gentry) not only to symbolize the suffering servant, with whom those on the bottom can identify in terms of passive acceptance of suffering; but also, because Christ is God, to symbolize the rulership of all that is established, the guardian and custodian of all human and "natural" resources. He is King of Kings. He is Lord of Lords. And he shall reign forever. The same Christ who can be for the poor a comforter and lowly brother is, for the rich, the God who knows what is best for his people, an icon created in the image of rulers.

This double-image/double-think has been called "paradox": both lowly and Lord; brother and God; human and divine. But the question that must be raised, I believe, about paradox is whether it does in this instance signal some deep truth about human and divine in relation (as Christian doctrine maintains) or—instead—some deep truth about power relations in human society. Is this paradox a conceptual tool of self-justification, employed by those who have shaped and perpetuated the paradoxical doctrine of the "God-man": namely, the theologians of the church, traditionally and still today white privileged males and those who are willing to represent them? White women and people of color are encouraged, as we know, to speak for and on behalf of white men—a marvelous and effective public relations tactic, of which white women and people of color had best beware.

It seems no coincidence that the powerless in each Western generation—the poor and often "darker" peoples—have been drawn to the image of a lowly brother Jesus, a friend in need, one of the despised. The Christ of the poor has been more the suffering servant, less the Christus Rex, except insofar as the poor have been taught by those with ecclesiastical and social power to look beyond the present world for what is most valuable, that heavenly privilege represented by Christ the King, the One who sits at the right hand of the Father and is himself divine. If Jesus Christ, a poor brother, is so exalted, so too may be the poor—in the Otherworld. White and black Christian feminists might benefit together from exploring the extent to which the Christendom of white male privilege has utilized cunningly the doctrine of Christ's divinity, the image of God's Eternal Son, the story of the King of Kings, as a political foil that serves to diffuse the power of the story of the human Jesus by exalting this power as that of an otherworldly spiritual man rather than as the power of oppressed people in history, a power that moves toward liberation and justice in this world. I suggest that female Christians, black Christians, poor Christians, and gay/lesbian Christians participate in the perpetuation of our own oppression insofar as we allow our visions and energies to be drawn toward a heavenly man and away from our human situation as sisters and brothers, by fixing our attention on the spiritual accomplishments of a divine Savior rather than on the spiritual possibilities of concerted human commitment that can be inspired by the Jesus story as a human story: a story of human faith, human love, and human possibility as the agency of divine movement in history.

I have been excited by this chance to present these reflections to a group of feminists who are both Christian and Jewish. My enthusiasm is steeped in my realization that Jesus' so-called divinity has been the major barrier to a common understanding between us of our radical historical relation, as people of the covenant: the covenant between God and humankind, as represented by the people of Israel, among whom Jesus stood as a faithful person.

I believe with increased faith that the doctrine of Jesus' divinity is false, as is any theological teaching that grows out of and feeds into unjust social relations. It is not that Jesus' "fully divine" nature was, once upon a time, an appropriate, truth-bearing doctrine that has simply passed its time, nor simply that we have moved beyond Greek metaphysics in our theoretical constructions of reality. It is rather that neither then nor now has this teaching represented justly the true and dynamic relation between God and *all* people, who may be Jews or Christians, Muslims or Hindus, Quakers or Unitarians, practitioners of Wicca or nonpractitioners of any religion.

Christian Relation to Jesus in Particular

Am I then suggesting that Christians should have no Christ? That "true religion" is simply a universalized consciousness or an awareness of a deity who is all-in-all, wherever and whatever we may name as divine, however we can best image her, or him, or it, or them? Does this suggest only a soft mishmash of religious affections, drawn here, drawn there, rooted nowhere in particular? Does my implicit salutation of ongoing revelation negate the particular revelations that are special and precious to Christian believers, to Jewish believers, or to those who find or are found by the Goddess in the particularity of female bonding?

I believe not. The primary danger of faith in nonspecific revelation of what is beautiful, true, and just is that any of us can locate, name, and attach ourselves to whatever we want, or believe, to be most ultimate, best, highest, "divine." To each his/her own: Aryan supremacy, male headship, white superiority, private property, and national security can float with equal ease under the banner of Christian commitment or the logos of any symbol we may choose to employ: symbols of light, cleanliness, racial or moral purity; symbols of being "God's chosen people," of possessing a "promised land" or "kingdom" as ours and ours alone; symbols of "femaleness" or "blackness" as signaling a morally superior way of being in history, in contradistinction to symbols of "maleness" and "whiteness" as representing a natural superiority in the world. These are violent symbols, sustained by those of us who make God anything we choose. The problem with a "natural" or "universal" religion in which Christians need no particular Christ or Jews need no particular promise is that we can attempt only to keep faith and find God *ahistorically*—outside of or "above" history, the *collective experience of human being* in this world; experience that includes, but is not contained within, our own autobiographical (or our own group's) lives, but rather is in relation to the lives and stories of those who have gone before, those who go with us today (known and unknown to us), and those who will come after. History is the realm of relation that reveals or signifies the corporate character of all religious faith and praxis.

Thus, to be Christian is to seek, find, and move *in relation to* others, all others, and, certainly, to *particular* others—real, specific persons, and groups of persons, with names, faces, stories to tell. This is the historical character of all religion, including Christianity.

Historical relation is a praxis of disjunctive relations and discontinuity, an arena of revolution and struggle, as well as of cohesion and continuity, which is to say that our relations are not unbroken. Frequently they do not seem "relational" at all in terms of responsibility and friendship. But as participants in history, we are bound to acknowledge, if not ever fully to understand, the relation of our own lives (hence, the relativity of our lives) to those who have gone before us and who live in the world with us today, with life experiences different from our own.

As *Christians* who participate in history, we are bound to acknowledge without fully understanding, I believe, the relation of our lives as Christians to those other Christians who live today with experiences and symbols different from our own; to those Christians who have gone before us; and to those Jews and Gentiles who gathered in wonder and amazement, confusion and hatred, adoration and rejection, around a particular teacher, healer, prophet, and companion, whom they knew as the son of Joseph, a carpenter from Nazareth, and of Mary, a young woman, who gave birth to this child, Jesus.

The fact that a *particular* person, Jesus, lived, died and is proclaimed, in faith, to have been raised from the dead by God is crucial to Christian faith and practice. The particularity of Jesus' life has been so fundamental to Christian faith that Jesus' life has borne the stamp of "Christ," a symbol both in continuity and discontinuity with Jewish history inasmuch as Christians make a messianic claim about Jesus, which did in fact for the early Jewish Christians signify a break in the continuity of Jewish expectation. Among Jesus' followers, the title "Christ" symbolized Jesus' chosenness, his special commissioning by God, his particular significance for the lives of those who knew or were otherwise touched by him. The messianic title "Christ" points, for Christians, directly and particularly to Jesus of Nazareth. This is a point of disjuncture between Jewish and Christian faith, a sharp and incisive difference in our corporate life experiences.

But the significant difference was not necessarily violent—supremacist and exclusive—until Christians began (in the first centuries of the church) to characterize this break with Judaism in the particularity of Jesus Christ as *God's* particular and unique interruption of Jewish history by entering history in human form, rather than as a messianic event rooted in *Jesus'* commitment to a way of life Jesus understood to be Jewish. Thus, while the disjuncture is there, now as before, between Jewish and Christian understandings of who/what the Messiah is, the oppressive character of the Christian claim (the theological manifestation of its violent praxis) is not in the Christian belief that Jesus was the Messiah, the Anointed One, the Christ, but rather in our orthodox treatment of this revelation as God's particular incarnation, rather than as a revelation of the power of human faith. And so "right-thinking" Christianity loses something of the power of religious faith that had marked so compellingly the people of Israel's efforts to do what is just in the world.

As I noted earlier, in the christological credo that Jesus is divine and that, as such, his power was unique among human beings, we who are Christians are lured from this world toward some other, from humanity toward God, from what we do to what Jesus did, in order to seek and find a justice and a peace that is not of this earth. The power of human being in faith (the power of one who was like us) is lost in the power of God (the supernatural power of one who was not like us). The strong faith commitment of the human Jesus becomes less important than the superhuman power of the Son of God, who is said to be God the Son.

Christian faith must, I believe, point directly and particularly to the human life, faith, and teachings of Jesus as Christ, rather than simply to a free-floating symbol of what is valuable to us. For symbols do not, in fact, float freely, but rather are reflections of what we value in our life together. When Christians lose sight of the particular message and mission of Jesus, we open the door to the making of anyone or anything into our "Christ," that which beckons us to allegiance on the basis of special interest, prejudice, or (as is often the case) greed, profit, and megalomania, such as in the case of a Hitler or of so many other religious or political gurus.

But cannot the same self-justifying or vicious liberties be taken with the life and teachings of Jesus of Nazareth? Can we not seek and find simply what we are looking for when we look at the biblical images of Jesus? A sweet conciliatory person or a revolutionary prophet? An angry radical or a pastoral counselor? A person of peace or one who came to set brother against sister, nation against nation? Are not all of these images present in scripture as well as in traditional historical and theological scholarship about who Jesus was and what he was doing?

Yes, indeed. It is as possible for Christians to manipulate the Jesus story to serve only our own special pleadings as it is for Jews to manipulate the story of Israel in such a way that it benefits only Jews, or special groups of Jews. Any person or group of believers can make mileage, doctrinally and otherwise, out of distorted and half true accounts of what we read as holy stories. The Jesus of history is open to twisting, co-optation, and manipulation, as has been demonstrated many times when Christian faith becomes little more than a mask for some personality disorder or political ideology. But we need to realize, and realize well, that religion—*all* religion—is ideological; that is to say, constructed on the basis of values, commitments, and ideas or mind-sets about the structures of human social relations that religion attempts to address, uphold, correct, or otherwise affect.

The point is not whether Christian faith can be misdirected and abusive, simply self-serving and unjust. Of course it can be. The point is whether or not there may be ways of seeking to live and profess a faith that is respectful of all human being, open and tolerant of pluralism in religion and other arenas of life, and, at the same time, a resource of commitment to whatever particular actions and values enhance the respect of all human being. Which is why the particularity factor—the particularity of Jesus; the particularity of the claim that in Jesus' life specific attitudes, words, actions, commitments touched people deeply—is so critical a factor in Christian faith.

Now we must recognize that nothing in particular that Jesus did or said can provide the answers to most of the urgent social questions we face today, dilemmas surrounding nuclear politics, procreative choice, and the relations between the United States and the USSR. But if Jesus was our human brother, friend and soul mate, someone long since deceased but with us in spirit, then it is not to the Jesus story that we must turn for answers to our questions, but rather to one another, here and now in the world, approaching one another in the *particular spirit we believe was revealed with such power, grace, and courage in the life of Jesus:* a particular way of engagement marked by openness to those who are "different," willingness to risk on behalf of our commitments, efforts to stand our ground without possessing it, and, most importantly, relentless faith in a God whom we, like Jesus, have met and come to know as the source and constant resource of love, which—in this world—is always actualized in justice. The Jesus story is about a person who knew and loved a God of justice. This is its particular message. This is its creative power. This is the only truly moral raison d'être for the Christian church, and a powerful and compelling one it is. They who have ears to hear, let them hear.

· 25 ·

Introduction to Feminist Theology: A Christian Feminist Perspective[1]

What is feminist theology? The term is used more often to denote a particular theological pursuit than to characterize a perspective that informs the method and content of the theological enterprise in general—a perspective distinct from the masculinist lessons taught most often in churches, synagogues, and seminaries. Both usages of the term are correct, insofar as they describe something that is happening among religious scholars currently at work. The former usage, that of particular theological pursuit, may be the more immediate and, for a time, the more critical; certainly, it is the most evident in theological curricula. The latter meaning of feminist theology, denoting a perspective that informs and shapes the entire theological enterprise, is, I believe, the more radical and, in the long run, the more effective. The former is today the more acceptable because it can be marginalized in the curriculum, while the latter understanding poses a challenge to most traditional assumptions about what theology is.

My purpose is to offer some suggestions as to what may constitute a feminist theological perspective, in relation both to particular courses in feminist theology and to the more general theological task. I can, and do, make no claim to speak definitively about what feminist theology is. I am *one* feminist theologian and, even in speaking these words, acknowledge implicitly the self-definitive character of who is and is not a feminist theologian. I am usually delighted when a person characterizes herself as a feminist theologian, whether or not I agree with her understanding of either feminism or theology. I am delighted because, in these antifeminist backlash times, to call oneself a feminist is to stand in defiance of the massive rock of masculinist assumptions about women, men, the world, and god.

Movements in theological thought tend to expand in terms of number and diversity of participants. Feminist theology is no exception. In what follows, I will attempt to cite points of significant divergence among feminist theologians and to be as candid as possible in my assessment of what may be at stake in the disagreements. I will also try to be clear about where *I* am in these differences. My expectation is not that all feminists be at the same place. To the contrary. If we were, the educational value of what we can teach and learn together would be grossly diminished. I expect to keep learning—just as I hope to keep teaching. What I say is steeped in value judgment. Put simply, I am stating my opinion, my point of view, which, although never shaped in an "incubator," is something for which I must take responsibility. What I believe is what I have appropriated as mine, something I value, rather than something about which I can pass the buck to Mary Daly, Tom Driver, Paul Tillich, Elie Wiesel, Friedrich Schleiermacher, or Jesus of Nazareth.

Theology is critical—important and carefully undertaken— reflection on and expression of the meaning and value of our experience of God: our ultimate concern? power of being itself? maker of justice? power in relation? creator/redeemer/sustainer? source and resource of love?

Who are *we* to do theology? We are the people of God. There is no universally correct theological system that can be applied to all people, everywhere, at all times. Thus, the more theology reflects the specific and particular experience of those who shape it, the more credible theology is to others, especially to honest people seeking an honest god. Good, constructive theology is done in the praxis of concrete situations, in which the doers of theology speak for and about themselves rather than for and about others or humanity in general by attempting to universalize their experiences of what is true or good.

Does this mean that theology cannot represent the life experience or faith commitments or values of anyone except the person or persons who are doing it? Not at all. It does mean that the universality in a given theological undertaking is rooted *both* in the depth and integrity of the particular experiences of God that it unfolds *and* in the openness and desire on the part of the theologian(s) for dialogue, sharing, new insights, and changes in perceptions and systems.

The gross predominance of Christian dogma and systematizing has been done by men who have reflected on and articulated the meaning and value of their experiences as the experiences of all men and women. A similar epistemological presumption has been made by white people (most often men) who have attempted to articulate the theological meaning and value of the lives of people of color. These presumptions fly implicitly under the banners of such assumptions as objectivity, science, value-free theorizing, bipartisan interest, and revelation. It is specifically in response to this epistemological error that white women and black men and women have suggested that God is, in fact, our mother/the goddess and/or that the messiah is black. What this means, methodologically, is that theology must be done modestly, in recognition that all theological images and patterns are limited—in terms of truth and intelligibility—by the boundaries of the life experiences of those who construct them.

What this may mean in terms of theological validity as borne out in the practice of ministry is this: For me, in the whiteness of my skin/psyche/life experience, the messiah may not be readily or easily as black to me as to sisters and brothers of color. But I am unable to say that the messiah is *not* black or that it really does not make any difference (is unimportant, trivial) what color the messiah is. It may in fact be unimportant to me to the extent that race and skin color do not make any difference to "enlightened" or liberal members of the ruling racial class. Our capacities to feel or think with integrity about our social/racial situation have been mystified by our racial privilege. But the color of God, messiah/liberator, is a matter of serious meaning and value to members of the subordinate racial classes.

Liturgically and otherwise, my business, as a white person, is to share as candidly as possible the meaning and value of my experience, which must include morally ongoing openness to and desire for sharing/dialogue/reciprocity where possible/ change *in relation to* what black sisters and brothers are willing and able to show me, tell me, share with me.

In a situation of oppression—such as in a racist society—it also is the epistemological privilege of the oppressed to lead in the naming and worship of god. What this means to me, as white, is that it may be my business to follow. Similarly, it is today the business of men to follow women's lead in the naming and worship of god. It may be that it is at this epistemological point (of how we know what we know) that feminists connect with what other liberation theologians are doing.

Feminism is an ideological perspective rooted in the recognition among many women and increasing numbers of men that "the common human experience" (David Tracey) of women in history is structurally that of subordination to men; and further-more, that this situation of domination (by men) and subordina-tion (of women) is linked structurally (via institutions, social arrangements and organizations, governments, and interfacings of assumptions about what is "natural," "true," and "right") to other human experiences of domination and submission, such as advanced capitalism and racism.

This is a "hard" definition of feminism (Beverly Wildung Harrison) in contrast to the "soft" feminism on which many (most?) white middle/upper-strata women who are feminists cut our teeth.[2] The difference between soft and hard feminism lies in whether or not we who call ourselves feminist recognize the *structural character of sexism.* Soft feminists tend to perceive the problem as primarily that of *individual* attitudes and opinions, which can be changed through persuasion. If we educate folks, show them how unjust sexism is, help them change their minds, we will be able to solve the problem of sexism. Hard feminists maintain that education is not enough and that social change happens when people are not only educated (and change their minds) but are moreover involved in a *restructuring* of society in such a way that the locus of social power is redistributed. Ten years ago many white feminists in this country were soft feminists: in the course of time we got ordained, got jobs in church/school/government, got raises in pay or help with our children. In attempting to participate in our new roles, many of us have become harder, postliberal feminists.

A soft feminist analysis informs my point of view in *A Priest Forever* (1976). I was interested to discover recently that a careful reading of this book reflects movement toward a more structural analysis. The struggle around the Philadelphia ordination had begun to push me beyond an individualized, educationally oriented expectation of what may be involved in the liberation of women, including my own liberation.

Currently, among Christian feminists, the soft feminist analysis is characteristic of many women and men who know that something is wrong in terms of the male-female relation. They may know, for example, that more women than men have trouble getting parish (or other) jobs; but they tend to believe that the "exceptional" woman will make it if she tries.

The hard feminist analysis attempts to unmask this interpretation as illusory. Among hard feminists there are at least three strong currents of theological movement, which diverge around the issue of the importance of male supremacy in relation to other structures of injustice. (1) Some feminists believe that sexism is the most devastating and thus most important and/or the oldest and most deeply rooted form of oppression in human history. Sexism must be undone before any significant justice will be made in this world. Mary Daly, Carol Christ, and Naomi Goldenberg move in this current. (2) Other feminists hold that the issue of which comes first—either in time or in importance—is a moot point both morally and strategically. These feminists cite the complexity of the interactive effects among gender, race, economic well-being, age. Rosemary Ruether, Elisabeth Schüssler Fiorenza, Delores Williams, and Judith Plaskow are among the women who take this position. (3) For other feminists, some other structural injustice may take immediate precedence over sexism in their work. Feminist theologian Dorothee Sölle, for example, has spent most of her time recently in the peace movement, both in Germany and in the United States.

Pauli Murray and some other black feminists cite the struggle of black people against racism as demanding priority in their daily lives and work. Women such as Sölle and Murray understand that male supremacy is related to economic injustice, racial oppression, and militarism.

The heart of feminist content beats strong in the theological method itself. The content reflects the method, and vice-versa. Anyone who reads Mary Daly *(Beyond God the Father* and *Gyn/Ecology)* and my *Redemption of God* may assume correctly that the difference in the substance of what we propose reflects a different methodology. Male theologians often ask us to tell them what feminist theology is, how it is done, and what all of us (feminists) agree on. We can only speak for ourselves and let other voices join us inasmuch as we sing the same songs. The general rises out of the particular and only on the terms of *each* particular voice. Here then are some methodological presuppositions in my work as a theologian.

1. I submit that *all* constructive theology is done in the praxis of life experience and that feminist theology pays special attention to life experience in sexist society. The experience of sexism provides the ground on which we stand as we reflect on, and articulate, theological meaning and value.

2. I believe that feminist theology is always "the second act" (Gustavo Gutiérrez), preceded by the recognition of a serious problem (the structure of sexual injustice) and the commitment to work toward its demise—in the creation of a just world.

3. As a feminist theologian, I grant justice a normative status in theology. Justice is right-relation between and among people, relation of mutual benefit, created by mutual effort. All theological resources—including Bible, doctrine, discipline, polity, systematics, and other fields—can be employed creatively only to the extent that they further human well-being in a just society.

4. Such theology is rooted in faith in a just god/ess. For some feminists, god is the source of justice; for others, the maker of justice; for others, justice itself: god *is* justice. These may reflect natural, moral, and humanistic interpretations, although among many feminist theologians there is no disjuncture, at times no difference, between so-called natural and moral categories.

5. This theology is a critical theology of liberation, done on

the basis of a "hermeneutic of suspicion" (Segundo). Feminist theology moves beyond the main streams of Latin American liberation theology, however, in explicating the physical human body as absolutely central to the "hermeneutical circle." All experiencing of our experiences (Nelle Morton), analyses of the social situations in which we live, critiques of the traditions we share, and constructions of theological affirmations (the four "points" of Segundo's circle) are done in relation to how we experience, feel, think about, and *live* as bodies. Because Christian tradition has been the forum for the denigration of the body—and especially the female body—women grant a primary place to our actual body experiences that most other liberation theologies, materialist though they are, have not assumed to be central as beginning and end of all our experiences of justice/god in the world.

6. Body-centered, feminist theology is sensual/sexual. Its spirituality is rooted in its sensuality/sexuality—that is, in our experiences of our body-yearnings/feelings/needs for relatedness/connectedness with other participants in the world.

7. Another way of articulating this relatedness/connectedness is to maintain, as I do, that feminist theology is fundamentally relational. "Our" experience is always in relation to the experience of others; so too is our theology. Thus, feminist theology is a broadly *ecumenical* enterprise of storytelling, celebration, critiquing of our traditions, delighting in them when they serve justice, re-forming them when they do not.

8. Such a feminist theology of liberation bears witness to the dynamic, changing character of relation, and hence of theology itself. Moreover, feminist theology moves in relation to a god who is relational (dynamic, changing, active). Like process theology, feminist theology recognizes this as true; unlike process theology, feminist theology presupposes no primordial and consequent bipolarity of natures in God, but rather might even suggest that god's nature (being) derives from god's activity (doing). Epistemologically, feminist theology moves from action to ideology, rather than vice-versa.

9. I would insist that no doctrine or belief is immune to the critique implicit in the above theses. Not god, not incarnation, not sin, not atonement. We feminists assume the prerogative to

transvaluate traditional Christian or religious norms, such as the assumption that pride is sin. As Valerie Saiving-Goldstein suggests in her 1960 essay, for most women, self-denial may be the greatest sin—and pride, an aspect of redemption.[3]

10. As long as we remain to any extent committed to our Jewish, Christian, or other predominantly masculinist religious traditions, feminist theologians share a vocation of bearing, as creatively as we can, the mighty contradictions between our faith commitments and theology and the practices and teachings of our various religious affiliations.

For example, one of the most difficult tensions Christian feminists encounter is between our life experience as feminists and the doctrine, discipline, and worship of a church founded on masculinist assumptions about the relation of a Father God to his Son Jesus who himself is God the Son, and who together reign in a Kingdom, in which power is "naturally" handed down from above—and only to those who submit to the omnipotence and omniscience of a Father who knows best. The Creator and Redeemer are experienced and conceptualized, explicitly, as being in the image of *men*. This is no historical accident, no metaphysical coincidence. Indeed, in the image of the prototypical and primary male-male relation (father-son), these doctrines are constructed and sustained/sanctified (by the third male-Spirit, the one who sustains and sanctifies) to benefit primarily *men* in their efforts to live meaningfully and well on earth.

The doctrines of the trinity and the incarnation, together with the atonement, provide the grist for the christological mill and constitute a particular scandal for christian feminists. I believe we must study these doctrines long and well. We must study these doctrines and we must study our lives if we do not want to relinquish either our senses of self or our roots in a religious tradition that we experience both as shamefully misogynist and as a place of friendship and solidarity in our search for meaning and value as women.

· 26 ·

On El Salvador*

Sisters and brothers, next time we do this (and there will be many next times), there should be ten thousand, twenty thousand of us here. And this platform should be filled with women of all colors and men of color, because a lot is happening among many women and many men of color, a lot that relates directly to what is happening in El Salvador. We must never let ourselves be fooled into believing the sexist, racist, classist, homophobic lies that the assaults being waged against human rights in this country are not purposely and systematically connected to the assaults being waged against the people of El Salvador.

I speak to you as a woman, a lesbian feminist, a socialist, and a Christian priest. I tell you these things because each of these words signals the locus of strong solidarity for the people of El Salvador. I speak to you in the name of God, and in the name of humanity. I do not have much to say, because our words should not be wasted.

---

*This essay is taken from a speech delivered at an El Salvador rally, Boston, MA, February 13, 1982.

The war being waged against the people of El Salvador by the junta and its military and paramilitary machine is a scandal against all that is just and respectful of human rights and dignity. This war, which could not be waged without the consent, support, and complicity of the United States, must be stopped. It will be stopped only when justice has been won; when the courageous *compañeras y compañeros* and those who stand with them have risen—like the phoenix from its ashes, like Jesus from the dead—as living witness to the irrepressible spirit that seeks and finds justice and that will not be overcome. Justice will not be overcome. Not in El Salvador. Not in the United States. Because those who cherish humanity will not allow it.

We do not have to be political scientists to see well the extent to which the United States is up to no good in Latin America, and most immediately and urgently in El Salvador. We do not have to be economists to see that what is happening in El Salvador is being planned and implemented, intentionally and carefully, by our government here in the United States in order to bolster our own economic interests. Every shot fired by the Salvadoran military is fired on behalf of wealth and power in the United States. Every child, woman, and man slaughtered by U.S. weapons in the hands of Salvadoran soldiers becomes another body upon which we here are building our empire. We do not have to be Christians or Jews, priests, rabbis, ministers, theologians, or religious people at all to see that what the United States is creating in El Salvador is an *evil* situation.

Listening to Alexander Haig talk about the security of El Salvador is like listening to a fox talk about the security of the chicken coup! It is not that our national leaders do not "have the facts." It is not that Congress is "confused." How can it be that citizens throughout this country know exactly what is happening in El Salvador and that the leaders of this country know too little to make a clear, definitive decision? We do not have to be communists, socialists, or even left-wing activists to understand that when people have been oppressed long enough, they will struggle for liberation! Our own nation was born of such a struggle. Ronald Reagan knows this. Our congresspeople know this. These people know as well as we do what is what, and the most powerful men in this nation have chosen to stand on the side of oppression, repression, and injustice against the courageous people of El Salvador.

The president and the Congress tell us that it is because of "communism," that communism is the enemy. When will they learn that *injustice* is the enemy—the only enemy of both humanity and God?

Please do not underestimate the weight of human *silence*—the damage being done this very minute by the silence, the complicity, of those in the United States and elsewhere who know that we are creating a monster in El Salvador and yet who sit silently, waiting for others to lead the way. Will we allow this evil situation to go unchecked? We will not. Will we wait quietly as Ronald Reagan, José Napoleón Duarte, and their co-conspirators dig ever deeper the graves of our sisters and brothers? We will not. I urge you to lead. To speak. To make no peace with this insidious, immoral outrage being perpetuated against the Salvadorans. It is going to get worse. We are citizens of a foolish nation obsessed by fear and greed. Our voices must be loud, uncompromising, angry, relentless. Our lives must be no less.

In this pitiful age, in which, in my opinion, the most narrow-minded, bigoted, christofascist people call themselves the "moral majority," it is time—high time, past time—for the rest of us religious folks to take to the streets, the legislative chambers, the White House, the voting booths, the pulpits and platforms, and anyplace else we can or must to make ourselves heard and our call heeded. Do not speak to us of God when you hate justice! *Cuando no hay justicia, no hay Dios!* (When there is no justice, there is no God!)

Injustice is the only enemy, and liberation, the only victory. Liberation it will be. The *compañeros/compañeras* will win, as surely as the sun is bound to rise some fine day. The question for those of us in the United States is, where will *we* be? Where are *we*?

With our voices, our anger, with our money, with our lives, may we be with the Salvadoran people. May we be there with the passion of an Oscar Romero. May we be there with the faith and work of an Ida Ford or a Jean Donovan. May we be there with the revolutionary commitment of an Enrique Alvarez. May we be there with all those whose names and faces we may never know, those who keep the fires burning for justice through the long, long night. And when the roll is called up yonder—and even more importantly, always more importantly, when the roll is called down here—may we, with these sisters and brothers, respond, *PRESENTE!*

Gracias.

· 27 ·

Compassion*

If I had only a single line today, it would be to plead with you to remain human—in spite of all temptations. And I would make this plea especially today to Mary, because of the temptation to allow oneself to be set apart from others in our common humanity; the temptation to minister down to others, believing that we who are ordained possess something (be it a special gift, a certain privilege, or even, within the ecclesial community, a right) by which we are able to bring God to people who look up to us to do so; the temptation to identify ourselves with what is holy, with what in fact is God. To do so, to try to be something other

*This sermon was given at the ordination of the Rev. Mary D. Glasspool to the priesthood at St. Paul's Episcopal Church, Chestnut Hill, PA, on March 6, 1982. It is included in this book because it reflects Heyward's effort to speak of *passion* as grounded in *com-passion*, or passion *with* others. As such, this sermon represents explicit theological movement from the earlier address, "Passion," pp. 19–23. It exemplifies also the author's attempt, in the context of a parish congregation, to help make the connections in as personal and particular a mode as possible. It is for that reason, to illustrate the relation between, for example, friendship and justice, that the references to the friendship of Carter Heyward and Mary Glasspool have not been omitted or altered.

than human, is, for the priest or the layperson, to hide under a bushel the one most valuable gift any of us can give another: our willingness to share what we need, what we yearn for, what we experience, what we believe, what we doubt, what we fear, what we cherish, what we create, what we celebrate, what we grieve for, the stuff that being human is made of. To rise above this precious openness and vulnerability to one another and to the world itself is to snuff out the possibility of meeting God in the world. I do not believe I am exaggerating when I suggest that the reason our world is on the verge of genocide, and possibly deicide (insofar as God's well-being is related to our own), is that so many, many of us are scrambling to rise above our common humanity. By way of money, power, reason; by way of some false notion of spirituality; by way of education, association, refinement, affiliation; by way of the sort of self-control that knows no strong feeling; by way of indifference and dispassion, many, many of us are deserting humanity, and in so doing, have turned our backs on God. Whatever we need most in our own lives is what we need most in the lives of these persons, like priests, whom we ordain to help us find what we are seeking. I believe that our charge to Mary should be that she remain human—in spite of all temptations—and that we could suggest to her that the sign of a person's real humanity is her compassion.

Compassion = *passion with*. Passion means suffering, as we know from the liturgical season of Passiontide, a reference to Jesus' suffering at the hands of an unjust world. What we often fail to see is that suffering does not refer simply to pain and distress. Rather, suffering means to bear up, to go with, to permit something that is happening. Jesus suffered God's inspiration. Jesus bore up God's movement in the world. Jesus gave license to God. Jesus' passion refers not simply to his death, but even more importantly to his life, in which God abounded God—the source and resource of human love, which takes the shape of justice (righteousness, right-relation) in our relationships, our commitments, our work. She, or he, who is passionate is the one who really experiences life, who drinks deeply from the wellspring of all that is given and all that is received.

The person who is passionate is, indeed, the one who not only remains human but who also takes pleasure in being human—a person whose laughter is plenty and whose tears flow freely, because in this world not to laugh and not to cry is to be cut off from realizing either the beauty of this earth and its resources (both human and other), or the shame and horror that mar our common home.

To live with passion is to live not above, or apart from, but within the dynamics of contradiction: in joy and sorrow, in caring and indifference, in courage and fear, in friendship and alienation, involved in the tensions that overload our senses and jar our sensibilities and push us toward that cynical point, at which we can glibly thank God for our many blessings as we go on our way assuming that the world is cursed and doomed by some maniacal force that is beyond both human and divine control. Passion is that fully human and fully divine spark which leaps in the face of cynicism and burns with a commitment that neither God nor humankind is finished!

Mary and I are both members of a generation cultivated to be cynical. We came into a world in which people pray for peace/ and build bombs; preach justice/and practice racism and sexism; praise the power of human creativity/and use this power to split atoms; teach sharing/and take from the poor; a society in which the most vocal Christians, those who speak most loudly and most often as being "pro life" seem to believe (to quote Congressman Barney Frank from Massachusetts) that "human life begins at conception and ends at birth." The temptation, the constant temptation, is to be cynical—to turn our backs on our common humanity, our brothers and sisters, because we cannot bear to face either them or our own senses of powerlessness, helplessness, and futility. "When he saw the crowds, he had compassion for them, because they were harassed and helpless [Matt. 9:36]."

Compassion is that attitude or quality of being that people of passion reflect in their relationships and work. A compassionate person lives in such a way that her passion for life, for human dignity, for God's justice manifests itself as a sturdy, unbreakable connection to other people. Passion *with* others. The passion you might feel if you were with your loved ones in a burning house. It is one thing to stand outside a house that is burning and know that your family is inside and that you must do what you can to get them out. That is passion, and that is good. But it is another thing altogether to be *in* the house *with* your loved ones and to know that while you yourself want out, there are others whose safety is as important to you as your own. That was the situation in which Jesus found himself. And that is compassion. To be involved, sharing the same world, the same dilemma, realizing that each person's destiny is bound up with one's own. The point at which radical self-interest and the willingness to give oneself/one's life, if necessary, coincide. Compassion, in which love is actually the love of one's neighbor as oneself.

Let me elaborate. Like so many moral virtues, compassion is commonly mistaken for a soft and indeterminate feeling: we feel sorry for someone who is in trouble, we offer sympathy, we pity the poor soul. We regret what has happened to this person. We are grateful it has not happened to us. But I think this is not what Jesus felt when he met the troubled, worried people. Jesus' engagement with those around him—those who touched him and were touched by him—was of such intensity that the boundaries which commonly separate people, which divide one person's self-interest from another's, were shattered. Whatever else we may find in the gospel narratives, we are met by the story of a human being, someone like us, who *acted* as if everyone he met were as significant as himself. A line between his own well-being and that of others was not there for Jesus. Not that he had no sense of himself—his faith, his needs, his yearnings, his vocations, his temptations, his friends and enemies. Not that he acted as if humanity were a large conglomerate of sameness, in which individuals had no place. To the contrary. Jesus acted as if every person mattered, as if every life were as deeply rooted in divine soil as every other human life, including his own. If, as we who are Christians believe (however differently we may image or express it), we see God in Jesus' life, then the God we encounter in Jesus is a power that moves us into relationships in which our own well-being is bound up in the well-being of others. These are relationships in which the needs and hopes of one person, or one race, or one nation, or one sex, cannot be extricated from the needs and hopes of all others. Jesus was someone who did not set himself apart from or above others. God is that holiest of spirits, which pulls, pushes, nudges, and yearns us toward a humanity that holds all things in common, a way of living together in which to be human, fully human, is to share.

And so, when Jesus looked with compassion on the anxious crowd, he was not looking down upon pitiful woebegone folks who, unlike him, were overwhelmed with the weariness of loss and grief, inequitable taxes and unjust laws, greed and indifference. Rather, he was looking upon people whose experiences in and of the world were his own. Common people with common experiences in a common world. To be sure, some of the people were undoubtedly more just than others; some more receptive to Jesus himself than others; some fairer, kinder, more personable than others. Different folks, different values and commitments. But Jesus acted as if each person, and each group of persons, were of the ultimate worth that *demands serious attention.* To pay serious attention to anyone is to encourage that person—indeed, to expect him/her—to meet you on common ground—holy ground. Jesus' compassion was grounded in his faithful realization that all human beings were his sisters and brothers; that their distress was his own, and his own was theirs; and that his relationships to them were as friend to friend—abundant with the expectation that they, no less than he, were responsible for going with God into the mutuality, reciprocity, and justice that is the only authentic form of love and that is God's only real presence in the world.

Seeing the crowd, feeling compassion—with them, knowing well himself the experience of a world like ours—so often cruel and cynical, Jesus said to his disciples, "The harvest is plentiful, but the laborers are few; pray therefore the Lord of the harvest to send out laborers into [the] harvest [Matt. 9:37–38]."

Pray that God will call people, other people, not only Jesus, to do what they can, with God, to empower and encourage those who are discouraged and feel powerless.

Pray that God will call forth from among us—we who are disheartened—people, friends, who can call us to open ourselves to the healing and liberating power of God, with which we too can participate in the mending of broken lives and a broken world.

Pray that God will show us those who share our distress, who know what it is to feel helpless and harassed and who, because they know these things, can be compassionate.

Pray that God will call from among us compassionate priests, and that we will have the wisdom to hear this call as it is spoken—and to go with God in the ordination of such persons as our priests.

We believe that God has called forth such a priest in Mary Glasspool, and that is why we are here today. Mary is one of the most compassionate people I have known, a woman *with* us in our ups and downs, a person who gives and receives, touches and is touched. Mary knows well the heights to which the human being can soar in love, happiness, humor, and pleasure, as well as the depths of our needs, our pain, our greed, and our indifference. To me, Mary (like so many of our seminary students) looks so young and fresh and innocent! Well, she is, in fact, a wise woman, who continues to teach me much about compassion.

I want to mention three things about compassion that Mary has helped me to realize. (Mary has also told me that Christians seem often, in our preaching, to have "Three" points to make!)

1. *Compassion and judgment go hand in hand.* Mary has helped me see the extent to which a person who is truly compassionate, truly with humanity as friend and advocate, is not timid in taking stands which, implicitly or explicitly, carry judgment about what is right and wrong, just and unjust, acceptable and unacceptable behavior. Christians often claim to be nonjudgmental. When we make this claim, I think we are either fools or liars, for all human beings make judgments, and all of us make moral judgments—which are bound to be offensive to some. We may be offensive in what we say or do. Or in refusing to do anything—refusing to get involved—we may be offensive in what we refuse to say or do. A compassionate person is not an inoffensive person, but rather is someone who realizes the bond, the commonness, between herself and those whose actions or attitudes she challenges, criticizes, or condemns. For

example, when a black person confronts me compassionately about my racism, telling me that something I have said or done is racist and unacceptable, the compassion in this judgment is in my black sister or brother's realization that we—both black and white—are in a racist society (the burning house) and that each of our well-being is bound up with the other's. Such compassion can help me begin to see that racism diminishes my well-being as well as the lives of people of color. Compassion and judgment go hand in hand.

2. *Compassion is a resting place.* Only those with compassion can be our true friends, pastors, teachers, soul mates, helpers. Because she is compassionate, Mary has helped me to learn to rest. Because when she is *with* me, she is *really* with me— intensely involved in the work and play of friendship. I have experienced time and again with Mary the comfort of knowing that I can relax, let my hair down, speak my mind, or say nothing, knowing well that when we part—however seriously we may have disagreed—I will have been nourished and will be rested. You at St. Paul's are fortunate. I miss this friend, who was so often a resting place.

3. *Compassion is a wellspring of transcendence,* or the movement of God not only between and among human beings, but also into and through the heights and depths of all that is. I teach a course at Episcopal Divinity School on the theological themes in the writings of Elie Wiesel, a survivor of the Holocaust who has written some twenty books that deal with God, humanity, evil, friendship, and solidarity. In one of Wiesel's books there is a character named Pedro, a favorite of both Mary's and mine.[1] Pedro is a Spanish smuggler, surely one of the most passionate characters in contemporary fiction. Pedro befriends Michael, a young survivor of the Holocaust whose Jewish faith has been destroyed and who has barely survived during his postwar years of meandering aimlessly, harassed and helpless, prisoner to his memories of the dead, unable and unwilling to make friends, to reach out or to be reached. It is a long story, in which Michael is propped at the edge of madness and will indeed go mad or maybe die unless he is somehow reached, gotten

through to, by someone. The someone is Pedro, who through many trials and desperate encounters begins to show Michael *the power in relation, power in friendship.* At the book's end, Pedro is dead or in prison, and Michael is confined to a small cell with one other person, a boy who is silent and catatonic. It has become clear to Michael that he will go mad unless he does something. He remembers Pedro, he remembers the power in his relation, and he sets out to relate to the catatonic boy. Days and weeks pass, there is no response, and yet Michael does everything he can—talks, touches, sings, makes faces, attempts to feed the boy, on and on, and finally says to him,

"One day the ice will break and you'll begin to smile. . . . You'll shake yourself. . . . You'll open your eyes and you'll say to yourself, 'I feel better, the sickness is gone, I'm different.' You'll tell me your name and you'll ask me, 'Who are you?' and I'll answer, *'I'm Pedro'*. . . . Later, in another prison, someone will ask you your name, and you'll say, *'I'm Michael.'* And then you will know the taste of the most genuine of victories."[2]

The most genuine of victories, to taste the power that transcends the boundaries of our own skins, to see our faces in the faces of Salvadoran peasants and battered women. This is to taste the fruits of the realm of God, to share, participate in, wonder at, and marvel at the power of the God whom we meet in human relations that are just. Compassion is a wellspring of this power, with which we are called to participate in the ongoing creation, liberation, and blessing of the world.

Mary, I have three brief charges.

1. In your compassion for all people, remember especially your sisters. In this broken world and broken church we have special need of you, and you of us. Women are not taken seriously in the church; and more importantly, most of us do not yet take ourselves seriously. We need strong sisters, strong in compassion and courage and faith, to be our advocates. You can be such a person, as indeed you are. You will also need such persons, such sisters and advocates, as indeed you have.

2. A wise Quaker woman, speaking to thousands of us at an El Salvador rally in Boston, said that there are two solutions to our feelings of powerlessness: (1) Do something. (2) Do it together. She is right. To act corporately as God's people—this is

the mission of the church. It is the shared vocation into which all of us are called and to which you are being ordained today as someone to help lead the way. Lead boldly, and do not hesitate to follow those who lead compassionately on behalf of justice, whatever their cause, whatever their sex, or race, or sexual orientation, or class, or religion, or age. Know that all people are your people, but choose your friends carefully, because you will need good friends if you are about God's business in the world. It is not a popular business, and your call is not to popularity, but to helping justice flow down like water, righteousness like an ever-flowing stream.

3. Finally, as the former bishop of this diocese, Bob DeWitt, is fond of saying, keep your courage. You will, of course, be afraid, if you remain human. But courage, as Tillich and others suggest, is the leap *in spite of* fear. Do not forget that you are not alone. Your passion is *with* others, and ours is *with* you. Come what may, the risks you take with and for others, here at St. Paul's, in the wider church and community, and in the world, will draw you as close as any of us will ever get to the heart of God.

Go well, sister.

Amen.

· 28 ·

Crossing Over: On Transcendence[1]

And our soul did magnify our God, who had blessed us, ordinary women.

Today we christian feminists are wiser, we trust, because we have been living attentively to this God whose movement we have learned to recognize among all persons and all other creatures who struggle for power—to live, to breathe, to choose. Therein is the link, both "natural" and "moral" in terms of traditional christian theology and ethics, between the movement for women's liberation and the many various movements around the world for the liberation of black people, poor people, indigenous people, racial/ethnic people everywhere, gay men and lesbians, religious minorities in any given social situation, and not only particular groups of people, but also for humankind and all creation. A "natural" and "moral" bond connecting feminist consciousness and commitment to nuclear disarmament, to ecological sanity, to diets for small planets, and to a restructuring of global economy to serve the many and not merely the few. The relation is "natural" because the power of mutual relation is, in fact, what makes us all one, relatives, interdependent, necessarily givers and recipients in the chain of life—whether or not we realize or accept this fact. Our realization and acceptance of this fundamental mutuality places our responsibility within what ethicists have called the "moral" dimension—in which what we choose, or refuse to choose, becomes crucial in the building up, or tearing down, of our common life.

Set in relation to this perspective, the complaint voiced frequently against feminist theology is that we have no place in our theology for "the transcendent."

It is time we respond to this charge, and we can begin by suggesting that, by the transcendent, these critics mean "God"—and most surely not the power of mutual relation but rather a power of hierarchical relation, a god at the top, he who has been imaged in christian tradition as "Father, Son, and Holy Spirit," who before the worlds began, before the curtain had been raised on the drama of salvation history (creation/fall/redemption), knew the plot, how it would begin, how it would end. An "Almighty God," the essence of whose power is control. This is the "transcendent God" whom many of us reject, not in the first instance because he is portrayed as male, but rather because he—reflecting that which generations of religious men have venerated—represents a use of power that neither we in our own lives today nor Western history itself from our perspective can testify to as creative or redemptive, this use of power as control, as knowing what is best for subordinates, as presumed master of children and slaves. At best, this deity is a benevolent ruler, who gives to his subjects what is good for us and whom we, in our eternal foolishness, have only to trust and obey. The problem with this view of transcendence is at least threefold.

1. Historically, to the rest of humankind, the dominant (white European) christian religious tradition has remarkably little which is creative or redemptive to show for its allegiance to a deity of benevolent, just, and merciful control. Christianity has reflected an enormity of control in its preaching and practices—but a dearth of benevolence, justice, and mercy—whether on the mission fields or in the bedroom. Control and domination in the name of "God" . . . From the earliest ecumenical councils of the church, faith in a divine master of domination and control, the predominant conservative "impulse" in this Euroamerican christian theology, has been to safeguard our

claims as those of an all-powerful "God," and our values as reflective of all that he values on the earth.

2. The second problem with this notion of transcendence, which relates to the first, is that it is a seriously limited view of actual transcendence. To transcend means, literally, to cross over. To bridge. To make connections. To burst free of particular locations. A truly transcendent God knows the bounds of no human life or religion. Such a God is not contained within holy scriptures or religious creedal formulations. No one person, no group of people, has a hot-line to a god who is actually transcendent, for God is too constantly, too actively, moving, crossing over from my life to yours, and from ours to theirs, to become our source of special privilege. No, the "God" of our Fathers, the one we are told is transcendent, is not, in fact, a transcendent god, but rather a projection of men who are stuck—concretized in their experience of what it means to rule and be ruled. So too is their god stuck, sealed fast by the limits of particular cultural movements and assumptions that have been historically shaped by male domination, white supremacy, and economic exploitation.

3. And so, finally, the problem with this patriarchal view of transcendence and the "God" who is said to be its essence is that it really has very little to do with transcendence, that fundamental relational power which moves to cross over from people to people, race to race, gender to gender, class to class, binding us into one Body of human and created beings, healing our wounds, breaking down the assumptions and structures that keep us divided, and, through it all, empowering us, each and all, to know and love ourselves and one another as participants in this transcendence. We have spent too many generations thinking of God's immanence as that "part" of God's being we can experience and of God's transcendence as that other "part," the unknownness, the mystery, the "God beyond God." Many of us are ready to proclaim, gladly and gratefully, that we, in our daily lives, experience a wonderfully mysterious power truly crossing over into and through and from our lives into the lives of all created beings—and that this power is indeed God, transcendent precisely in the fullness and radicality of her immanence among us.

I submit that this traditional, historical failure either to experience or to understand God's transcendence is related directly to the church's teachings against sexuality. And not only against homosexuality—against sexuality, period. Since we have not been permitted theologically to believe in a radically transcendent God, whose very character is to carry us beyond the boundaries of our own skins into mutual relation with sisters and brothers, we have not been able to experience this very natural and moral stirring in ourselves, between and among us, as good—related to God, of God, empowered by God. To the contrary, we have grown up, century upon century, we who are Christians, on the assumption—legitimated by both church and state—that this human desire to touch and be touched deeply, at the core of our bodyselves, is wrong—contrary to the "will" of our "Father." Church and state have conspired, since the fourth century when the two first joined hands officially, to proscribe sexual license as, on one hand, destructive to "God's" plan for us and, on the other, dangerous to the state's economic plan for us. What has been good for "God" has been good for the national fiscal policy. And sexual inhibition has been good for both. Small wonder that the "family" has been maintained as the central christian image of how life is supposed to be lived in "God's" world; and that the prevailing view of family (which has changed historically and only recently, in postindustrial capitalist society, has meant "nuclear" family) tends to reflect theologically whatever is in the best interests of the economic status quo.

If we are to appreciate ourselves as sexual beings, really appreciate ourselves and learn more and more how to enjoy ourselves/our bodies and those of other people in ways that are mutually empowering and creative, we who are christians are going to have to participate in articulating and offering some quite radical theological alternatives to what we have been given by our fathers. For the predominant traditional images—of an "Almighty God," the icon of domination and submission, the beginning and the end of self-control and control over others— however benevolently he is perceived to operate—cannot be tolerated, except within our grossly dis-integrated personalities, by those of us who have experienced, and who believe in, the power of mutual relation as the locus of all that is creative and redemptive. The power of mutual relation is creative sexual power, which is redemptive of our isolation and brokenness in its carrying us into relation with others. Sexual power not only carries us into lovemaking with our partners, but is moreover present and active in all creative, mutually empowering relations we have, whether in our one-to-one relations or in our efforts to cross over the various boundaries we have tolerated between us as people of different races, genders, nations, classes, and religions. Do not imagine that it is merely coincidental that churchmen often dismiss christian feminists as a bunch of lesbians, nor that it is mere chance that many of us are. For what these churchmen often intuit, frequently without realizing it, is that women are *making the connections* between the power of mutual relation and sexuality. We are making the connections in our daily lives, in our relationships, and in our work. Coming out, we are testifying to that power crossing over among us and all that lives. Coming out, we are calling public attention to what we so strongly believe to be true. Once we have begun to come of age, there can be no return to our "Father's" realm—except as witnesses to an empty tomb. No longer dead, we are rising together.

· 29 ·

Living in the Struggle*

"The harvest is plentiful, but the laborers are few [Matt. 9:37]."

We at the Episcopal Divinity School attempt to shape our common life around the assumption that our own lives are our basic educational resources. By taking our gifts and our goals seriously, we are better able to notice the seeds of God's harvest as they grow, even now, among us. And we realize that Christian vocation is not something we are simply preparing for, or helping others prepare for, but is rather the stuff of our daily lives. This is, in brief, our educational philosophy.

But I wonder how well we see the theological implications of what we are about in this school. Do we understand that to take human initiative, human goals, human competence, human confusion seriously as spiritual resources is, in fact, to bear witness to a cooperative, co-creative relation between what we believe to be human and what we believe to be divine? I submit that it is precisely this—the implications of our theological witness—that makes Episcopal Divinity School outstanding among theological schools, and a lightning rod in the wider

---

*This was the text of a commencement sermon given at Episcopal Divinity School, May 26, 1983.

Episcopal community. It is scary business—taking ourselves seriously as God's people.

And so, we tend often to avert our eyes from this unnerving vision of Christian vocation. It makes us nervous, because, insofar as we share it, there is no easy escape hatch from the possibility of our own conversion—of having our priorities, our plans, our relationships turned completely around. Our ministry becomes not simply something we do for others, but rather is rooted in the likelihood that we ourselves will be touched, transformed, transfigured much in the spirit of Jesus himself. Understandably, the strong temptation among us is to resist, to pull out all the controls, and, with all the force we can muster, to put the brakes on the opportunity of our conversion.

It is, after all, one thing to teach or study the prophets, Pentecost, the Reformation, process thought, liberation theology, the church at the end of the twentieth century. It is quite another thing to *be* this church; to *speak* words of denunciation and annunciation; to *feel* passionately about God, humanity, or anything else; to *commit* ourselves to processes of reform and liberation. And so we are apt to find ourselves walking around like a bunch of prickly porcupines, fending off defensively the likely consequences of what might happen to us if we actually believed ourselves to be shaped by, and shapers of, the common-wealth of a God who loves justice and likes surprises.

To the extent, however, that we turn our backs on our life together as the harvest of God, allowing the small places of our loves and fears and work to be trivialized by our notions of "more important issues," we render ourselves impotent. For to make light of our own lives—romanticizing "real Christianity" as something "out there" in liberation movements, emergency rooms, monasteries, urban missions—is to lop off the roots of our best energy. Cut off from the wellspring of spiritual power, we find ourselves depressed, a debilitated people whose boredom can barely conceal our rage—at ourselves, the world, and God—for sticking us here, glued to our sense of powerlessness, left wallowing in the passivity bred among those who are out of touch with the value of their own lives.

The greatest danger facing us here and elsewhere in the church is that of our passivity and depression—not our pains, or our conflicts. The struggles on this campus are, in fact, a sign of our health and our hope, for they signal our connection to brothers and sisters throughout the world. Why should we be exempt from the effects of white supremacy, male gender superiority, homophobia, economic injustice, when these forces are at war against the vast majority of God's people on the earth? In our society, I would suggest that the three prevailing images of the Christian God have become that of the christofascist white male ruler on one hand, the dark-skinned revolutionary woman on the other, and the denominational bureaucrat—the objective mediator—standing somewhere in the middle. In this context, what right have we to imagine that we in this school should be able simply to come together and worship the same god? How dare we hope that, somehow, we will be able to escape the various destructive dependencies—on people, alcohol, and a myriad of other externalized authorities, including fixed, closed symbol structures—which people throughout the globe fall back on as coping mechanisms? Christians are not, and ought not to be, immune to the effects of living in the world. And it is only an uninviting arrogance that would lead us to believe that we should be "better," "more together," than others because we profess the name of Jesus Christ. To labor in the harvest is to live in the struggle.

Thus, I believe we are blessed here at Episcopal Divinity School, and I would pray this blessing upon all graduates. May you remember the opportunities we have been given to wrestle no less fiercely than Jacob with an array of ornery angels. They have greeted us with uncompromising demands that we study our lives so that we may see more clearly how we are seen by others, and so that we may know more fully which god we do, in fact, worship with our lives. These angels invite us to realize that *we are the harvest of God* and that our conflicts and confusion, no less than the many happy blessings we can name, hold the seeds of the harvest that is ours to cultivate. Surely we are sinners, but the most deadly of our sins is not the deed we do, or fail to do, but rather the *denial of ourselves* as God's harvest.

Now, what has any of this to do with the doctrine, discipline, and worship of the church? Forty years ago, Dietrich Bonhoeffer suggested that only a "religionless Christianity" would do in a "world come of age." Only a church, he contended, that is wed first not to its own life, but rather to human well-being, could do God's work in the world. I think Bonhoeffer was right, up to a critical point. Certainly, he wrote prophetically that the church must re-prioritize its commitments: Human need must set the agenda. The doctrine, discipline, and worship of the church must emerge as reflectors of the church's commitment to human life. But because Bonhoeffer, like so many, tended to place the church—the essence of its gospel—*above* the world, rather than *in* and *of* it, he did not understand the radical extent to which the church's doctrine, discipline and worship are themselves responses to human need, instruments by which the whole human family is served well, or poorly. Bonhoeffer did not seem to grasp the extent to which our theology, our symbols, our words and images *do* matter. How we speak of God matters a great deal.

Yes, it *does* make a difference if our christology is anti-Semitic. It made a terrible difference in 1943.

Yes, it *does* make a difference if our liturgies serve, generation upon generation, to venerate—in principle and in fact—a Father God/a patriarchal icon, in relation to whom the possibility of womanpower is historically anathema.

And yes, it makes a *world* of difference that images of lightness, whiteness, and Anglo-American fixations on order, obedience, and imperial authority are employed theologically in contradistinction to darkness, dirt, death, chaos, spontaneity, sexuality, paganism, tribalism, and other images held sacred among peoples of diverse cultures and histories.

What the church does, or does not, teach about God may make all the difference in the world. And it is our vocation to teach, preach, and worship a God who is actually the source of all creation and all redemption of all humanity.

To maintain that ours is a "world come of age" is to blaspheme against the processes of aging. Ours is a world come of madness—and so was Bonhoeffer's Nazi Germany. And we are not called into a "religionless" Christianity, but rather into a radicalized Christianity. Our task is not to devalue, or play down, our religious system and symbols—but rather to recognize that the value of our religion is ours to determine—and ours to determine its doctrine, discipline, and worship accordingly. The more seriously we value human well-being—our own and that of others—as the ground upon which we, the church, must stand, the more valuable the Christian religion will be; the more humane our doctrines; the more empowering our discipline; the more compelling our worship.

The more we value ourselves as the Body of Christ, the better we will be able to see that, just as Jesus was both priest and victim, we harassed and helpless people are empowered to live as people of the compassionate One, able to take the plight of humankind seriously because it is our own. To realize our own fields of labor as fertile patchworks in the larger harvest is to dip into a knowledge of transcendence, an experience of that One whom we worship as God: She who crosses over among us. He who invites us to a meal from which no one is excluded. They who pull us beyond the boundaries of our own skins into solidarity with the whole creation. It is a matter of our life and our death, and I mean that quite literally.

For, finally, I hear the warning that some of you have signaled boldly among us. With many of you, I believe that the threat of nuclear holocaust cannot be interpreted by Christian laborers as anything but the most insidious symbol of evil, our gross neglect of God's harvest. If, in the face of this demon, we do not hear the trumpet call to a passionate faith on behalf of human well-being, we are dead—and the harvest wasted. For our collective paralysis at the altars of our idols, as surely as it destroys us all, will pin the very power of love onto a cross from which there may be no raising up again of life in this world.

My question to you, and ours to one another, must always be: *How seriously do we take our own lives and those of others as resources in the work of creation and redemption?*

It is time to go now—and we move on. And if we say to the mountains before us, "Be taken up and cast into the sea [Matt. 21:21]," and do not doubt in our hearts, but believe that it may come to pass, it will be done for us.

May we approach the mountains boldly.

May our lives spill over with the power of God's movement and compassion among all those lives. May our lives reflect an intense love for humanity and for all created life.

And, my graduating friends—among whom are those who have taught me much of what I have just shared—may you go well.

Amen.

Eucharistic Prayer for Peace[1]

"Peace I give to you. My own peace I leave with you. Peace, not as the world gives, but of God." Let us present ourselves, as living gifts, to God's work of peace.

May God be with us.
God is with us.
Let us open our hearts to God.
We open them to God and to one another.
Let us give thanks to God.
It is right to give God thanks and praise.

ALL:
For touching our lives, for bearing with us, for calling us to remember your face in the faces of our sisters and brothers, we thank you, Holy Mother. We remember you burning in Hiroshima.

For giving us this bounteous earth as our home, and for blessing us as one family throughout the world, we thank you, Merciful Father. We remember you naked in Auschwitz.

For spreading the table before us and cushioning our bodies with rest, for bringing us in from the storms and lighting your fire to warm us when we are cold or afraid, we thank you, Loving Sister. We remember you screaming at My Lai.

For assuring us that your presence is closer to us than our next breath, and that our presence makes all the difference in the world, we thank you, Faithful Brother. We remember you mutilated in Sabra and Shatilla.

For taking us into your heart, giving us your hands, walking tedious roads and treacherous steps with us, showing us your way of peace, and teaching us that peacemakers must struggle for justice, we thank you, courageous friend and neighbor, you who are our God, creator and redeemer and lover of all human-kind.

We remember that on the night before our brother Jesus was handed over to be executed for his faithfulness to you, O God, he shared food with his disciples and asked them to remember him. Taking bread, he blessed it, and gave it to them, and said, "Take. Eat. This is my Body, which will be broken for you. Whenever you eat it, remember me." Then he took a cup of wine, blessed it, gave it to them, and said, "Drink this, all of you. This is my Blood which will be shed for you. Whenever you drink it, remember me."

And we have not forgotten Jesus. By the power of the Holy Spirit, we are bound to remember his life, death, and resurrec-tion, as sign and promise that all men and women, all creatures and living things, which have been dis-membered by our greed, selfishness, and indifference, will be remembered by us and by you, O God, as we work with you to restore this earth, our home.

Send your Spirit upon this bread and wine, gracious one, making them for us the Body and Blood of Jesus Christ—*our* Body, *our* Blood, and that of *all* your people—so that in sharing this holy food, we share ourselves, as gifts to you, one another, and the world.

All this we ask in the name of Jesus Christ whom we re-member, but also in the memory of the millions whom we forget. On their behalf we ask you to acccept the gifts of our lives, even as we thank you for the gift of yourself. Amen.

Notes

Preface

1. See Rosemary Ruether, *Sexism and God-Talk: Toward a Feminist Theology* (Beacon, 1983), for usage of the term God/ess.
2. Beverly Harrison's forthcoming book, *Making the Connections: Essays in Feminist Social Ethics* (Boston: Beacon Press, 1984), elaborates, from an ethical perspective, many of the themes addressed in this volume. Her work is fundamental to much of my own.

2 / Feminist Theology

1. This essay is taken from an address given at Colgate-Rochester-Bexley Hall, Crozier Theological Seminary, Rochester, NY, December 8, 1977.
2. Quoted in Carter Heyward, *A Priest Forever: The Formation of a Woman and a Priest* (New York: Harper & Row, 1976), p. 132 (italics added).
3. Sarah Bentley Doely, ed., *Women's Liberation and the Church: The New Demand for Freedom in the Life of the Christian Church* (New York: Association Press, 1970).
4. Emily C. Hewitt and Suzanne R. Hiatt, *Women Priests: Yes or No?* (New York: Seabury Press, 1973).

5. Leonard Swidler, "Jesus Was a Feminist," *The Catholic World*, January 1971, pp. 177–83.

6. Linda Brebner, Bonnie O'Brien, and Ruthann Swaincott, "A Questioning Theology." Project for Feminist Credo course, Episcopal Divinity School, Cambridge, MA, December 6, 1977.

7. Mary Daly, *Beyond God the Father: Toward a Philosophy of Women's Liberation* (Boston: Beacon Press, 1973), p. 73.

8. Ibid.

9. Ibid., p. 71.

10. Suzanne R. Hiatt, "God Is an Equal Opportunity Employer," *Radcliffe Quarterly*, December 1977, p. 13.

11. Ntozake Shange, *For Colored Girls Who Have Considered Suicide When the Rainbow Is Enuf* (New York: Macmillan, 1975), p 63.

4 / The Enigmatic God

1. Elie Wiesel, *Night* (New York: Avon, 1960), p. 76.

5 / Lesbianism and the Church

1. This essay is based on an address to women seminarians at a conference on sexuality held at Andover-Newton Theological School, Newton Centre, MA, spring 1977.

6 / Theological Explorations of Homosexuality

1. Adapted from an address to the Conference on Homosexuality cosponsored by the Diocese of Massachusetts' Church and Society network and the Diocesan Ministries Commission, October 1977. A nearly identical adaptation of the address was published in *The Witness*, June 1979, pp. 13–15. Used by permission.

7 / Blessing the Bread: A Litany

1. Written to be shared as a litany in a service commemorating International Women's Year, Lafayette Park, Washington, DC, spring 1978.

1. This essay originally appeared in *Christianity and Crisis*, April 2, 1979, pp. 66–72, and is reprinted with permission.

2. Mary Daly, *The Church and the Second Sex*—with a New Feminist Postchristian Introduction by the author (1968; San Francisco: Harper & Row, 1976) p. 223.

3. See Mary Daly, *Gyn/Ecology: The Metaethics of Radical Feminism* (Boston: Beacon Press, 1978).

4. See Rosemary Radford Ruether, *Liberation Theology: Human Hope Confronts Christian History and American Power* (New York: Paulist Press, 1972), and *New Woman/New Earth: Sexist Ideologies and Human Liberation* (New York: Seabury Press, 1975).

5. Cf. Daly's terms in *Gyn/Ecology*.

6. Carter Heyward, *A Priest Forever: The Formation of a Woman and a Priest* (New York: Harper & Row, 1976), p. 74.

7. Carol P. Christ, "The New Feminist Theology: A Review of the Literature," *Religious Studies Review* 3 (1977): 203–12.

8. Mary Daly, *Beyond God the Father: Toward a Philosophy of Women's Liberation* (Boston: Beacon Press, 1973), p. 6 (italics added).

9. Daly, *Gyn/Ecology*, pp. 423–24.

10. Ibid., p. 24.

11. Ibid., pp. 43–106.

12. Ibid., p. 1.

13. See, for example, Ruether's work on the anti-Semitism in Christian theology. Rosemary Radford Ruether, *Faith and Fratricide: The Theological Roots of Anti-Semitism* (New York: Seabury Press, 1974).

14. See Rosemary Radford Ruether, *Mary: The Feminine Face of the Church* (Philadelphia: Westminster Press, 1977).

15. Ruether, *Liberation Theology*, p. 7.

16. Beverly Wildung Harrison, "Sexism and the Language of Christian Ethics," in *Making the Connections* (Boston: Beacon Press, 1984).

17. See especially Ruether, *New Woman/New Earth*.

18. For example, J.J. Bachofen and Elizabeth Gould Davis.

19. Ruether, *New Woman/New Earth*, p. 5.

20. Ibid.

21. Ruether, *Liberation Theology*, p. 22 (italics added).

22. Daly, *Beyond God the Father,* p. 2.
23. Daly, *Gyn/Ecology,* p. 5.

9 / Looking in the Mirror

1. This article appeared originally in *The Witness,* January 1979, pp. 14–16. Reprinted with permission.
2. *New York Times,* November 26, 1977.
3. Dorothee Sölle, *Beyond Mere Obedience* (New York: The Pilgrim Press, 1982), p. 20.

10 / Coming Out

1. See chapter 6 in this book.

11 / Sexuality, Love, and Justice

1. This article is adapted from an address delivered at the Integrity Convention, Denver, CO, September 1979. Earlier versions were published in *Integrity Forum* (Advent 1979), and as Appendix F in *The Redemption of God: A Theology of Mutual Relation* (Lanham, MD: University Press of America, 1983), copyright © 1983 by University Press of America and reprinted by permission.

13 / Latin American Liberation Theology

1. This essay is taken from a lecture given at the Convocation of Episcopal Divinity School and Weston School of Theology, Cambridge, MA, March 11, 1980.
2. Quoted in Penny Lernoux, "The Long Path to Puebla," in *Puebla and Beyond,* edited by John Eagleson and Philip Scharper (Maryknoll, NY: Orbis Books, 1979), p. 3.
3. Jose Miguez Bonino, *Doing Theology in a Revolutionary Situation* (Philadelphia: Fortress Press, 1975), p. 16.
4. Robert McAfee Brown, *Theology in a New Key: Responding to Liberation Themes* (Philadelphia: Westminster Press, 1978), p. 70.
5. Ernesto Cardenal, *Apocalypse and Other Poems* (New York: New Directions, 1977), p. 30. Used by permission of the author.
6. Ibid., p. 16. Used by permission of the author.

7. Quoted in Brown, *Theology in a New Key*, op. cit., p. 93. See John Gerassi, ed., *Revolutionary Priest: The Complete Writings and Messages of Camilo Torres* (New York: Vintage Press, 1971).

8. Quoted in Miguez Bonino, *Doing Theology*, pp. 43–44.

9. Ibid., pp. 44–45.

10. Gustavo Gutiérrez, "Liberation Theology and Progressivist Theology," in *The Emergent Gospel: Theology from the Underside of History*, edited by Sergio Torres and Virginia Fabella (Maryknoll, NY: Orbis Books, 1978), p. 240.

11. Gustavo Gutiérrez, "Liberation Praxis and Christian Faith" (revision of *Praxis de liberacion y fe cristiana*), in *Frontiers of Theology in Latin America*, edited by Rosino Gibellini (Maryknoll, NY: Orbis Books, 1979), p. 16.

12. Gustavo Gutiérrez, *A Theology of Liberation: History, Politics and Salvation* (Maryknoll, NY: Orbis Books, 1973), p. 177.

13. Ibid., p. 173.

14. Gutiérrez, "Liberation Praxis," p. 15.

15. Gutiérrez, *Theology of Liberation*, p. 175.

16. Ibid., p. 200.

17. Ibid., p. 205.

18. Ibid., p. 202.

19. Gutiérrez, "Liberation Praxis," p. 20.

20. Gutiérrez, *Theology of Liberation*, p. 201.

21. Ibid., p. 195.

22. See ibid., pp. 232–34.

23. Gutiérrez, "Liberation Theology and Progressivist Theology," p. 233.

24. See Max Echegaray, "Central America 'Backfire' " in *National Catholic Reporter*, February 8, 1980.

14 / Redefining Power

1. See Sheldon Kopp, *If You Meet the Buddha on the Road, Kill Him* (Palo Alto, CA: Science and Behavior Books, 1972).

15 / Till Now We Had Not Touched Our Strength

1. This essay is taken from an address delivered at Gay, Lesbian and Christian Conference at Kirkridge, Bangor, PA, June 13, 1980. Part

of this address was included in a presentation at the Consultation on Ministry with Gay and Lesbian Community, College of Preachers, Washington, DC, December 18, 1980, and was published as Part IV ("Power and Sexuality"), "In the Beginning Is the Relation: Toward a Christian Ethic of Sexuality," *Integrity Forum* (Lent 1981). Used with permission of the author.

2. The lines from "Phantasia for Elvira Shatayev" from *The Dream of a Common Language: Poems 1974–1977*, by Adrienne Rich, are reprinted by permission of W.W. Norton & Company, Inc. Copyright © 1978 by W.W. Norton & Company, Inc.

3. Ibid., p. 4.

17 / Liberating the Body

1. See chapter 11, "Sexuality, Love, and Justice," pp. 83–93.

18 / A Eucharistic Prayer

1. This prayer was written for services at the Episcopal Divinity School, Cambridge, MA, 1980; revised 1982.

19 / Limits of Liberalism

1. See Peggy Ann Way, "An Authority of Possibility for Women in the Church," in *Women's Liberation and the Church*, edited by Sarah Bentley Doely (New York: Association Press, 1970), pp. 77–94.

2. See Beverly Wildung Harrison, *Our Right to Choose: Toward a New Ethic of Abortion* (Boston: Beacon Press, 1983), for a superb, detailed analysis of the moral basis and dimensions of procreative choice.

3. *Boston Globe*, March 20, 1981, p. 3 (italics added).

4. Dorothee Sölle first used this term in the spring of 1979 in response to a presumably well-intended—and unconsciously anti-Semitic—sermon given by a Christian priest.

5. See Zillah Eisenstein, *The Radical Future of Liberal Feminism* (New York: Longman, 1981).

6. Ibid., p. 6 (italics added).

7. See John MacMurray, *Self as Agent* (New York: Harper & Bros., 1957), and *Persons in Relation* (1961; Atlantic Highlands, NJ:

Humanities Press, 1979). Astute philosophical/theological works on the social/relational ground of personhood.

8. See Mary Daly, *Beyond God the Father: Toward a Philosophy of Women's Liberation* (Boston: Beacon Press, 1973), and *Gyn/Ecology: The Metaethics of Radical Feminism* (Boston: Beacon Press, 1978).

9. Beverly Wildung Harrison, "The Power of Anger in the Work of Love," *Union Seminary Quarterly Review* 36 (Suppl. 1981): 48.

21 / Gay Pride Day

1. I do not know the source of this story. I have heard it many times in different forms.

24 / Must "Jesus Christ" Be a Holy Terror?

1. See Mary Daly, *Beyond God the Father: Toward a Philosophy of Women's Liberation* (Boston: Beacon Press, 1973).

2. See Rosemary Radford Ruether, *Faith and Fratricide: The Theological Roots of Anti-Semitism* (New York: Seabury Press, 1974). This is an important account of the historical/theological roots of Christian anti-Semitism.

25 / Introduction to Feminist Theology

1. This essay is taken from a lecture given at the first meeting of the course "Jesus: Feminist Perspective," Episcopal Divinity School, Cambridge, MA, February 4, 1982.

2. Beverly Wildung Harrison first used this term in conversation with me in 1979.

3. See Valerie Saiving-Goldstein, "The Human Situation: A Feminine View," *The Journal of Religion*, April 1960.

27 / Compassion

1. Elie Wiesel, *The Town Beyond the Wall* (New York: Holt, Rinehart & Winston, 1964).

2. Ibid., pp. 177–78.

1. This essay is excerpted from an address given at Wellwoman, Philadelphia, PA, March 1983; Theological Opportunities Program, Harvard Divinity School, Cambridge, MA, April 1983; and Conference on Some Basic Issues in Christian Feminism, Auburn Theological Seminary, New York, NY, July 1983.

30 / Eucharistic Prayer for Peace

1. This prayer was written in protest of nuclear weapons and of U.S. militarism and, specifically, for a service celebrating the witness of Episcopal Divinity School students against the building at Groton, CT, of the Trident nuclear submarines on Good Friday, April 1, 1983.